SO, YOU THINK YOU KNOW SPORTS?

SO, YOU THINK YOU KNOW SPORTS?

By Ron Smith

The Sporting News
PUBLISHING CO.

Efrem Zimbalist III, President and Chief Executive Officer, Times Mirror Magazines; **James H. Nuckols,** President, The Sporting News; **Francis X. Farrell,** Senior Vice President, Publisher; **John D. Rawlings,** Senior Vice President, Editorial Director; **John Kastberg,** Vice President, General Manager; **Kathy Kinkeade,** Vice President, Operations; **Steve Meyerhoff,** Executive Editor; **Ron Smith,** Associate Editor; **Craig Carter,** Statistical Editor; **Dave Sloan,** Associate Editor; **Marilyn Kasal,** Production Director; **Mike Bruner,** Prepress Director; **Michael Behrens and Christen Webster,** Macintosh Production Artists. Computer illustrations by **Jack Kruyne and Nancy Hinds.**

A Times Mirror
Company

Contents

Introduction

A party discussion, an office debate, a bar-room bet, a computer chat—sports trivia is the stuff of which conversations are made. It's becoming harder and harder to escape any kind of social situation without absorbing the sports minutiae of our past and present—and, of course, sharing a little minutiae of our own.

The great thing about trivia is that it's, well, trivial. It's not meaningful in the overall scheme of life's events, it doesn't have any particular use, it lacks function and it has no basis or form. But despite those obvious limitations, trivia is hot, it's hip, it's "in" and, in a more universal language, it's fun.

When THE SPORTING NEWS decided to take its third plunge into the trivia pool (TSN published two baseball trivia books and one football trivia book in the 1980s), the operative word was "fun." The mandate was to publish a sports trivia book that was challenging, interesting, creative, informative and entertaining—not necessarily in that order. What follows is the result of that mandate and an opportunity for sports fans to discover just how much minutiae has collected and multiplied in the moldy recesses of their brains.

If you can recognize a silhouette of Sandy Koufax throwing a baseball; if you can name the only rookie to win a baseball batting title; if you can remember a mechanical rabbit named Harvey or a running back named Beattie Feathers; if you can identify actor James Dean in his high school basketball uniform ... then there's probably more than enough to handle this trivial exercise.

This trivia book covers the Big Six sports—baseball, pro and college football, pro and college basketball, and hockey—and challenges the reader with a variety of word and visual tests. There are individual chapters for each sport, combined chapters for the professional and college sports and visual chapters covering a wide spectrum, from sports venues to sports movies. Everything is up to date through the 1996-97 basketball and hockey seasons.

So get comfortable, fasten your seatbelts and open your memory banks so all that long-stored trivia finally can be put to use. Let the games begin.

—Ron Smith

Where's Yogi?

Can you find Yogi Berra in this crowd? His location is revealed on page 287.

Mystery Guest

Can you name the athlete and sport? Answer, page 286.

1. As a child of the '60s, I never could have imagined the '70s and '80s. With Dad calling the shots, my brothers and I fired up bricks and laid the foundations for our futures. It didn't take me long to realize I wanted to move into a faster lane.

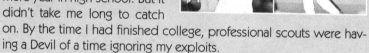

2. I never thought much about sports until my sophomore year in high school. But it didn't take me long to catch on. By the time I had finished college, professional scouts were having a Devil of a time ignoring my exploits.

3. Round 1 of my professional career went fine. But the later rounds have been a real gas. I quickly discovered that I don't like crowds and need my space. So I spend most of my time making sure I get it. When I do, I score big points with the fans.

4. I'm a numbers freak: 49, 80, 100 and 1,000 are four important ones in my life. So is 7, the number of years I studied at the Montana School of Sports Music. I love records and have amassed quite a collection over the years.

5. I also love to be the best in my field and I have reached that pinnacle, both from a personal and team perspective, many times. I'm like the Energizer Bunny: I just keep going ... and going ... and going. ... And I pity all those poor guys chasing me and my shadow.

6. Everyone knows I'm a bomb expert. It's no secret and I openly defy anybody who wants to stop me. You might be able to cut me off at the pass occasionally, but more often than not you'll get blown away.

7. Although I've grown older and wiser in the 1990s, I've also been revitalized by my Young friend. When he throws a party, it's usually a doozy. He has reaffirmed my belief that it's better to receive than to give.

8. Sometime before I retire, I want to rekindle that Super feeling and pad my incredible record collection. If I do, I'll hang a championship banner from the Golden Gate Bridge. And I'll leave my heart when I go back home to Mississippi.

Firsts

Warming up

1. In 1973, the American League began its noble experiment with the designated hitter. What New York Yankees player went down in history as the first official DH?

2. This future Hall of Fame pitcher hit a home run in his first major league at-bat in 1952. Over his next 21 seasons, he never hit another. Who was this outstanding reliever?

3. In 1973, this former Pittsburgh right fielder, who had died only months earlier in a tragic plane crash, became the first Hispanic player to be elected to the Hall of Fame. Name him.

4. Jackie Robinson broke baseball's color barrier in 1947 when he played in an opening day game for the Brooklyn Dodgers. Who broke the American League color barrier in July 1947 for the Cleveland Indians?

5. What American League power swept through the first three A.L. Championship Series (1969-71) with a 9-0 record?

6. The Astros have always been located in Houston. But Houston has not always been known as the Astros. What was the National League team's first nickname?

7. Where was the first All-Star Game played in 1933 and who hit the first All-Star home run?

8. The first World Series grand slam and the first World Series home run by a pitcher occurred in the same 1920 game. What Cleveland Indians outfielder and pitcher gained prominence with their Game 5 feats?

9. The first major league team to head west was not from New York or Brooklyn. What N.L. team started the franchise-shift ball rolling in 1953?

10. What team won the first World Series in 1903?

Did You Know

That three of the American League's longest-running franchises have career home run leaders who were still active in the 1997 season? Frank Thomas is Chicago's career leader, Albert Belle is Cleveland's all-time leader and Mark McGwire tops the Athletics charts.

Mark McGwire

Chapter 1 answers begin on page 287.

Getting serious

Each of the following dates represents a significant baseball "first." Identify the event:

1. April 15, 1947.
2. May 24, 1935.
3. July 6, 1933.
4. October 1, 1903.
5. April 12, 1965.
6. April 15, 1958.
7. April 8, 1975.
8. August 26, 1939.

9. August 9, 1988.
10. April 14, 1953.
11. October 8, 1956.
12. August 16, 1920.
13. April 14, 1969.
14. April 10, 1961.
15. October 4, 1969.

Lasts

Warming up

1. This team's frustrated fans have not enjoyed a World Series champion since 1908 or a World Series appearance since 1945. Name the team.

2. Babe Ruth's first and last major league duty came in the same city for different teams. Name his "first and last" employers.

3. From 1992 through 1996, the Dodgers boasted five straight National League Rookie of the Year winners. What Houston star won in 1991, setting the stage for the Dodgers' run?

4. The last time an American League team produced multiple 20-game winners was 1990. Who were the two Oakland Athletics righthanders who turned the trick?

5. Who was the last rookie to win 20 games? This lefthander performed the feat for Cincinnati in 1985.

6. In 1967, this future Hall of Famer completed his own Impossible Dream and captured baseball's last Triple Crown. Who was he?

7. The last player to hit four home runs in a game also tied the major league single-game record with 12 RBIs. Name the Cardinals star who enjoyed one of baseball's monster games in 1993.

8. What Minnesota Twins outfielder was the last (and only) rookie to win a 20th century batting championship?

9. After recording its fifth World Series championship in 1918, this team has not won another since. What long-frustrated franchise has gone almost eight decades without a title?

10. Who was the last catcher to lead the American League in triples? Hint: He actually tied for the league lead while playing for the Red Sox in 1972.

Getting serious

Each of the following game descriptions represents a baseball "last" —either a significant finale or the last time something was accomplished. Identify:

1. Danny McDevitt pitched a shutout for the home team, which won 2-0. Elmer Valo and a third baseman named "Hodges" drove in the only runs against Pittsburgh. The home team also used another third baseman, named "Reese."

Danny McDevitt contributed to a memorable 'last' in a different city.

2. Reggie Jackson homered twice, but the home team defeated the A's, 5-4, thanks to Willie Horton's game-ending ninth-inning single. The winning rally was enough to make someone Dizzy.

3. Fred Caligiuri recorded one of his two major league victories, but he got a Splinter in the process. His 7-1 victory for the A's in the nightcap of a doubleheader split was overshadowed by the final big-league appearance of Hall of Fame pitcher Lefty Grove and another significant achievement.

4. Veteran righthander Carl Mays fired a three-hitter, outdueling Chicago's Lefty Tyler in a 2-1 victory. The game was noteworthy beyond its status as a "significant last." A young lefthanded pitcher was used in the contest as a left fielder.

5. The Red Sox defeated the Orioles, 5-4, in a late-season 1960 game at Fenway Park. The game had no bearing on the American League pennant race, but it was memorable for another reason—a solo home run off pitcher Jack Fisher.

6. As a major league debut, it lacked dramatics. But Pumpsie Green will be remem-

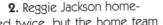

Did You Know

That on the same July day in 1966 when Braves pitcher Tony Cloninger made baseball history by hitting two grand slams, driving in nine runs and pitching Atlanta to a 17-3 victory over the Giants, teammate Felipe Alou was celebrating the birth of son Moises, a future major league All-Star? And, oh yeah, Felipe also homered in that memorable game.

Rich Reese made an out that will be remembered forever.

bered well beyond what his performance as a pinch runner and one-inning shortstop merits. For the record, the White Sox recorded a 2-1 victory over the Red Sox in this July 1960 game at Comiskey Park.

7. The 1972 Pirates, cruising to their final 11-game victory over Chicago in the N.L. East Division, posted a 5-0 victory over the Mets at Three Rivers Stadium. Much more momentous than the final score was the performance of one player, who would be thrust into a different kind of spotlight a few months later.

8. The Brewers pounded out a 6-2 victory over California in a midseason game at Milwaukee. One player added his own Bicentennial touch to the season and a career with a little help from pitcher Dick Drago.

9. The final day of the season—a 5-3 victory over Minnesota—punctuated an Impossible Dream, for both a team and a player. The player finished the season-closing series on a 7-for-8 tear and, in the process, became the last member of an exclusive club.

10. Minnesota's Rich Reese pinch-hit in this May 8, 1968, game and made an out. But he forever will be remembered for his role in one of baseball's most cherished moments.

Famous Home Runs

Warming up

1. When Roger Maris hit a record 61 home runs in 1961, who finished second on the major league homer chart with 54?

2. Name the young Oakland slugger who hit the moonshot home run that struck the light tower atop the grandstand at Tiger Stadium, an estimated 520 feet from home plate, in the 1971 All-Star Game. The home run helped the American League end the National League's All-Star winning streak at eight games.

3. Name the New York shortstop who delivered a three-run, seventh-inning homer that helped the Yankees defeat Boston, 5-4, in a one-game playoff to decide the 1978 East Division title.

4. When Atlanta rookie Andruw Jones hit home runs in his first two 1996 World Series at-bats, he duplicated the 1972 feat of an Oakland catcher against the Cincinnati Reds. Name the catcher.

5. St. Louis first baseman Jack Clark brought a sudden end to the 1985 N.L. Championship Series with a dramatic three-run, ninth-inning home run. What Dodgers reliever served up the Game 6 homer?

6. Name the Red Sox outfielder who drilled a dramatic two-out, ninth-inning home run, rescuing his team from the brink of elimination in the 1986 A.L. Championship Series. He later delivered an 11th-inning sacrifice fly to help Boston defeat California.

7. George Brett's infamous "Pine Tar" homer of 1983 eventually resulted in a 5-4 Kansas City victory over New York. Name the Yankees pitcher who was victimized by the blast.

8. Duplicating the 1954 feat of St. Louis' Stan Musial, this San Diego slugger belted five home runs in a 1972 doubleheader, driving in 13 runs. Name the young outfielder.

9. What legendary slugger hit his final three career home runs in the same game against the Pittsburgh Pirates?

10. When Bobby Thomson hit his Shot Heard 'Round the World to give the Giants a 1951 pennant-playoff victory over Brooklyn, what rookie outfielder and future Hall of Famer was kneeling in the on-deck circle?

Did You Know

That Mike Schmidt's 500th career home run provided a storybook ending to a game against the Pirates? Schmidt connected in the ninth inning of an April 18, 1987, game with two runners on base, giving the Phillies an 8-6 victory.

Mike Schmidt

Getting serious

The following list is made up of people who witnessed baseball's most famous home runs from a different vantage point. Identify the historic blasts and where the witness(es) was located:

1. Yogi Berra.

2. Clint Hartung.

3. Tom House.

4. Paul Molitor.

5. Sal Durante.

6. Mike Davis.

7. Johnny Bench.

8. Miller Huggins.

9. Charlie Root.

10. Manny Trillo, Rod Carew, Robin Yount.

One Brief, Shining Moment

The following achievements describe a player who had little major league success before or after his big moment. Identify:

1. On September 14, 1951, I became the first player to hit home runs in my first two major league at-bats, although the rest of my 12-year career was nondescript. I played for seven big-league teams.

2. I finished my career with 35 victories and seven shutouts, but Dodgers fans will never forget me. In 1966, I faced them five times and fired five shutouts, allowing 24 hits in 45 innings.

3. In my first major league starting assignment, I made history by pitching a 6-0 no-hitter against the Athletics. That May 6, 1953, victory was the first of three I would record in my only major league season.

4. My 19-29 major league career was not exactly noteworthy. But my performance on September 12, 1962, raised eyebrows because I struck out a major league-record 21 Orioles hitters in a 16-inning game.

Detroit pitcher Floyd Giebell enjoyed his one brief, shining moment.

5. In an otherwise nondescript career, I will forever be remembered as the man who replaced Lou Gehrig in the Yankees lineup on May 2, 1939. I upheld Gehrig's successful tradition that day by hitting a home run and a double in a 22-2 victory over Detroit.

6. I hit 86 career home runs, but a record-tying four of them came in a July 18, 1948, game against the Athletics. I also drove in seven runs in the 11-inning contest.

7. I was a respectable player over an 11-year career, but I didn't exactly attract the spotlight. Except, that is, for that special

September day in 1975 when I became the first player in this century to collect seven hits in a nine-inning game. Fittingly, my team beat the Cubs, 22-0.

8. You might not remember me, but Indians ace Bob Feller certainly does. One of my three major league victories was a 2-0 shutout in a matchup against Feller—and it clinched the 1940 American League pennant.

9. Don't look for my name in any record books, but it will always be there when great World Series moments are discussed. My moment came in 1947 when I robbed Joe DiMaggio with a Game 6-saving catch. Ironically, it was the final major league game of my career.

10. My name might not be easy to spell, but it is memorable. My respectable 13-year career was defined by the unassisted triple play I pulled off in the 1920 World Series.

11. Yeah, I admit it. I was a journeyman outfielder. But you can't take away my one major league claim to fame: I am the only player in modern major league history to get three hits in one inning. I did it on June 18, 1953, when my team scored 17 runs in the seventh inning against the Tigers.

12. I appeared in only one major league game, so I'm a little short on statistics. But every baseball fan has heard of me. My fame is a product of Bill Veeck's imagination and my moment in the sun came on August 19, 1951.

13. I was no slouch as a pitcher. But I spent only four seasons in the major leagues and had one brush with immortality. That came in the 1919 World Series when, while all my teammates were cheating, I was pitching my heart out and winning two games.

14. I played 15 years, batted .281 and got three World Series rings. But what am I known for? A lousy headache that kept me out of the lineup on June 2, 1925, and started Lou Gehrig on his record streak.

15. I never ranked among baseball's foremost hit men. But I was pretty good with a glove. My seven-year career was defined by the outfield catch I made in Game 7 of the 1955 World Series, saving the championship for my team and some pretty happy fans.

By the Numbers

Baseball's all-time top 5 in All-Star Game RBIs (through 1996):

1. Ted Williams 12
2. Fred Lynn 10
Stan Musial 10
4. Willie Mays 9
5. Hank Aaron 8
Rocky Colavito 8

Did You Know

That Cincinnati outfielder Art Shamsky hit three home runs in a 1966 game against Pittsburgh—and he didn't enter the game until the eighth inning. Shamsky, a defensive replacement, hit a two-run homer in the bottom of the eighth, a game-tying solo shot in the 10th and a game-tying two-run blast in the 11th. Pittsburgh finally won in the 13th, 14-11.

Seasonal Offerings

The following events and performances all occurred in the same baseball season. Identify the year:

1. ◆ Kansas City fans lit matches and sang to 60-year-old pitcher Satchel Paige, who was brought out of mothballs by owner Charles O. Finley to pitch three innings against the Red Sox.

◆ Willie Mays, en route to an N.L.-leading 52 home runs, connected for No. 500 in a September game at Houston.

◆ The National League won the All-Star Game, 6-5, and took its first-ever lead in the midsummer classic.

◆ Chicago catcher Smoky Burgess gave new meaning to the art of pinch hitting, collecting his career major league-record 115th in that role.

◆ Broadcaster Lindsey Nelson called a Mets-Astros game from a gondola, 208 feet above second base at Houston's Astrodome.

The year was: 1965 1966 1968

2. ◆ 23-22. The Phillies pounded out a dizzying victory in an 11-home run, 50-hit marathon at Chicago's windswept Wrigley Field.

◆ The National League won another All-Star Game on a bases-loaded walk to Lee Mazzilli.

◆ Atlanta knuckleballer Phil Niekro tied for the N.L. lead with 21 victories and led the league with 20 losses.

◆ A Disco Demolition Night promotion backfired on White Sox owner Bill Veeck when unruly fans rioted between games of a doubleheader against Detroit and forced Chicago to forfeit the nightcap.

◆ Champagne corks popped after Oakland pitcher Matt Keough defeated Milwaukee September 5, ending his 18-game losing streak and his record-tying 14-game skid to open the season.

The year was: 1978 1979 1980

3. ◆ Joel Youngblood made history when he became the first player to collect hits for two different teams—and off two future Hall of Fame pitchers—on the same day.

◆ Gaylord Perry won his 300th game, Pete Rose passed Hank Aaron on the all-time hit list and the National League won its 11th consecutive All-Star Game.

◆ Twins righthander Terry Felton completed the season with an 0-13 record and brought his career mark to 0-16—the longest losing streak to open a career in baseball history.

◆ California's Doug DeCinces blasted three home runs in a 5-4 loss to the Twins—and three more five days later in a 9-5 victory at Seattle.

◆ Owners voted not to renew the contract of 14-year commissioner Bowie Kuhn during a meeting at Chicago.

The year was: 1980 1982 1983

4. ◆ Young Cleveland lefthander Herb Score was struck in the eye by a line drive off the bat of Yankee Gil McDougald, an injury that would ruin a promising career.

- A thick fog shrouded Ebbets Field in the second inning of a game against the Cubs, forcing one of the more unusual postponements in baseball history.

- Commissioner Ford Frick, upset by the ballot-stuffing antics of Cincinnati fans, replaced three N.L. starters for what would have been an all-Reds starting line-up in the All-Star Game.

- When John Kennedy (not the future president) entered a game against Brooklyn as a pinch runner, the Philadelphia Phillies became the last National League team to break the color barrier.

Herb Score was never the same after getting hit by a line drive.

- Boston's Ted Williams, at age 39, batted .388 and became the oldest batting champion in baseball history, but he lost another close MVP vote to Yankees slugger Mickey Mantle.

The year was: 1955   1956   1957

5. - A baseball first: Philadelphia manager Eddie Sawyer resigned after watching his Phillies drop a 9-4 opening day decision to the Reds. He was replaced by Gene Mauch.

- Another first: Detroit sent manager Jimmie Dykes to Cleveland for manager Joe Gordon in a midseason trade.

- An impressive, high-kicking righthander named Juan Marichal made his major league debut for the Giants and allowed one hit in a 2-0 victory over Philadelphia.

- A Chicago insurance tycoon purchased 52 percent of the Kansas City Athletics for just under $2 million, beginning a colorful and controversial association with baseball.

- Ebbets Field, the Brooklyn home of the Dodgers for 44 years, was laid to rest by a wrecking ball.

The year was: 1959   1960   1961

Baltimore's Mike Cuellar receives his 1969 co-Cy Young Award.

Honors

Warming up

1. Name the "original 16" franchise that has never produced a Cy Young Award winner.

2. What Detroit Tigers outfielder batted .340 in 1955 and became the youngest player in big-league history to claim a batting championship?

3. What Pittsburgh and St. Louis stars shared National League MVP honors in 1979—the first and last time that has happened?

4. Name the two four-time winners of the Cy Young Award.

5. What former Cincinnati and Baltimore outfielder is the only player to win MVP awards in both leagues?

6. Stan Musial, Roy Campanella and Mike Schmidt are three-time MVPs. So is one other player who still is active. Name him.

7. Name the only man to claim three Manager of the Year awards. Hint: He's trying to win a fourth in a different league.

8. What slick-fielding former third baseman and pitcher share the major league record for Gold Gloves with 16 each?

9. What National League team has cornered the market on Rookie of the Year winners with 16?

10. In 1969, Baltimore lefthander Mike Cuellar shared the A.L. Cy Young with a righthander who had won the award the previous season in noteworthy fashion. Who was the Detroit player who went on to disgrace and infamy rather than fame and fortune?

Getting serious

Each of the following "award" groupings have a common thread. Identify what the players have in common:

1. Jim Konstanty, Rollie Fingers, Willie Hernandez, Dennis Eckersley.

2. Ty Cobb, Walter Johnson, Christy Mathewson, Babe Ruth, Honus Wagner.

3. Jose Rijo, Jack Morris, Pat Borders, Paul Molitor, Tom Glavine, John Wetteland.

4. Frank Frisch, Lefty Grove, Don Newcombe, Jackie Robinson, Tom Lasorda, Tony La Russa.

5. Don Newcombe, Sandy Koufax, Denny McLain, Bob Gibson, Vida Blue, Rollie Fingers, Willie Hernandez, Roger Clemens, Dennis Eckersley.

6. Albie Pearson, Bob Allison, Tony Oliva, Rod Carew, John Castino, Chuck Knoblauch, Marty Cordova.

7. Sandy Koufax, Bob Gibson, Reggie Jackson.

8. Fernando Valenzuela, Fred Lynn.

9. Willie Mays, Steve Garvey, Gary Carter.

10. Jimmie Foxx, Hal Newhouser, Yogi Berra, Ernie Banks, Mickey Mantle, Roger Maris, Joe Morgan, Mike Schmidt, Dale Murphy, Barry Bonds, Frank Thomas.

11. Earl Averill, Lou Boudreau, Larry Doby, Mel Harder, Bob Feller.

12. Carl Morton, Andre Dawson, Buck Rodgers, Felipe Alou.

13. Ty Cobb, Honus Wagner, Rod Carew, Rogers Hornsby, Stan Musial, Tony Gwynn, Ted Williams, Wade Boggs, Dan Brouthers.

14. Steve Garvey, Dave Stewart.

15. Steve Carlton, Greg Maddux, Sandy Koufax, Tom Seaver, Bob Gibson, Jim Palmer, Roger Clemens, Denny McLain, Gaylord Perry.

Did You Know

That Richie Zisk was the first player to hit home runs in Canada as both a National Leaguer and an American Leaguer? Zisk homered at Montreal's Jarry Park while playing for the Pirates and at Toronto's Exhibition Stadium as a member of the White Sox.

Richie Zisk

Laugh-In

If Rosemary Casals married Don Beebe her name would be Rosemary Beebe.

Did You Know

That former Cardinals great Stan Musial is the all-time home run leader among players who never won a league homer title? Musial finished his career with 475 home runs.

Stan Musial

By the Numbers

Baseball's all-time top 5 in steals of home (through 1996):

1. Ty Cobb   50
2. Max Carey   33
3. George Burns   28
4. Honus Wagner   27
5. Sherry Magee   23
   Frank Schulte   23

Milestones

Warming up

1. These two superstars reached their biggest career milestones during games played a continent apart on the same day—August 4, 1985. Name the Chicago White Sox righthander who joined the 300-win club and the California Angels star who collected his 3,000th hit.

2. Name the former Kansas City Royals star who in 1990 became the first player in baseball history to win batting championships in three decades.

3. Baseball's top all-time career basestealer also holds another distinction: He was Nolan Ryan's milestone 5,000th strikeout victim. Name him.

4. Name the San Diego Padres first baseman who dislocated his thumb while sliding into home during a July 29, 1983 game at Atlanta, ending his National League-record ironman streak at 1,207 games.

5. What former St. Louis Cardinals great joined the exclusive 3,000-hit fraternity and claimed the career basestealing record in 1979—his final big-league campaign?

6. This six-time batting champion enjoyed a record-tying two Triple Crown seasons—and finished second in the MVP voting both years. Name him.

7. Name the only player post-1900 to hit four home runs in a game that his team lost. The four-homer feat has been accomplished only one time since.

8. This Hall of Famer holds distinction as the winningest and losingest pitcher in baseball history. Who was he?

9. When Babe Ruth ended his career in 1935 with 714 home runs, he had more than twice as many as his closest pursuer. Name the second-place slugger who eventually would reach the 500 plateau and earn Hall of Fame distinction.

10. Baseball has produced eight 300-save pitchers, but only one has reached the 400 plateau. Name him.

Babe Ruth clearly was the home run king of his era.

The following initials fit players who are members of exclusive baseball clubs. Name the milestones they have reached:

1. P.R., T.C., H.A., S.M., T.S., C.Y., H.W., E.C., W.M.. N.L., E.M., G.B., P.W., R.Y., D.W., R.C., L.B., P.M., A.K., R.C.
2. J.C., B.B.
3. B.L., E.D., L.G., C.K., P.S., G.H., J.A., R.C., W.M., M.S., B.H., M.W.
4. C.Y., W.J., G.A., C.M., W.S., K.N., P.G., T.K., S.C., J.C., E.P., N.R., D.S., P.N., G.P., T.S., C.R., M.W., L.G., E.W.
5. P.R., T.C.
6. N.L., T.C., H.Z., R.H., J.F., C.K., L.G., J.M., T.W., M.M., F.R., C.Y.
7. B.R., H.A., W.M.
8. J.D., W.K., P.R., B.D., G.S., T.C.
9. C.Y., W.J.
10. H.A., B.R., W.M., F.R., H.K., R.J., M.S., M.M., J.F., W.M., T.W., E.B., E.M., M.O., E.M.
11. N.R., S.C., B.B., T.S., D.S., G.P., W.J., P.N., F.J., B.G.
12. R.H., L.B., V.C., M.W.

Getting serious

Peripheral Visions

The following plays recreate memorable moments in baseball history. One player was the focus of each moment, but others played key peripheral roles. Identify the peripheral players:

1. Game 3 of the 1975 World Series, 10th inning. The Reds batter, attempting to sacrifice, drops a bunt and hesitates in front of the plate. Red Sox catcher Carlton Fisk collides with the batter, picks up the ball and throws wildly into center field, setting up a key Cincinnati victory. Fisk's cries of interference go unheeded. Who was the batter?

2. Game 4 of the 1941 World Series. Two out, nobody on base in the ninth inning with the Dodgers leading the Yankees 4-3. Yankee slugger Tommy Henrich swings and misses at strike three, but Dodgers catcher Mickey Owen lets the ball get away and Henrich reaches first base. The Yankees break loose for four runs and an unlikely 7-4 victory. Who threw the strikeout pitch to Henrich?

3. July 17, 1941. Yankee center fielder Joe DiMaggio fails to get a hit during a game at Cleveland's Municipal Stadium, ending his record 56-game hitting streak. What Indians third baseman made two fine defensive plays to rob DiMaggio of potential hits?

4. Game 6 of the 1975 World Series at Boston's Fenway Park. Bottom of the 12th inning, score tied 6-6. Red Sox catcher Carlton Fisk hits a dramatic, game-ending home run, high off the left-field foul pole. Name the Boston

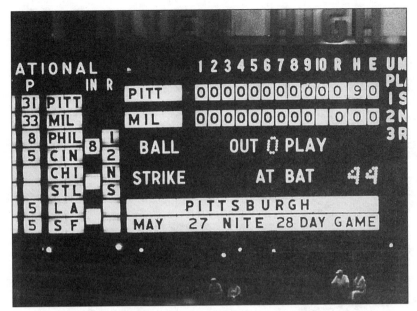

The scoreboard tells the story of Harvey Haddix's near-perfect effort.

pinch hitter who tied the game with a three-run, eighth-inning home run off Cincinnati's Rawly Eastwick?

5. Game 6 of the 1977 World Series. Yankees slugger Reggie Jackson ties Babe Ruth's fall classic record by hitting three home runs in a Series-ending victory over the Dodgers. Name the three Los Angeles pitchers who surrendered Jackson's dramatic home runs?

6. August 1, 1978. Two out, ninth inning, Braves leading the Reds, 16-4, at Atlanta Fulton-County Stadium. Pete Rose, trying to extend his National League record-tying 44-game hitting streak, swings and misses at a 2-2 changeup, ending the game. Name the Braves pitcher who struck out Rose.

7. Game 7 of the 1946 World Series. Bottom of the eighth inning, scored tied 3-3 and St. Louis' Enos Slaughter stationed on first base. When Harry Walker hits a double to left-center field, Slaughter makes his mad dash around the bases to score the winning run in the Cardinals' Series-ending victory. Name the Red Sox shortstop who hesitated on the relay, allowing Slaughter to scamper home.

8. May 26, 1959, at County Stadium in Milwaukee. Pittsburgh lefthander Harvey Haddix unveils the most incredible pitching performance in baseball history, retiring 36 consecutive Braves over a perfect 12 innings. But the Pirates can't give Haddix a run and his performance is scarred in the 13th when Felix Mantilla reaches on an error, Hank Aaron walks and the next batter hits the ball over the right-center field fence. Who delivered the only hit off Haddix?

By the Numbers

Baseball's all-time top 5 in World Series victories by a manager (through 1996):

1. Joe McCarthy   7
     Casey Stengel   7
3. Connie Mack   5
4. Walter Alston   4
5. Sparky Anderson 3
     Miller Huggins   3
     John McGraw   3

Yogi Berra

Did You Know

That Hall of Fame catcher Yogi Berra has collected 21 World Series rings—14 as a player for the New York Yankees, 1 as manager of the Yankees, 4 as coach of the Yankees, 1 as manager of the New York Mets and 1 as a Mets coach?

9. Game 5 of the 1956 World Series. Yankees righthander Don Larsen becomes the first pitcher in World Series history to throw a perfect game. Who was the Dodgers pitcher who allowed only five hits in a 2-0 loss?

10. September 15, 1969, at St. Louis' Busch Memorial Stadium. Cardinals lefthander Steve Carlton strikes out a modern-record 19 New York Mets—but loses the game, 4-3. Who hit a pair of two-run homers to hand Carlton the disappointing loss?

Memorable Numbers
Warming up

1. In the 10-year period from 1949-58, the New York Yankees won nine American League pennants. But their only 100-win season (103) during that period came in 1954—and they finished in second place, eight games behind what team?

2. In 1978, the only pitchers to beat this New York Yankees lefthander were named Mike—Mike Caldwell, Mike Flanagan and Mike Willis. Name the A.L. Cy Young winner who finished with a 25-3 record.

3. Two players have accounted for six of baseball's eight 100-steal seasons. One reached that mark three times for the Oakland Athletics, the other did it three times for the St. Louis Cardinals. Name them.

4. Baltimore, New York and Oakland won three American League pennants apiece in the 1970s. What team accounted for the 10th?

5. Cincinnati (4), Los Angeles (3) and Pittsburgh (2) captured nine N.L. pennants in the 1970s. What team accounted for the 10th?

6. Name the matchup for the only World Series in the 1950s that did not involve a New York team.

7. The years 1971 and 1983 have special meaning within the context of a 21-year period of baseball's All-Star Game. What was special about those two years?

8. The 1976, '77 and '78 seasons marked the last hurrah for Cincinnati's Big Red Machine and a resurgence for the Yankees and Dodgers. Name the teams that finished as bridesmaids in their respective leagues each of those three seasons.

9. From 1972-80, the Boston Red Sox produced the only American League batting champion not named "Carew" or "Brett." Who was he?

10. 1908, 1917, 1918, 1948 and 1954 were the last years that five of baseball's "original 16" franchises won World Series championships. Hint: Three are American League teams, two are in the National League.

The following dates and number sequences are important to baseball history. Identify the patterns:

1. 1955, 1959, 1963, 1965, 1981, 1988.
2. 1961, 1962, 1969, 1977, 1993, 1998.
3. 130, 118, 110, 109, 108, 107, 104, 100.
4. 190, 184, 183, 175, 175.
5. 1903, 1969, 1995.
6. 5,714, 4,136, 3,701, 3,640, 3,574, 3,534, 3,509.
7. 1946, 1948, 1951, 1959, 1962, 1978, 1981, 1995.
8. 54, 59, 35, 41, 46, 25, 47, 60, 54, 46.
9. 1894, 1896, 1932, 1936, 1948, 1950, 1954, 1959, 1961, 1976, 1986, 1993.
10. 1903, 1912, 1915, 1916, 1918.
11. .356, 36, 137, .343, 32, 114.
12. 1907, 1908, 1909, 1910, 1911, 1912, 1913, 1914, 1915, 1917, 1918, 1919.
13. 1941, 1947, 1949, 1952, 1953, 1955, 1956, 1963, 1977, 1978, 1981.
14. 1, 3, 4, 5, 7, 8, 9, 10, 15, 16, 32, 37, 44.
15. 1901, 1909, 1912, 1922, 1925, 1933, 1933, 1934, 1937, 1942, 1947, 1956, 1966, 1967.

Getting serious

Chapter 1 answers begin on page 287.

Mystery Guest

Can you guess the athlete and sport? Answer, page 286.

1. No, I was not born on a mountaintop and I didn't kill a bear when I was only 3. But, like that other Tennessean, I did find the path to fame and fortune. I call it good fortune because I've always been able to do what I want.

2. I've always been the best I can be and I don't intend to change. Even when I was a little tyke, I said my prayers, worked hard in school and got passing grades. Developing a winning attitude wasn't hard because I almost always won. My dad preached hard work and I listened to him at least once a week.

3. Baseball was one of my early religions. So were football and basketball. I was a standout in all three sports and my high school has the state championship trophies to prove it. I was armed and dangerous when I jilted my state university and warmed up to a college career that only Walter Mitty could have conceived.

4. I was a record lover in college and I dug Graves. When I threw caution to the wind, all America took note. My whole career was like a fairy tale—Sugar and Orange and everything nice. And when it was over, I claimed my biggest prize.

5. I felt like a statue at the professional level—I mostly just stood around and watched. Oh well, these things happen. I never could get into a groove and I got my first taste of life as a spectator. It was hard to take, but I look at it now as a learning experience. I might have spent a lot of time in San Francisco, but trust me, I didn't leave my heart there.

6. It's hard to keep a good man down, and I finally found my way back into the spotlight. After a few more years of study, I made out like a Bandit and played Devil's advocate en route to my dream job. Everywhere I went, young men wanted to meet me at the pass—and I was glad to oblige.

7. Who said you can never go home again? I did, sort of, and now everybody loves me. I'm not on the firing line any more, but when I speak everybody listens. The success I'm experiencing now is different than the old days, but it's just as rewarding. Maybe more.

8. Everybody listened to me last year and they're glad they did. We passed every challenge and brought our fans a long-awaited championship. Whoever said winning is everything was right on target. Now we'll try, try again. See you later, alligator!

2 Who Are These Guys?

Silhouettes in the Shade

Athletes often are identifiable by their throwing, running and shooting style, a distinctive swing or unusual physical features and habits. Test the hypothesis that a picture is worth a thousand words by identifying the athletes in their silhouette form on the following pages. Some will jump out at you and others will come after momentary study—or not at all.

1.

Chapter 2 answers begin on page 289.

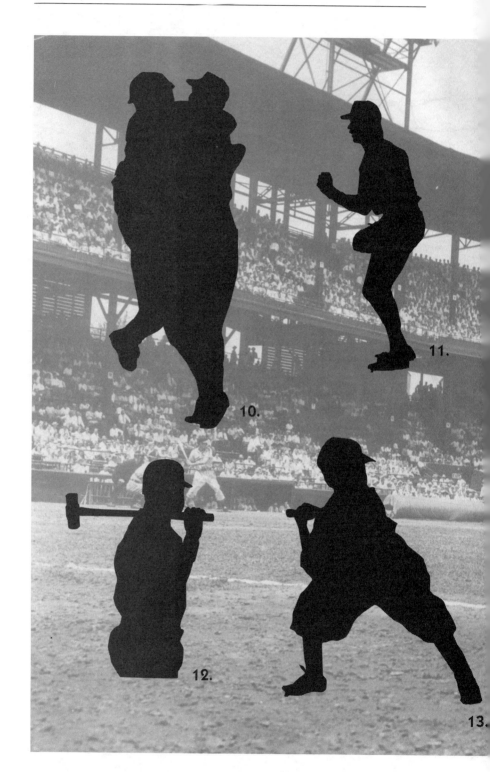

22.

23.

24.

28.

29.

30.

31.

43.

44.

45.

46.

51.

52.

53.

57.

58.

59.

60.

61.

62.

63.

64.

65.

66.

67.

68.

69

70.

71.

72.

73.

74.

75.

76.

77.

78.

79.

80.

Chapter 2 answers begin on page 289.

Mystery Guest

Can you guess the athlete and sport? Answer, page 286.

1. When I look back at my early years, I'm amazed at my naivete. My mom told me to shoot for the stars and I took her literally. It wasn't until my career had ended that I realized what she really meant.

2. There never was much doubt what I was meant to do when I grew up—the only question was where. And how well. I bounced around from college to college and my first year was a waste. My second was simply boring. I rebounded after that and passed every obstacle.

3. Magic was in the air on that wonderful spring day when my career really took off. I scored big points with all my critics and set the stage for a bright future. It was kind of fun being the center of attention, even though I really wasn't.

4. My roots are French but my luck is Irish. And no, contrary to popular opinion, I couldn't fly. I didn't need to. Some of my enemies could, but that didn't bother me. I brought them back to earth with hard work, determination and a will to succeed.

5. If you like championships, you should have hung around me. Life was one big Garden party during my career and my net worth grew considerably. So did my reputation and my flair for the dramatic. When I took my best shot, everybody listened.

6. I played inside. I played outside. And I weathered every storm. Sometimes it wasn't easy because a lot of my enemies were bigger than I was. But I never backed down. At least not until the end of my career, when I didn't have any choice.

7. I had a dream. And I had a team. When I combined them at the end of my career, they gave me a medal. Oh well. It was fun while it lasted, even if I missed more often than I succeeded.

8. I hate to brag, but I notice that my old team has hit the skids since my departure. And the Garden of Eden has been destroyed. I'm not sentimental by nature, but I do hate to see all that tradition bite the dust. It just makes me want to jump through the rafters.

Firsts

Warming up

1. This team defeated New Orleans, 33-14, for its first NFL victory, ending its record franchise-beginning losing streak at 26 games.

2. In 1973, Buffalo's O.J. Simpson became the first 2,000-yard single-season rusher in NFL history. Who became the second 11 years later?

3. The first coach in Cincinnati Bengals history had previously been the first coach for another franchise. Who was this Hall of Famer?

4. This defensive tackle became the Cowboys' first draft pick, their first member in the Ring of Honor and their first Hall of Famer. Who was he?

5. Quarterback John Elway has spent his entire NFL career with the Denver Broncos. But he actually was drafted by a different team. Name his "real" first NFL team.

6. Bo Jackson was the first overall pick of the 1986 draft, but he spurned his NFL suitor to begin a baseball career with the Kansas City Royals. Name the team that drafted him.

7. What team, quarterbacked by the legendary George Blanda, defeated the Chargers to capture the first American Football League championship?

8. In 1980, the NFL took its traveling Pro Bowl show to a non-league city, where it found a permanent home. Name the site.

9. On January 3, 1983, this Dallas running back recorded the NFL's first 99-yard touchdown run in a game against Minnesota. Name the record setter.

10. Name the two future Hall of Famers the Chicago Bears landed in the first round of the 1965 draft.

Getting serious

Each of the following names, sites and team matchups represent an important pro football first. Identify the event or accomplishment:

1. Beattie Feathers, 1934.
2. Jay Berwanger, 1936.
3. Cleveland Browns vs. New York Jets, 1970.
4. Cliff Battles, 1933.
5. Green Bay 35, Kansas City 10, 1967.
6. Joe Auer, John Gilliam, 1966, 1967.
7. Pete Gogolak, 1964.
8. Lionel Taylor, 1961.
9. Emlen Tunnell, 1967.
10. Michigan Panthers, 1983.
11. Broncos 35, Steelers 35, 1974.
12. Don Hutson, 1942.

By the Numbers

The NFL's first 10 1,000-yard rushers:
1. Beattie Feathers, Chicago, 1934.
2. Steve Van Buren, Philadelphia, 1947.
3. Tony Canadeo, Green Bay, 1949.
4. Steve Van Buren, Philadelphia, 1949.
5. Joe Perry, San Francisco, 1953.
6. Joe Perry, San Francisco, 1954.
7. Rick Casares, Chicago, 1956.
8. Jim Brown, Cleveland, 1958.
9. J.D. Smith, San Francisco, 1959.
10. Jim Brown, Cleveland, 1959.

Out Patterns

Warming up

Alabama QB Joe Namath spurned the NFL.

1. Who was the starting quarterback for Miami in Super Bowl XVII—a few months before the Dolphins grabbed Dan Marino in the NFL draft?

2. One Hall of Fame quarterback was the ninth-round draft pick of the Pittsburgh Steelers in 1955. Another was the 17th-round selection of the Green Bay Packers a year later. Name them.

3. When Joe Namath elected to sign with the American Football League's New York Jets in 1968, he spurned an NFL team that could have used his services. Name the team.

4. In the only Super Bowl appearance of Johnny Unitas' outstanding career, he came off the bench. Name his team and the starting quarterback he was backing up.

5. In 1951, Rams quarterback Norm Van Brocklin became the first passer to top the 500-yard single-game barrier when he buried the New York Yanks with 554. In 1982, another Rams quarterback joined the exclusive fraternity with 509. Name him.

6. What balding Giants star became the fourth quarterback to throw seven touchdown passes in a game? He performed the feat against Washington in 1962.

7. Name the former Cleveland quarterback who led the Browns to seven championships and 10 title game appearances—four in the All-America Football Conference and six in the NFL—in his 10-year career.

8. As a quarterback for the Redskins in the 1930s and '40s, he directed two NFL championships. But he also was an outstanding defensive back and record-setting punter. Name him.

9. Name the scrambling Chicago Bears quarterback who set an NFL season record in 1972 when he rushed for 968 yards.

10. Name the three quarterbacks who were picked 1-2-3 overall in the 1971 NFL draft. They were picked out of Stanford, Mississippi and Santa Clara.

Rams quarterback Norm Van Brocklin

Getting serious

So you think you know your quarterbacks? Find the common thread that pulls together the following groupings:

1. John Elway, Todd Blackledge, Jim Kelly, Tony Eason, Ken O'Brien, Dan Marino.

2. Dan Marino, Fran Tarkenton, Dan Fouts, Warren Moon, John Elway, Joe Montana, Johnny Unitas.

3. Sid Luckman, Adrian Burk, George Blanda, Y.A. Tittle, Joe Kapp.

4. Norm Van Brocklin, Warren Moon, Dan Marino, Phil Simms, Vince Ferragamo, Y.A. Tittle.

5. Cotton Davidson, Mike Livingston, Steve Fuller, Bill Kenney, Todd Blackledge, Steve DeBerg, Dave Krieg.

6. Bart Starr, Joe Namath, Len Dawson, Roger Staubach, Terry Bradshaw, Jim Plunkett, Joe Montana, Phil Simms, Doug Williams, Mark Rypien, Troy Aikman, Steve Young.

7. Ken Stabler, Steve Young, Mark Brunell, Jim Zorn, Scott Mitchell, Boomer Esiason.

8. Eddie LeBaron, Craig Morton, Steve Pelluer, Danny White.

9. Fran Tarkenton, John Elway, Jim Kelly.

10. George Izo, Joe Namath, Steve Pisarkiewicz, Kelly Stouffer.

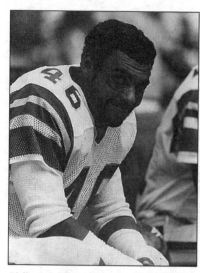

Philadelphia's Herman Edwards

Famous Plays

Warming up

1. Name the Minnesota Vikings defensive end who picked up a San Francisco fumble in a 1964 game and advanced the ball 60 yards to the end zone—only to discover he had run the wrong way.

2. Name the controversial Oakland Raiders defensive back who jazzed up a 1972 game against Green Bay by scooping up a Packers end zone fumble and returning the ball 104 yards for a record-setting touchdown.

3. What Chicago Bears running back scored on an 85-yard fourth-quarter punt return in a 1965 game against San Francisco, putting the icing on his record-tying six-touchdown performance?

4. With 1:05 remaining in the 1987 AFC championship game, this Cleveland Browns running back, apparently heading for a game-tying touchdown, fumbled the ball, ensuring a Broncos' victory and a berth in the Super Bowl. Name the running back.

5. Name the 1982 New England coach who waved the snow-plow driver onto the field to clear a path for John Smith to kick the winning field goal in a 3-0 regular-season victory over Miami at wintry Schaefer Stadium.

6. With less than a minute remaining and his team out of timeouts in a 1978 game at Giants Stadium, Philadelphia defensive back Herman Edwards picked up a New York fumble and ran 26 yards for a game-winning touchdown. Name the Giants quarterback who, under orders from his bench, attempted the ill-fated handoff when he could have fallen on the ball and run out the clock.

7. His playoff record-tying fifth field goal of the day, a 42-yarder as time expired, gave the Giants a 15-13 victory over the 49ers in the 1990 NFC championship game at San Francisco's Candlestick Park. Name the kicker.

8. Name the former LSU star who caught an 88-yard touchdown bomb from George Blanda, sealing Houston's 24-16 victory over the Los Angeles Chargers in the American Football League's first championship game.

9. When his wind-blown pass out of the end zone struck the goal post, the Cleveland Rams were awarded a first-quarter safety that proved to be the difference in their 15-14 NFC championship game victory in 1945. Name the unfortunate Washington quarterback who threw the pass.

10. With 20 seconds remaining in a 1996 Monday Night Football game at

Irving, Texas, the Cowboys angered Green Bay coaches and players by taking a timeout so their placekicker could boot his record-tying seventh field goal. Name the kicker who scored all of Dallas' points in a memorable 21-6 victory.

Getting serious

The following players were key figures in some of pro football's most memorable plays. Identify the famous games in which they occurred:

Green Bay's Bart Starr

1. Bart Starr and Jerry Kramer.
2. Terry Bradshaw, Jack Tatum and Franco Harris.
3. Joe Montana and Dwight Clark.
4. Roger Staubach, Drew Pearson, Nate Wright and Terry Brown.
5. Earl Morrall and Jim O'Brien.
6. Ken Stabler, Pete Banaszak and Dave Casper.
7. Johnny Unitas and Alan Ameche.
8. Garo Yepremian, Bill Brundige and Mike Bass.
9. Joe Scarpati and Tom Dempsey.
10. Joe Montana and John Taylor.

Milestones

Warming up

1. This former Cleveland Browns running back/turned actor led the NFL in rushing a record eight times.
2. When Jerry Rice caught his record-setting 101st career touchdown pass in 1992, he broke the pass-receiving TD record set by this former Seattle star three years earlier. Identify him.
3. Professional football's first 4,000-yard single-season passer performed his feat in the American Football League. Name the charismatic, strong-armed quarterback.

> ### Did You Know
>
> That the winning quarterback in nine consecutive Super Bowls—VI through XIV—wore uniform No. 12? Pittsburgh's Terry Bradshaw (4), Dallas' Roger Staubach (2), Miami's Bob Griese (2) and Oakland's Ken Stabler (1) were the Dirty Dozens.

4. In 1984, these two major single-season milestones were passed by the Dolphins' Dan Marino and the Rams' Eric Dickerson. Name them.

5. When Dallas' Emmitt Smith rushed for a record 25 touchdowns in 1995, he broke the 12-year-old record of this Hall of Famer. Name the former Washington star who ran for 24 TDs in 1983.

6. Fran Tarkenton, who ranks second in career passing yardage and touchdown passes, played two long shifts for the Vikings. Name the NFL team that employed Tarkenton between his Minnesota stints.

7. Until 1984, former Cleveland star Jim Brown held the NFL career rushing record with 12,312 yards. Name the three players who have since passed him on the list.

8. Name the Hall of Fame quarterback who threw touchdown passes in a record 47 consecutive games from 1956 to 1960.

9. Name the former Minnesota star who played in an NFL-record 282 consecutive games.

10. These two former Kansas City kickers rank 1-2 on the career field goal list. Name them.

Getting serious

The milestones listed below are followed by initials of the players who have reached them. Identify the players:

1. 100 career touchdowns: J.R., M.A., J.B., W.P., J.R., E.S., L.M., D.H., S.L., F.H.
2. 1,500-point career scorers: G.B., N.L., J.S., G.A., M.A.
3. 10,000-yard career rushers: W.P., E.D., T.D., J.B., F.H., M.A., B.S., J.R., O.J.S., T.T., O.A., E.S.
4. 40,000-yard career passers: D.M., F.T., D.F., W.M., J.E., J.M., J.U.
5. 250 career touchdown passes: D.M., F.T., J.U., J.M., D.K., S.J., D.F., W.M., J.E.
6. 750 career receptions: J.R., A.M., S.L., H.E., A.R., J.L., C.J.
7. 120 career sacks: R.W., L.T., R.J., R.D., B.S., K.G.
8. 4 career touchdowns in Super Bowl: J.R., E.S., F.H., R.C., T.T.
9. 20 seasons in NFL: G.B., E.M., J.M., J.S.
10. 4-time rushing champions: J.B., S.V.B., O.J.S., E.D., E.S.

Laugh-In

If Billie Jean King married Jeff George her name would be Billie Jean King-George.

Super Intense

Warming up

1. These three men have coached losing teams in the Super Bowl four times. Name them.

2. Name the first wild-card team to advance through the playoffs and win a Super Bowl. This team won Super Bowl XV.

3. Name the first team to appear in five Super Bowls. That distinction was attained in Super Bowl XIII.

4. What quarterback claimed Super Bowl MVP honors a record three times?

5. When Green Bay defeated New England in Super Bowl XXXI, it extended the NFC's dominance over the AFC to 13 games. Name the last AFC team to win.

6. The Buffalo Bills, four-time Super Bowl losers, had a chance to win Super Bowl XXV when this kicker missed on a game-ending 47-yard field goal attempt. Name the player whose miss allowed the Giants to post a 20-19 victory.

7. Name the Washington quarterback who fired a record four touchdown passes in the second quarter of Super Bowl XXII—a 42-10 romp over Denver.

8. Name the Dallas Cowboys linebacker who was named MVP in Super Bowl V—the first MVP chosen from a losing team.

9. Name the two Cowboys defenders who shared MVP honors in Super Bowl XII—a 27-10 Dallas victory over Denver.

10. Name the two men who earned Super Bowl rings as a player, assistant coach and head coach.

Getting serious

Winning Super Bowl teams are listed below with the contributions of a key performer. Identify the player:

1. Los Angeles Raiders (Super Bowl XVIII); 191 rushing yards, 2 touchdowns.

By the Numbers

The famous quarterback draft class of 1983 is 0-9 in Super Bowl appearances. Buffalo's Jim Kelly was 0-4 in the big game, Denver's John Elway 0-3, Miami's Dan Marino 0-1 and New England's Tony Eason 0-1. Ken O'Brien and Todd Blackledge never played in a Super Bowl.

Jim Kelly

Did You Know

That until 1985 when O.J. Simpson and Roger Staubach gained election, the Pro Football Hall of Fame had never inducted a former Heisman Trophy winner?

2. Washington Redskins (Super Bowl XXII); 204 rushing yards, 2 touchdowns.

3. Miami Dolphins (Super Bowl VII); 2 interceptions, MVP.

4. Green Bay Packers (Super Bowl I); 7 receptions, 138 yards, 2 touchdowns.

5. Dallas Cowboys (Super Bowl VI); 95 rushing yards, 1 touchdown.

6. Pittsburgh Steelers (Super Bowl XIII); 3 receptions, 115 yards, 2 touchdowns.

7. Oakland Raiders (Super Bowl XV); 13-of-21, 261 yards, 3 touchdowns.

8. San Francisco 49ers (Super Bowl XIX); 58 rushing yards, 77 receiving yards, 3 touchdowns.

9. Miami Dolphins (Super Bowl VIII); 145 rushing yards, 2 touchdowns.

10. Washington Redskins (Super Bowl XXVI); 18-of-33, 292 yards, 2 touchdowns.

11. New York Jets (Super Bowl III); 121 rushing yards, 1 touchdown.

12. Dallas Cowboys (Super Bowl XXX); 2 interceptions, MVP.

Don Shula shot down the Papa Bear's record for career victories.

Memorable Numbers

Warming up

1. How many AFC coaches directed teams to Super Bowl championships during the 1980s?

2. Before Don Shula claimed the NFL record for coaching victories in 1993, Chicago's Papa Bear, George Halas, held the mark. How many wins did Halas record in his four long stints as Bears coach?

3. What point totals have been compiled most often by Super Bowl winners and losers?

4. What numbers were worn by Hall of Fame quarterbacks Bart Starr and Johnny Unitas?

5. How many former players and founding fathers were inducted into the Pro Football Hall of Fame in its 1963 charter class?

6. Through the January 1997 game, how many Super Bowls have been played?

7. How many times did Kansas City linebacker Derrick Thomas sack Seattle quarterback Dave Krieg in a record-setting November 11, 1990, performance at Kansas City?

8. How many different head coaches have led the Cowboys to Super Bowl victories? Name them.

9. When Miami quarterback Dan Marino set his single-season pass-yardage record in 1984, he also set a record for touchdown passes. How many did he throw?

10. The Miami Dolphins were the first team to appear in three straight Super Bowls. What consecutive years did they reach the big game?

Getting serious

Associate the following numbers with an important pro football fact, player, coach or accomplishment:

1. 2,003.
2. 53$\frac{1}{3}$.
3. 73-0.
4. 82:40.
5. 17-0.
6. 63.
7. 275.
8. 347.
9. 5,084.
10. 0-4, 0-4, 0-4.

Bears coach George Halas (left) and quarterback Sid Luckman.

Did You Know

That former Minnesota coach Bud Grant caught 56 passes in his NFL playing career—and all came in the same season? Grant, an end, made all of his catches in 1952 for the Eagles before moving to the Canadian Football League.

Bud Grant

By the Numbers

Leaders in 200-yard rushing games:
1. O.J. Simpson, 6.
2. Jim Brown, 4.
   Earl Campbell, 4.
4. Ricky Bell, 3.
   Eric Dickerson, 3.

Seasonal Offerings

The following events and performances all occurred in the same football season. Identify the year:

1. ◆ A young quarterback named Warren Moon scored a pair of touchdowns and drove the Edmonton Eskimos to the winning field goal in a 26-23 victory over Ottawa in the Canadian Football League's Grey Cup final.

   ◆ Joe Delaney, an unheralded running back out of Northwest Louisiana, finished his rookie season in Kansas City with 1,121 rushing yards.

   ◆ New York, New York. The Jets (11 years) and the Giants (17) ended long playoff droughts by clinching postseason berths on the season's final day.

   ◆ The defending Super Bowl-champion Oakland Raiders, who had not been shut out in 15 seasons, were held scoreless by the Lions, Broncos and Chiefs on consecutive weekends.

   ◆ Six rookies—George Rogers, Joe Delaney, Lawrence Taylor, Ronnie Lott, Everson Walls and Cris Collinsworth—earned spots on the Pro Bowl squads.

   The year was: 1980   1981   1982

2. ◆ Colorful Bears coach Mike Ditka made headlines when he said Washington's Dexter Manley had the "IQ of a grapefruit" and knocked the Minneapolis Metrodome as a "Rollerdome."

   ◆ Washington "replacement player" Lionel Vital ran for 346 yards in three games and ranked 21st in the final NFC rushing statistics.

   ◆ Kansas City Royals outfielder Bo Jackson took up a hobby when he signed a five-year contract with the Los Angeles Raiders.

   ◆ Back-to-back kickoffs resulted in touchdowns when Atlanta's Sylvester Stamps ran 97 yards and the 49ers' Joe Cribbs answered with a 92-yard return.

Kansas City's Joe Delaney rushed into prominence with a big rookie season.

Chicago's George Halas, late in his fourth stint as Bears coach.

◆ Instant replay got the owners' thumbs-up for a third season.
   The year was: 1985   1986   1987

3. ◆ Controversial Dallas running back Duane Thomas called team president Tex Schramm "sick, demented and completely dishonest." He called director of player personnel Gil Brandt "a liar." And he labeled coach Tom Landry "a plastic man."

◆ While making his NFL coaching debut with the Green Bay Packers, Dan Devine went down in a pileup near the team bench and suffered a broken leg.

◆ Pittsburgh wide receiver Dave Smith, apparently headed for a touchdown after catching a fourth-quarter pass from Terry Bradshaw, spiked the ball at the 5-yard line and it rolled through the end zone, giving Kansas City a touchback.

◆ Jets quarterback Joe Namath, forced to make a touchdown-saving tackle during an exhibition game, suffered torn ligaments in his left knee.

◆ Based on a Louis Harris poll, NFL commissioner Pete Rozelle declared that pro football had replaced major league baseball as the nation's favorite sport.
   The year was: 1970   1971   1973

4. ◆ NBC, not wanting a long NFL game to delay its scheduled telecast of the movie "Heidi," drew the wrath of millions of football fans when it cut away from the last 1:01 of a Jets-Raiders contest that was decided when Oakland scored two late touchdowns for a 43-32 victory.

Did You Know

That Adrian Burk, the Philadelphia quarterback who threw seven touchdown passes in a 1954 game, was the back judge 15 years later when Minnesota's Joe Kapp became the last of five players to match the feat in a game against the Colts?

Minnesota's Kapp was no ordinary Joe.

◆ Chicago founder George Halas announced his retirement, completing his fourth and final stint as Bears coach.

◆ The Houston Oilers left Rice Stadium for the Astrodome, becoming pro football's first "indoor" team.

◆ The expansion Cincinnati Bengals made Tennessee center Bob Johnson their first-ever draft pick.

◆ Denver's Marlin Briscoe became the first black quarterback to start as many as five games in a season.

The year was: 1966   1967   1968

5. ◆ Notre Dame Heisman Trophy winner Leon Hart became the NFL's first overall draft pick when he was selected by the Detroit Lions.

◆ Chicago Cardinals quarterback Jim Hardy threw eight interceptions against the Eagles in the season opener and six touchdown passes against the Colts a week later.

◆ Los Angeles Rams receiver Tom Fears caught an NFL-record 18 passes, good for 189 yards, in a game against Green Bay.

◆ Unlimited free substitution was instituted, opening the door for two-platoon and specialization football.

◆ Curly Lambeau, founder of the Green Bay Packers and the team's coach since 1921, resigned under fire.

The year was: 1950   1951   1953

Double and Triple Vision

Warming up

Identify the teams that featured the following quarterback-wide receiver-running back combinations:

1. Steve DeBerg-Kevin House-James Wilder.
2. Gary Hogeboom-J.T. Smith-Earl Ferrell.
3. Chris Miller-Shawn Collins-John Settle.
4. David Whitehurst-James Lofton-Terdell Middleton.
5. Joe Ferguson-Frank Lewis-Joe Cribbs.

Bobby Douglass was not a Bear when he teamed with Galbreath and Muncie.

6. Mike Pagel-Bernard Henry-Curtis Dickey.
7. Bobby Douglass-Tony Galbreath-Chuck Muncie.
8. Richard Todd-Bruce Harper-Scott Dierking.
9. David Klingler-Jeff Query-Harold Green.
10. Jim Plunkett-Reggie Rucker-Sam Cunningham.

Getting serious

Now that you've warmed up with some of the more obscure passing-receiving-running combinations, try your luck with some of the more memorable groupings. Name the leading receiver and running back for the championship teams and quarterbacks listed below.

1. 1982 Redskins, Joe Theismann QB.
2. 1976 Raiders, Ken Stabler QB.
3. 1977 Cowboys, Roger Staubach QB.
4. 1969 Chiefs, Len Dawson QB.
5. 1989 49ers, Joe Montana QB.
6. 1986 Giants, Phil Simms QB.
7. 1983 Raiders, Jim Plunkett QB.
8. 1992 Cowboys, Troy Aikman QB.
9. 1968 Jets, Joe Namath QB.
10. 1966 Packers, Bart Starr QB.
11. 1987 Redskins, Doug Williams QB.
12. 1984 49ers, Joe Montana QB.

Chiefs quarterback Len Dawson had a nice supporting cast in 1969.

John Riggins (left) and George Rogers share an impressive NFL record.

Running In Place

Warming up

Name the AFC and NFC rushing leaders who match up with the years and teams below:

1. NFL, Cleveland 1957, 1958, 1959, 1960, 1961, 1963, 1964, 1965.
2. NFC, Chicago 1976, 1977, 1978, 1979, 1980.
3. AFC, Houston 1978, 1979, 1980, 1981.
4. AFC, Buffalo 1972, 1973, 1975, 1976.
5. NFC, Rams 1983, 1984, 1986
   AFC, Indianapolis 1987, 1988.
6. NFL, Chicago 1966, 1969.
7. AFC, Buffalo 1990, 1991, 1993.
8. NFL, Philadelphia 1945, 1947, 1948, 1949.
9. NFC, Dallas 1991, 1992, 1993, 1995.
10. NFC, Green Bay 1971, 1973.
11. NFC, Detroit 1989, 1990, 1994, 1996.
12. AFC, Denver 1970, 1971.

Getting serious

The following running backs are grouped because they are the lone members of an exclusive club. Match the groups with their accomplishments:

1. Tony Dorsett-Andy Uram-Bob Gage
2. O.J. Simpson-Eric Dickerson
3. Marcus Allen-Walter Payton
4. Walter Payton-Eric Dickerson
5. Ernie Nevers-Jim Brown-Cookie Gilchrist
6. O.J. Simpson-Walter Payton
7. O.J. Simpson-Earl Campbell
8. Eric Dickerson-Barry Foster
9. Eric Dickerson-George Rogers-Ottis Anderson
10. John Riggins-George Rogers

A. The only players to rush for 270 or more yards in a single game.
B. The only players to rush for 100 or more yards 12 times in a single season.
C. The only players to top 1,600 yards in their rookie season.
D. The only players to rush for 200 yards in consecutive games.
E. The only players to rush for 110 or more career touchdowns.
F. The only players with 13,000 or more career rushing yards.
G. The only players to make runs of 97 or more yards from scrimmage.
H. The only players to rush for touchdowns in 13 consecutive games.
I. The only players to rush for five or more touchdowns in a game.
J. The only players to top 2,000 rushing yards in a single season.

Chapter 3 answers begin on page 290.

Mystery Guest

Can you guess the athlete and sport? Answer, page 286.

1. As a skinny Illinois kid with demanding parents, I never had any big ideas. In fact, I never had many ideas at all beyond school, work at the restaurant and piano lessons. I did collect shooters, agates, pee wees and cat's-eyes, thanks to my one competitive outlet. I was the undisputed marble champion of Will County.

2. I wish I could say I was one of those all-everything high school athletes who had college recruiters knocking down their door. But the truth is I never played sports in high school—and they didn't have a marbles team. I was planning to play basketball my senior year, but a badly broken leg took care of that and I entertained ideas of studying for the priesthood.

3. I guess you can say I grew out of that idea. While my leg mended, my body expanded. So did my competitive desire. I decided to take my best shot and finally found a Ray of hope. Hard work, determination and my sizeable appetite for a challenge turned me into a college demon.

4. I always looked at the world through rose-colored glasses and it's a good thing I did because there was a war going on out there. My personal war was fought in the trenches and I took a lot of abuse. That's all right because it only made me tougher. I don't want to NIT-pick, but I usually got the last laugh.

5. I also got a lot of attention, everywhere I traveled. I was big—Babe Ruth didn't have nuthin' on me. I turned professional but changed Gears after one season. And it's a good thing I did. I recorded a big save long before that statistic became accepted. I was raw power in a world that operated on finesse.

6. How intimidating was I? People ducked when they saw me coming and people whistled at me with disapproval. They even changed the rules so others could bring me down, but I still thrived. When they threw something new at me, I simply would get mad and try to make a point. I usually won my battles, but then who's keeping score?

7. If you like rings, I've got more than the Olympic Games. I've also got the scars to prove that people picked on me. Oh well, I'm a big man and I can take it. I guess you can say I dished out a few scars, but what's an elbow or two? When I retired, I passed a bar and began a whole new career.

8. You might remember me in more recent time as the Commish. You know, back when life was as simple as ABA. But if you look back in history, you're sure to run across my name in the record books. The city where I played no longer has a team, but my old franchise is still going strong. And the trends I started still loom big in today's game, by George.

The Eyes Have It

So you're a travelin' man and a connoisseur of ballparks, stadiums and arenas where people play. If so, the images throughout this chapter should trigger instant recognition of venues past, present and future. If not, well most of them still should be easy to place. Identify the ballpark, stadium or arena with which the person, mascot or thing is closely associated:

1.

2.

3.

4.

6.

7.

8.

10.

9.

11.

13

12.

14.

15.

16.

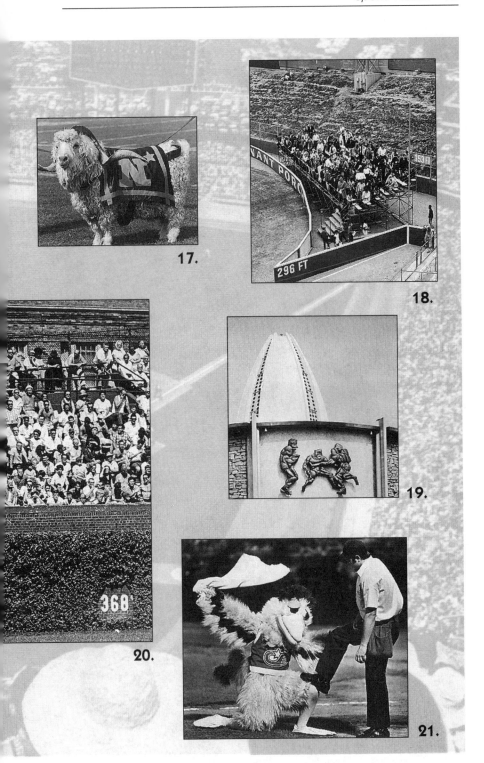

17.

18.

19.

20.

21.

This ballpark is a composite of 10 different major league stadiums—seven that are no longer in use and three active parks that were built before 1925. The elements range from obvious to subtle and include outside landmarks as well as architectural features. Identify as many of the ballparks represented here as you can and name the park that served as the base for the composite.

22.

23.

24.

25

26.

27.

28.

29.

30.

31.

32.

3.

34.

35.

36.

37.

38.

39.

40.

41.

42.

43.

44.

45.

46.

47.

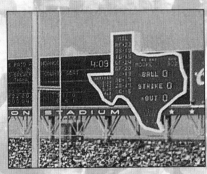

48.

49.

50.

51.

52.

53.

54.

55.

56.

57.

58.

Chapter 4 answers begin on page 292.

This ballpark is a composite of 10 different major league stadiums that still were being used in the 1990s. The elements range from obvious to subtle and include outside landmarks as well as architectural features. Identify as many of the ballparks represented here as you can and name the park that served as the base for the composite:

Mystery Guest

Can you guess the athlete and sport? Answer, page 286.

1. I guess it's only fitting that I'm a baby boomer because I grew up to become an adult boomer. And I had a blast or two along the way.

2. I don't like to brag, but I was an incredible high school athlete who lettered in baseball, basketball, football and track. In 1964, I heeded Horace Greeley's advice to "go west, young man."

3. I had it Kushy in the early years of my college career and received passing grades. But I really hit the jackpot after I got into the swing of campus life.

4. As a young and naive professional, I powered my way into the national spotlight with wondrous athletic feats and non-stop feuds with my mule-headed boss. If nothing else, give me A's for effort and perseverance.

5. My reputation spread from coast to coast in 1976 and I landed my first gig on Broadway a year later. I struck out a few times, but overall I was a smash hit. I stirred up controversy and emotions in the country's most infamous zoo.

6. I was so successful over a five-year run that friends and writers began addressing me as "Mr." My summers were OK, but I much preferred the fall.

7. I admit I was never an angel during my most productive seasons, but I was from 1982-86. After leaving George, Billy, Sparky and my other friends behind, I did some California dreamin' and joined the elite "500 Club" in 1984.

8. How do I look back on my career? I hit some moonshots, struck out more than any other athlete in the history of my sport, performed heroic deeds and never failed to excite the fans—in both positive and negative manners. Like O.J. Simpson, my glove never fit very well, but I more than made up for it with my charismatic play. Five years after my retirement, I got a standing ovation at Cooperstown.

5 Pro Basketball

Firsts

Warming up

1. Wilt Chamberlain became the NBA's all-time leading scorer on Valentine's Day in 1966 when he recorded his 20,881st point. Name the Hall of Fame St. Louis forward who was the first to reach the 20,000-point plateau.

2. The Pipers defeated the Buccaneers in the ABA's first championship series in 1968. What cities did the Pipers and Bucs represent?

3. On February 16, 1972, Lakers center Wilt Chamberlain became the first player to reach what lofty career scoring plateau?

4. This Boston player justified his selection as the NBA's first black coach by guiding his team to two championships in three seasons. Who was he?

5. The NBA's first three-time scoring champion also was the league's original superstar big man. Who is this former Lakers center?

6. The 1971-72 Los Angeles Lakers won an NBA-record 33 consecutive games. Name the Kareem Abdul-Jabbar-led team that had become the first to win 20 straight the year before.

7. On October 24, 1960, the Lakers dropped a 111-101 decision to New York. What was the historical significance of the game?

8. It seems only fitting that this Celtics marksman would win the first three 3-point shooting contests staged in conjunction with the NBA All-Star Game. Name him.

9. This red-headed former UCLA star guided the Portland Trail Blazers to their first—and only—championship in the 1976-77 season. Name him.

10. When the Basketball Association of America, the forerunner to today's NBA, began play in 1946, it's first game, ironically, was played outside the continental United States. What was the site of the BAA inaugural, which was won by the New York Knickerbockers.

By the Numbers

The top five left-handed scorers (ABA/NBA combined) in professional basketball history (through 1996-97):

1. Artis Gilmore, 24,941 points, 18.8 average;
2. Bob Lanier, 19,248, 20.1;
3. Gail Goodrich, 19,181, 18.6;
4. Nate Archibald, 16,481, 18.8;
5. Billy Cunningham, 16,310, 21.2;

Chapter 5 answers begin on page 295.

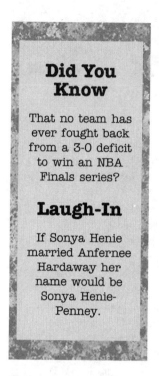

Did You Know

That no team has ever fought back from a 3-0 deficit to win an NBA Finals series?

Laugh-In

If Sonya Henie married Anfernee Hardaway her name would be Sonya Henie-Penney.

Getting Serious

Identify the following pro basketball firsts. Most of the descriptions contain subtle clues:

1. March 2, 1951, at Boston Garden. The NBA's star rises.
2. October 13, 1967. Oaks 134, Amigos 129.
3. October 12, 1979. Boston's Chris Ford earns a long-range niche in NBA history.
4. August 29, 1974. A young, young Virginian finds his Promised Land.
5. March 1, 1996. The No. 1 Hawk is grand.
6. October 30, 1954. A timely victory for the Rochester Royals.
7. April 13, 1957. A 125-123 double over-time thriller is the start of something big.
8. April 22, 1947. It's Joe Fulks Day in Philadelphia.
9. February 17, 1968. A big day for some dedicated people.
10. July 1, 1947. Beggars can be choosers.

Numero Uno

Warming up

1. In Wilt Chamberlain's second professional season, this Hall of Fame forward set an NBA single-game scoring record that Chamberlain eventually would top numerous times. Name the former University of Seattle star who scored 71 points in a game against the New York Knicks.

2. From February to April of 1996, this expansion team set a single-season record for futility. Name the team that lost 23 consecutive games.

3. Name the Hall of Fame point guard who averaged 34.0 points and 11.4 assists per game for the Kansas City/Omaha Kings in 1972-73, the only time in history a player has led the NBA in both categories.

4. Bill Russell played on 11 championship teams for the Boston Celtics. Name the Celtics guard who ranks second on the championship list with 10.

5. Only one player in NBA history has topped 2,000 points in a season 10 consecutive years. Name the record-setter, who is a current NBA power forward.

6. Which one of the following players has never led the NBA in a major statistical category: Dominique Wilkins, Chris Gatling, Bill Walton, Ernie DiGregorio, Patrick Ewing, Michael Cage.

7. This former Cincinnati Royals guard is the only player to record a triple-double in his first NBA game.

8. Name the only player to be selected in the first round of both the NBA and Major League drafts. He currently plays for the Golden State Warriors.

9. Name the New York Knicks forward who won his only scoring title in 1984-85, Michael Jordan's rookie season with Chicago.

10. Michael Jordan won seven consecutive scoring titles from 1986-87 to 1992-93. Name the San Antonio star who won in 1993-94, Jordan's one full season of temporary retirement?

Chicago's Michael Jordan

The following numbers carry a special significance in NBA history. Identify the significance or special memory associated with each:

1. 100.
2. 19-18.
3. 1966-67.
4. 50.4.
5. 16.
6. 72-10.
7. November 5, 1971 to January 7, 1972.
8. 38,387.
9. 12-1.
10. 7-foot-7

Getting serious

Uniformity

Warming up

1. Name two of the four players who have had the same number retired by two different teams.

2. Name one of the two players who have had different numbers retired by two different teams.

3. Two NBA teams, located a continent apart, retired the No. 1 in honor of their longtime owner. One of the teams is obvious, the other is not. Name the teams.

4. The New York Knicks retired No. 613 in honor of former coach Red Holzman. What is the significance of the number?

5. The Portland Trail Blazers retired No. 77 in honor of former coach Jack Ramsay. What is the significance of the number?

6. The Dallas Mavericks have retired only one number—15. Name the player who wore it.

7. In addition to the plethora of uniform numbers retired by the Boston Celtics, the franchise also has retired a "microphone" and the nickname "Loscy." Name the former announcer and player receiving the honors.

8. The Sacramento Kings retired the No. 6, but it wasn't to honor a player, coach or owner. What was the significance assigned to the number?

9. Name the former DePaul University and Lakers center who earned his way into the Hall of Fame wearing No. 99.

10. After sporting No. 32 through his career with the Trail Blazers and Clippers, Bill Walton changed in 1985 when he joined the Celtics. His new number was a real handful. What was it?

Getting serious

Uniform numbers have always given players a special identity beyond their names and skills. Provide a Hall of Fame name for each of the numbers listed below:

1. Celtics: 6, 14, 17, 33.
2. Lakers: 13, 22, 33, 44.
3. Knicks: 10, 15, 19, 24.
4. 76ers: 6, 13, 15.
5. Nuggets: 2, 33, 44.

6. Bucks: 1, 4, 33.
7. Bullets: 11, 41.
8. Pistons: 16, 21.
9. Jazz: 7, 35.
10. Hawks: 9, 23.

Did You Know

That on the November 5, 1971, day the Lakers began their record 33-game winning streak, Los Angeles players, coaches, front-office personnel and fans were preoccupied with the sudden retirement of All-Star forward Elgin Baylor?

Offensive Patterns

Warming up

1. Two players have won NBA Rookie of the Year and MVP honors in the same season. Name the former Philadelphia Warriors and Washington Bullets stars.

2. Only one player has won league MVP, All-Star MVP and NBA Finals MVP citations in the same season. Name the former New York Knicks star.

3. Name the only player who was a teammate of Boston Celtics stars Bill Russell and Larry Bird.

4. Chicago's Michael Jordan and Boston's Larry Bird are the only players to win regular-season and NBA Finals MVP awards in the same season more than once. Name two of the other four players who have earned this honor—in 1970, 1971, 1987 and 1994.

5. Four players have gone from an NCAA championship team one year to an NBA championship team the next. One went from the University of San Francisco to the Boston Celtics; another from UCLA to the New York Knicks; another from Michigan State to the Los Angeles Lakers; and another from Louisville to the Lakers. Name the players.

6. After battling in the 1979 NCAA championship game, former Michigan State star Magic Johnson and former Indiana State star Larry Bird renewed their rivalry in the NBA. How many times did Johnson's Lakers and Bird's Celtics meet in the NBA Finals during the 1980s?

7. After winning three consecutive league scoring championships in the mid-1970s with the Buffalo Braves, this player earned his first NBA championship ring as a role player for the 1981-82 Los Angeles Lakers. Name the former North Carolina sharpshooter.

8. Name the only player to win scoring championships in the NBA and ABA. He performed his feat for the 1966-67 San Francisco Warriors and the 1968-69 Oakland Oaks.

9. Name the only player to win rebounding titles in the NBA and ABA. He performed his double for the 1974-75 San Antonio Spurs and the 1979-80 San Diego Clippers.

10. Name the only player to win assist titles in the NBA and ABA. He won his titles in consecutive seasons for the 1975-76 Indiana Pacers (ABA) and the 1976-77 Pacers (NBA).

Getting serious

Each of the following groupings has a common thread. Identify what each has in common:

1. Dave Cowens, Artis Gilmore, Bob Lanier, Willis Reed, David Robinson, Bill Russell.

2. Frank Ramsey, John Havlicek, Larry Siegfried, Don Nelson, Bill Walton, Kevin McHale.

3. Connie Hawkins, Rick Barry, Spencer Haywood, Dan Issel, Charlie Scott, Julius Erving, George McGinnis.

Connie Hawkins

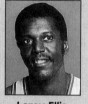
4. Wilt Chamberlain, Wilt Chamberlain, Wilt Chamberlain, Wilt Chamberlain, David Thompson, Wilt Chamberlain.

5. Larry Costello, Don Nelson, Del Harris, Frank Hamblen, Mike Dunleavy, Chris Ford.

6. Muggsy Bogues, Gheorghe Muresan.

7. Michael Jordan, Larry Bird, Magic Johnson, Charles Barkley, Karl Malone, David Robinson, Patrick Ewing, Scottie Pippen, Clyde Drexler, Chris Mullin, John Stockton, Christian Laettner.

8. Nick Anderson, Dennis Scott, Brian Williams, Stanley Roberts, Shaquille O'Neal, Chris Webber, Geert Hammink, Brooks Thompson, David Vaughn, Brian Evans.

9. Stags, Packers, Zephyrs, Bulls.

10. Bobby Jones, Jerry Sloan, Dennis Johnson, Michael Cooper, Tom (Satch) Sanders.

That's Final

Warming up

1. Only one player has recorded a 60-point game in NBA Finals history. Name the Los Angeles Lakers forward who notched 61 in an April 14, 1962, game against Boston.

2. With their 1997 victory over Utah, the Chicago Bulls lifted their NBA Finals record to 5-0. Only one other active franchise is undefeated in NBA Finals play, and its lone appearance came more than four decades ago when it played in a different city with a different nickname. Identify the current team.

3. Six different teams have swept opponents in a best-of-seven NBA Finals. But one team has been a victim three times—1959, 1983 and 1989. Name the team.

4. Name the only coach to guide two different franchises to NBA championships.

5. Through 1984, the Lakers had lost all eight of their NBA Finals matchups with the Celtics. Name the 38-year-old star who earned MVP honors in a six-game Finals victory over Boston in 1985, ending the 25-year jinx.

6. Name the teams that met in both the 1978 and 1979 NBA Finals, each winning its first championship.

7. Name the team that won three of the nine ABA championships.

8. This Lakers guard averaged 37.8 points per game in the 1969 NBA Finals—but his team still lost. Name the only player to capture Finals MVP honors for a losing team.

9. Before the Bulls won in 1991, this was the last NBA franchise to win a championship in its first NBA Finals appearance. The team has since lost twice in the 1990s.

10. The Boston Celtics have won a record 70 NBA Finals games and the Lakers rank second with 66 victories. Name the team that ranks a distant third with 23.

Boston's Bill Sharman

Getting serious

Each of the NBA championship teams listed below is followed by four-fifths of its starting lineup. Name the missing member of each lineup.

1. 1969-70 New York Knicks: Walt Frazier, Dick Barnett, Willis Reed, Bill Bradley.

2. 1966-67 Philadelphia 76ers: Wali Jones, Hal Greer, Wilt Chamberlain, Billy Cunningham.

3. 1956-57 Boston Celtics: Bob Cousy, Bill Sharman, Bill Russell, Jim Loscutoff.

4. 1971-72 Los Angeles Lakers: Jerry West, Jim McMillian, Wilt Chamberlain, Happy Hairston.

5. 1989-90 Detroit Pistons: Isiah Thomas, Joe Dumars, Mark Aguirre, James Edwards.

6. 1970-71 Milwaukee Bucks: Oscar Robertson, Greg Smith, Kareem Abdul-Jabbar, Jon McGlocklin.

7. 1978-79 Seattle Super-Sonics: Dennis Johnson, Fred Brown, Jack Sikma, Lonnie Shelton.

8. 1982-83 Philadelphia 76ers: Andrew Toney, Julius Erving, Moses Malone, Marc Iavaroni.

9. 1985-86 Boston Celtics: Dennis Johnson, Danny Ainge, Larry Bird, Robert Parish.

10. 1991-92 Chicago Bulls: Michael Jordan, Scottie Pippen, Bill Cartwright, John Paxson.

11. 1977-78 Washington Bullets: Kevin Grevey, Mitch Kupchak, Wes Unseld, Bob Dandridge.

12. 1986-87 Los Angeles Lakers: Magic Johnson, Byron Scott, Kareem Abdul-Jabbar, A.C. Green.

Seasonal Offerings

The following events and performances all occurred in the same year. Identify the year:

1. ◆ The Los Angeles Lakers and Milwaukee Bucks, weakened by the retirements of Jerry West and Oscar Robertston, sank to the bottom of the Pacific and Midwest divisions.

◆ The ABA's San Diego Conquistadors defeated the New York Nets, 176-166, in the highest-scoring regulation game in professional history.

◆ Larry O'Brien succeeded Walter Kennedy as NBA commissioner.

◆ The rebuilding Bucks changed the NBA's balance of power when they sent 7-2 center Kareem Abdul-Jabbar to Los Angeles in a blockbuster six-player trade.

◆ Portland player-coach Lenny Wilkens concluded his 15-year NBA career with 17,772 points, the 11th-best total in league history.

The year was: 1974   1975   1976

2. ◆ The Naismith Memorial Basketball Hall of Fame opened in Springfield, Mass.—the site where Dr. James Naismith invented the game more than three-quarters of a century earlier.

◆ Philadelphia's Wilt Chamberlain stunned fans and critics by averaging a league-leading 8.6 assists per game—the first center in history to lead the NBA in that category.

◆ The 76ers, unhappy with their inability to win a championship and Chamberlain's salary demands, traded him to Los Angeles in a blockbuster deal for three players and an undisclosed amount of cash.

◆ The NBA expanded its roster to 14 teams with the addition of Milwaukee and Phoenix.

◆ Detroit's Dave Bing averaged 27.1 points per game and became the first guard to lead the league in scoring in more than two decades.

The year was: 1966   1967   1968

By the Numbers

The winningest teams in the nine-year existence of the ABA:

1. Kentucky Colonels, 448-296;
2. Indiana Pacers, 427-317;
3. New York Nets, 338-328;
4. Denver Rockets, 288-288;
5. Utah Stars, 265-171;
6. Carolina Cougars, 215-205;
7. Dallas Chaparrals, 202-206;
8. Virginia Squires, 200-303;
9. San Antonio Spurs, 146-106;
10. Memphis Sounds, 139-291.

3. ◆ The NBA voted to expand to 27 teams with future franchise additions in Miami, Charlotte, Orlando and Miami.
   ◆ The NBA added a third referee for all games.
   ◆ The league reduced its annual draft from seven to three rounds.
   ◆ Rising Chicago star Michael Jordan claimed his second consecutive scoring title with a 35.0 average.
   ◆ Jordan captured his second straight slam-dunk championship in pre-All-Star Game festivities and punctuated his growing reputation with a 40-point performance in the mid-season classic.
   The year was: 1986 1987 1988

4. ◆ In a wild final-day shootout, San Antonio's George Gervin scored 63 points in a night game against New Orleans after Denver's David Thompson had scored 73 in a day game against Detroit, claiming the closest scoring title in NBA history—27.22 to 27.15.
   ◆ An unprecedented trade: John Y. Brown and Harry Mangurian handed over their Buffalo Braves team for Irv Levin's Boston Celtics.
   ◆ The Celtics, aware they would have to endure another difficult season before gaining his services, selected junior-eligible Indiana State forward Larry Bird with the sixth pick of the draft.
   ◆ Buffalo guard Randy Smith enjoyed an incredible All-Star Game performance—11-of-14 from the floor, 27 points and long buzzer-beating jumpers at the end of the first and second quarters.
   ◆ After being honored at every NBA arena in a grand farewell tour, Celtics star John Havlicek ended his 16-year career in an emotion-filled season finale at Boston Garden.
   The year was: 1978 1979 1980

5. ◆ Oscar Robertson and Jerry West, who would go on to Hall of Fame careers in the NBA, were the first two players picked in the annual draft of college players.
   ◆ Philadelphia center Wilt Chamberlain muscled his way to a still-standing NBA-record 55 rebounds in a 132-129 loss to Boston.

Buffalo's Randy Smith

Jerry West: A hot-shot draft pick out of West Virginia.

◆ Chamberlain's 23-point, 25-rebound performance stole the All-Star spotlight, but Philadelphia teammate Tom Gola clinched the East victory with four straight fourth-quarter baskets.
◆ The Lakers opened their first West Coast season with a 140-123 loss at Cincinnati.
◆ The New York Knickerbockers drew an all-time attendance high of 332,578 fans in 30 dates at Madison Square Garden.
The year was: 1959 1960 1961

Sites and Sounds

Warming up

Everybody needs a place to play. Match the following players and images to an NBA arena—past or present.

1. Parquet floor. Championship banners hanging from the rafters. Red, Russell, Cooz, Hondo and a Bird.

2. Showtime. Dancing girls. Jack Nicholson. Magic and Kareem. Purple and gold.

3. Madison Street. The Barton Organ. Blue-collar basketball. Michael and Scottie.

4. Small and quiet. 810 consecutive sellouts. 1977. Walton, Lucas, Hollins and Gross.

5. "The World's Most Famous Arena." Spike Lee and Donald Trump. 1970 and 1973. Clyde, Willis, Dollar Bill and Patrick.

6. Broad Street. 1983. Billy ball. Dr. J, Moses, Chocolate Thunder and Sir Charles.

7. A Clipper joint. Showtime with a blue collar. Billy Crystal. Danny, Loy and years of futility.

8. A Capital investment. The league's first luxury skyboxes. 1977-78. Big Wes, the Big E and big disappointments.

The Summit

Name the NBA teams that call the following arenas home.

1. The Omni.
2. ARCO Arena.
3. General Motors Place.
4. America West Arena.
5. The Summit.
6. FleetCenter.
7. Reunion Arena.
8. The Palace of Auburn Hills.

9. The Rose Garden.
10. Delta Center.
11. KeyArena.
12. Gund Arena.
13. Bradley Center.
14. Market Square Arena.
15. CoreStates Center.

Did You Know

That 1987 first-round draft picks Reggie Williams (Clippers), Muggsy Bogues (Bullets) and Reggie Lewis (Celtics) were once prep teammates at Baltimore's Dunbar High? Another Dunbar teammate was David Wingate, a second-round pick in 1986.

Reggie Williams

Muggsy Bogues

Reggie Lewis

Feeling a Draft

Warming up

1. In 1990, the Sacramento Kings became the first team in history to make four first-round draft selections, picking players from La Salle, Texas, Temple and Saint Louis University. Name two of the four.

2. In 1985, the New York Knicks were awarded the first overall pick in the draft's new lottery system. Name the player selected by the Knicks.

3. In 1969, the future of the Milwaukee Bucks franchise was determined by a coin flip. The Bucks won the rights to UCLA star Lew Alcindor (Kareem Abdul-Jabbar) and won a championship in his second NBA season. Name the coin-flip loser that ended up with the second pick and Neal Walk.

4. The draft had a sizeable impact for the Houston Rockets, who grabbed 7-footers with back-to-back No. 1 overall picks in 1983 and 1984. Name the Twin Towers the Rockets selected.

5. The Orlando Magic reaped the same kind of benefits when they used back-to-back No. 1 overall lottery picks in 1992 and 1993 to get Shaquille O'Neal and Anfernee Hardaway. But Hardaway was not actually a Magic draft pick. Name the player Orlando picked No. 1 in 1993 and then sent to Golden State in a blockbuster draft-day trade for Hardaway and three future No. 1 picks.

6. The Boston Celtics made a shrewd gamble in 1978 when they used the sixth overall pick on Indiana State forward Larry Bird, a junior-eligible forward who already had announced he would stay in school for his senior season. In 1987, an NBA team gambled with the first overall pick by selecting a player who would not be available for two years because of a military commitment. Again the maneuver paid big dividends. Name the 1987 NBA team and its pick.

Golden State draft pick Chris Mullin: Was he or wasn't he?

7. The 1956 draft yielded two important pieces to Boston's incredible championship machine—Tom Heinsohn and Bill Russell. But Russell was actually drafted by another team and obtained by Boston in a draft-day trade. Name the team that drafted Russell.

8. Only one of the following players was a No. 1 overall pick in the 1966-84 coin-flip era: Dave Bing, Elvin Hayes, Bob McAdoo, Darrell Griffith, Isiah Thomas.

9. Only one of the following players was a No. 1 overall pick in the 1985-present lottery era: Chris Mullin, Danny Ferry, Gary Payton, Larry Johnson, Alonzo Mourning.

10. Since Wilt Chamberlain played collegiately at Kansas, why was Philadelphia allowed to claim him in 1959 as a territorial draft pick?

Getting serious

The following groups, covering the first 10 years of the NBA's draft lottery, are listed according to perceived impact they have had on the league—in retrospect. Take a stab at re-arranging the names in their actual order of selection.

1. 1985: Patrick Ewing, Chris Mullin, Xavier McDaniel, Wayman Tisdale, Joe Kleine, Jon Koncak, Benoit Benjamin.

2. 1986: Brad Daugherty, Chuck Person, Roy Tarpley, Kenny Walker, William Bedford, Chris Washburn, Len Bias.

3. 1987: David Robinson, Scottie Pippen, Kevin Johnson, Armon Gilliam, Reggie Williams, Kenny Smith, Dennis Hopson.

Did You Know

That Kareem Abdul-Jabbar was born on April 16, 1947—the day the Chicago Stags and Philadelphia Warriors squared off in the opening game of the first NBA Finals?

Kareem Abdul-Jabbar

4. 1988: Mitch Richmond, Hersey Hawkins, Rik Smits, Danny Manning, Charles Smith, Chris Morris, Tim Perry.

5. 1989: Glen Rice, Sean Elliott, Danny Ferry, George McCloud, Tom Hammonds, Stacey King, J.R. Reid, Pervis Ellison, Randy White.

6. 1990: Gary Payton, Derrick Coleman, Dennis Scott, Kendall Gill, Tyrone Hill, Chris Jackson, Rumeal Robinson, Willie Burton, Felton Spencer, Lionel Simmons, Bo Kimble.

7. 1991: Dikembe Mutombo, Stacey Augmon, Kenny Anderson, Terrell Brandon, Larry Johnson, Steve Smith, Luc Longley, Brian Williams, Billy Owens, Doug Smith, Mark Macon.

8. 1992: Shaquille O'Neal, Alonzo Mourning, Christian Laettner, Clarence Weatherspoon, Tom Gugliotta, Jimmy Jackson, Robert Horry, LaPhonso Ellis, Adam Keefe, Walt Williams, Todd Day.

9. 1993: Anfernee Hardaway, Vin Baker, Chris Webber, Jamal Mashburn, Allan

Maryland star Len Bias (left) never got to live up to his lofty draft status.

Houston, J.R. Rider, Shawn Bradley, Calbert Cheaney, Rodney Rogers, Lindsey Hunter, Bobby Hurley.

10. 1994: Grant Hill, Eddie Jones, Juwan Howard, Glenn Robinson, Jason Kidd, Brian Grant, Lamond Murray, Sharone Wright, Donyell Marshall, Eric Montross, Carlos Rogers.

Odds and Ends

Warming up

1. Name the former Los Angeles Lakers star whose silhouette adorns the NBA's logo.

2. This well-traveled coach made NBA history when he became the first coach to direct two different teams in the same season. Name the man who guided San Antonio to a 21-17 record and the Los Angeles Clippers to a 23-12 mark in 1991-92.

3. On March 1, 1987, the Boston Celtics defeated Detroit and became the first team to reach this lofty victory plateau. What was the magic number?

4. This former 76ers star won three scoring titles in the ABA, but never finished higher than fourth in 11 NBA seasons. Name him.

5. When Lakers star Magic Johnson won the first of his three MVP awards in 1987, he became the first guard to win the award since 1964 and only the third overall. Name the Boston and Cincinnati stars who won in 1957 and 1964.

6. Name the Philadelphia forward who led the NBA in rebounding in 1986-87, becoming the first player 6-foot-6 or shorter to accomplish that feat since 1954.

Detroit's Dennis Rodman

Did You Know

That over the last nine seasons, Dennis Rodman has compiled more rebounds than points, and for his career he has collected almost twice as many rebounds (10,324) as points (6,225)?

Calvin Murphy (right) was short on stature, but not on ability.

7. Name the only two coaches who played on an NCAA championship team and coached an NBA championship team. They were teammates, both in college and in the NBA.

8. The San Antonio Spurs made a record 35-game improvement from 21-61 in 1988-89 to 56-26 in 1989-90. What was the biggest reason for that surge?

9. This talented playmaker has topped 1,000 assists in seven NBA seasons. No other player has reached that figure more than once. Name the NBA's top passing fancy.

10. When the Toronto Raptors began play in 1995-96, they became the first franchise located outside the continental United States since the league's inaugural season. What city did the 1946-47 Huskies call home?

Getting serious

List the following players from shortest to tallest:

1. Artis Gilmore, Shawn Bradley, Ralph Sampson, Hakeem Olajuwon, David Robinson.
2. Calvin Murphy, Dana Barros, Muggsy Bogues, Mister Jennings, Tiny Archibald.
3. Julius Erving, Dave Cowens, Moses Malone, Patrick Ewing, Walt Frazier.
4. Reggie Miller, Bob Cousy, Doc Rivers, Joe Dumars, Oscar Robertson.

We provide the conference, you provide the schools the players and former players attended:

5. Big Ten: Quinn Buckner, Ronnie Lester, John Havlicek, Derek Harper, Gary Grant, Greg Kelser.
6. Southeastern: Rex Chapman, Bob Pettit, Chris Morris, Dominique Wilkins, Dwayne Schintzius, Allan Houston.
7. Atlantic Coast: Sam Perkins, David Thompson, Cherokee Parks, Dennis Scott, John Lucas, Bryant Stith.
8. Big Eight: Fred Hoiberg, Anthony Peeler, Jo Jo White, Rolando Blackman, Eric Piatkowski, Wayman Tisdale.

We name the award, you name the only player who did not win it:

9. Rookie of the Year: Magic Johnson, Ralph Sampson, Michael Jordan, Patrick Ewing, David Robinson.
10. MVP: Kareem Abdul-Jabbar, Bill Walton, Moses Malone, Charles Barkley, Jerry West.
11. NBA Finals MVP: Jerry West, Rick Barry, Cedric Maxwell, Julius Erving, Isiah Thomas.
12. Coach of the Year: Cotton Fitzsimmons, Don Nelson, K.C. Jones, Doug Moe, Lenny Wilkens.

Chapter 5 answers begin on page 295.

Mystery Guest

Can you guess the athlete and sport? Answer, page 286.

1. I was born and raised in Florida, but don't let that fool you. I did my best athletic work in the Northeast and still consider that home. I have always been a straight shooter with fan appeal. That's an offshoot of my exciting style and boyish charm.

2. If you go back to 22 B.C., you'll find a reference for my incredible success. My fans considered me a miracle man and I must admit that I analyzed my accomplishments with more than a passing interest. I had the ability to jump-start my team and I was deadly from long range.

3. I broke through the starting gate my freshman year. Was I surprised? Just a little. I didn't view myself as a big deal, but I wasn't exactly living in a small world, after all. I was operating in a land of giants and sometimes they would try to step on me. But that was a catch 22 proposition.

4. In my college career, I had a ball—and more than a few airballs. I didn't always connect with my friends, but more often than not, we were on the same wavelength. It kind of got me down when things didn't go right. But I must admit, that didn't happen very often.

5. Some people considered me a deep thinker, but I don't agree with that assessment. I could be that way when I had to, but usually I just liked to pass the little tests and take my chances. I can see how I developed that reputation. I performed a few of my miracles when everybody was watching and I even calmed a hurricane when nobody thought I had a prayer.

6. Yeah, I was a media sensation. All America loved me and so did my eagle-eyed fans. Everybody wanted to give me a medal for my heroics, but I settled for a trophy. As a record collector of more than passing renown, I played a big part in my school's rise to national prominence.

7. The rest of my career reads like a short story. I played my Trump card and challenged the $6 Million Dollar Man, but that was a General failure. My next stop was a bear and I never felt comfortable watching Patriot Games. So I headed north and tried to put the fun back into my game.

8. In retrospect, the school of hard knocks has helped make me a bigger man. I was never afraid of height, but my critics seemed to be obsessed with it. My sport has given me a lot of wonderful memories and plenty of money in my pocket. And, of course, a statue that tells me I was the absolute best for at least one brief, shining moment.

☆ 1 ☆

onty Stratton

☆ 2 ☆

Joe Hardy

☆ 3 ☆

Roy Hobbs

6 Sports Movies

The following pages list names of characters from some prominent and not-so-prominent sports movies. Identify the movie and, if you're really sharp, the name of the actor/actress who played the character. The photos should provide an additional challenge.

☆ 4 ☆

Jimmy Piersall

☆ 5 ☆

Dizzy Dean

☆ 6 ☆

Willie Mays Hayes

Robert Redford put on a baseball uniform in 1984 and began filming one of the most famous baseball movies of all time. Identify the real stadium where action sequences for *The Natural* were filmed.

Chapter 6 answers begin on page 297.

Larry Semon (right), a talented actor/comedian who was popular in the silent-movie era, donned his best athletic attire in 1923 and asked one of baseball's all-time greats for his autograph. Identify the object of Semon's attention.

☆ 12 ☆
Billy Hoyle

☆ 11 ☆
Norman Dale

☆ 10 ☆
Jake Taylor

☆ 9 ☆
Harriet Bird

☆ 8 ☆
Annie Kinsella

☆ 7 ☆
Jimmy Dugan

☆ **13** ☆
Brian Piccolo

☆ **14** ☆
Gordon Bombay

☆ **15** ☆
Max Mercy

☆ **16** ☆
Billy Clyde Puckett

Robert De Niro (left) and Michael Moriarty teamed up in *Bang the Drum Slowly,* a 1973 film that focuses on the tragic relationship between two players on a fictional New York baseball team. Name the positions played by the De Niro and Moriarty characters.

☆ **17** ☆
Amazing Grace Smith

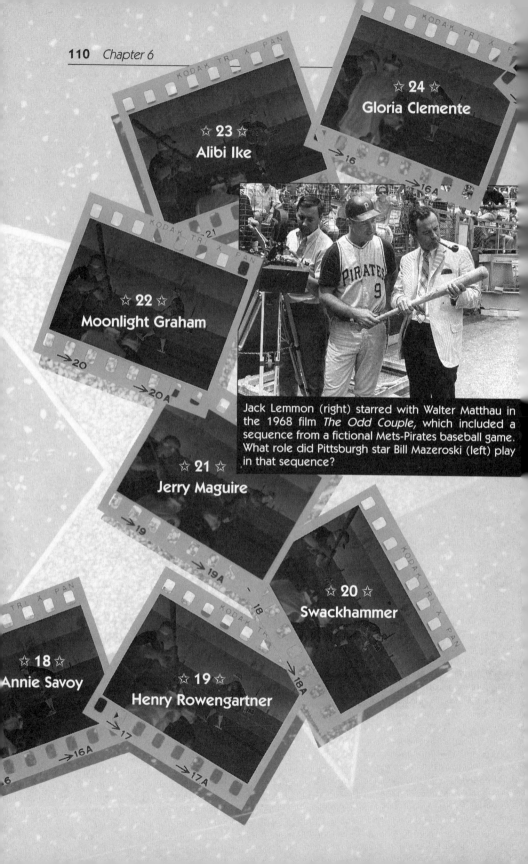

☆ 24 ☆
Gloria Clemente

☆ 23 ☆
Alibi Ike

☆ 22 ☆
Moonlight Graham

☆ 21 ☆
Jerry Maguire

☆ 20 ☆
Swackhammer

☆ 18 ☆
Annie Savoy

☆ 19 ☆
Henry Rowengartner

Jack Lemmon (right) starred with Walter Matthau in the 1968 film *The Odd Couple,* which included a sequence from a fictional Mets-Pirates baseball game. What role did Pittsburgh star Bill Mazeroski (left) play in that sequence?

☆ **25** ☆
gie Dunlop

☆ **26** ☆
Spearchucker Jones

☆ **27** ☆
Shooter

☆ **28** ☆
Dottie Hinson

☆ **29** ☆
Branch Rickey

Jackie Robinson (left) played himself in *The Jackie Robinson Story*, which also starred actors Minor Watson (center) and Richard Lane (right). What role did Watson play—to critical acclaim?

In a scene from the 1952 movie *The Pride of St. Louis,* Cardinals players gather around a fallen teammate. Name the pitching brothers, portrayed by Richard Crenna (sitting) and Dan Dailey (kneeling right), who were the focus of the film.

☆ **36** ☆
Rod Tidwell

☆ **35** ☆
Hans Lobert

☆ **34** ☆
Knute Rockne

☆ **30** ☆
Ty Cobb

☆ **31** ☆
Mickey Gordon

☆ **32** ☆
The Whammer

☆ **33** ☆
Tanner Boyle

☆ 37 ☆
o Paris

☆ 38 ☆
Ethel Stratton

☆ 42 ☆
Al Stump

☆ 39 ☆
Professor Vernon
Simpson

☆ 41 ☆
Neon

☆ 40 ☆
Barbara Jane
Bookman

Tab Hunter donned a Washington uniform in 1958 and led the Senators to great heights in the musical *Damn Yankees*. What price did Hunter's character have to pay for his success?

☆ **48** ☆
Moses Guthrie

☆ **43** ☆
Ron LeFlore

☆ **47** ☆
George Gipp

☆ **44** ☆
Paul Crewe

☆ **46** ☆
Lola

☆ **45** ☆
Monk Lanigan

The 1938 Western musical *Rawhide* featured some shoot-'em-up, saloon-brawling sequences that provided an unusual diversion for a famous athlete. Identify the athlete-turned-actor (white hat), who is taking his lumps in this photo from a room full of bad guys.

☆ **49** ☆
Bingo Long

☆ **50** ☆
Roger Dorn

☆ **51** ☆
Engelberg

☆ **52** ☆
Gavin Grey

☆ **53** ☆
Sidney Deane

☆ **54** ☆
Doris Murphy

In the 1962 film *Safe at Home*, Roger Maris (left) appeared as the affection of a young baseball fan played by Bryan Russell (center). Name the veteran actor (right) who appeared in the movie as the character Bill Turner.

Gary Cooper (right) and director Sam Wood (center) received plenty of expert instruction for *The Pride of the Yankees*. Identify the consultant (left) who had good, first-hand knowledge of the film's subject.

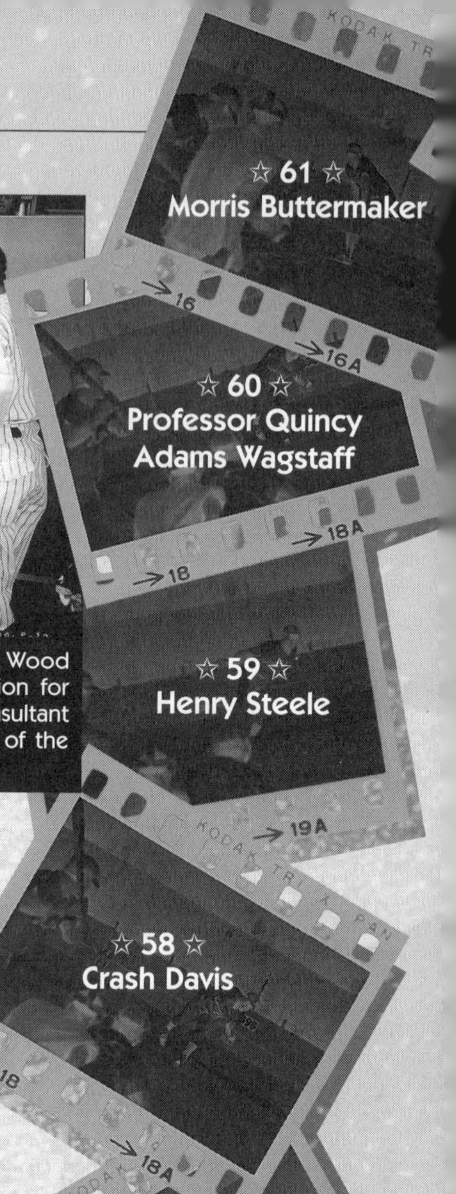

☆ 61 ☆
Morris Buttermaker

☆ 60 ☆
Professor Quincy
Adams Wagstaff

☆ 59 ☆
Henry Steele

☆ 58 ☆
Crash Davis

☆ 57 ☆
Montgomery
Brewster

☆ 56 ☆
Gale Sayers

☆ 55 ☆
Ray Kinsella

☆ **62** ☆
Paul Dean

☆ **63** ☆
Guffy McGovern

☆ **64** ☆
Rudy Ruettiger

☆ **65** ☆
Two-Call Johnson

☆ **66** ☆
Brother Mathias

☆ **67** ☆
Terence Mann

Actor Gary Cooper (left) receives batting instructions from major leaguers Babe Herman (center) and Lefty O'Doul (right). Name the baseball star Cooper was preparing to portray in a 1942 movie *The Pride of the Yankees*.

Will the real Babe Ruth please stand up? Former Yankees star Ruth (no uniform) advises actors from the 1948 movie *The Babe Ruth Story* as the man who will portray him listens (in Yankees uniform). Name the Babe Ruth wannabe.

☆ **74** ☆
Edwina "Eddie" Franklin

☆ **73** ☆
Larry "Pop" Cooper

☆ **72** ☆
Iris Gaines

☆ **68** ☆
Mae Mordabito

☆ **69** ☆
Warden Hazen

☆ **71** ☆
Myra Fleen

☆ **70** ☆
Babe Ruth

☆ **75** ☆
ge Halas

16A

☆ **76** ☆
Phil Brickman

→ 16

☆ **80** ☆
Applegate

→ 20

☆ **77** ☆
Jack Elliot

☆ **79** ☆
Rickie Vaughn

→ 17   → 17A

☆ **78** ☆
Reno Hightower

→ 18   → 18A

The real and fake Babe Ruths are charmed by actress Claire Trevor, who co-starred in *The Babe Ruth Story*. What part did Trevor play?

☆ 81 ☆
Bruce
Pearson

☆ 82 ☆
Shoeless Joe
Jackson

☆ 83 ☆
Pete Bell

☆ 84 ☆
Shake Ti

☆ 85 ☆
Paul Blake

☆ 86 ☆
Karin Kinsella

Actors Edward G. Robinson (center) and Jeff Richards (left) receive technical advice from Hall of Fame pitcher Carl Hubbell during filming of the 1953 movie *Big Leaguer*. What was the job of Robinson's character in the film?

☆ 87 ☆
nda Whurlizer

☆ 88 ☆
H.S./Halsey Tilson

☆ 89 ☆
Joy Piccolo

☆ 90 ☆
Kabakov

☆ 91 ☆
Pop Fisher

This actress, better known for her work in the movie *White Christmas*, donned a baseball uniform for her part in the film *Big Leaguer*. Name the actress.

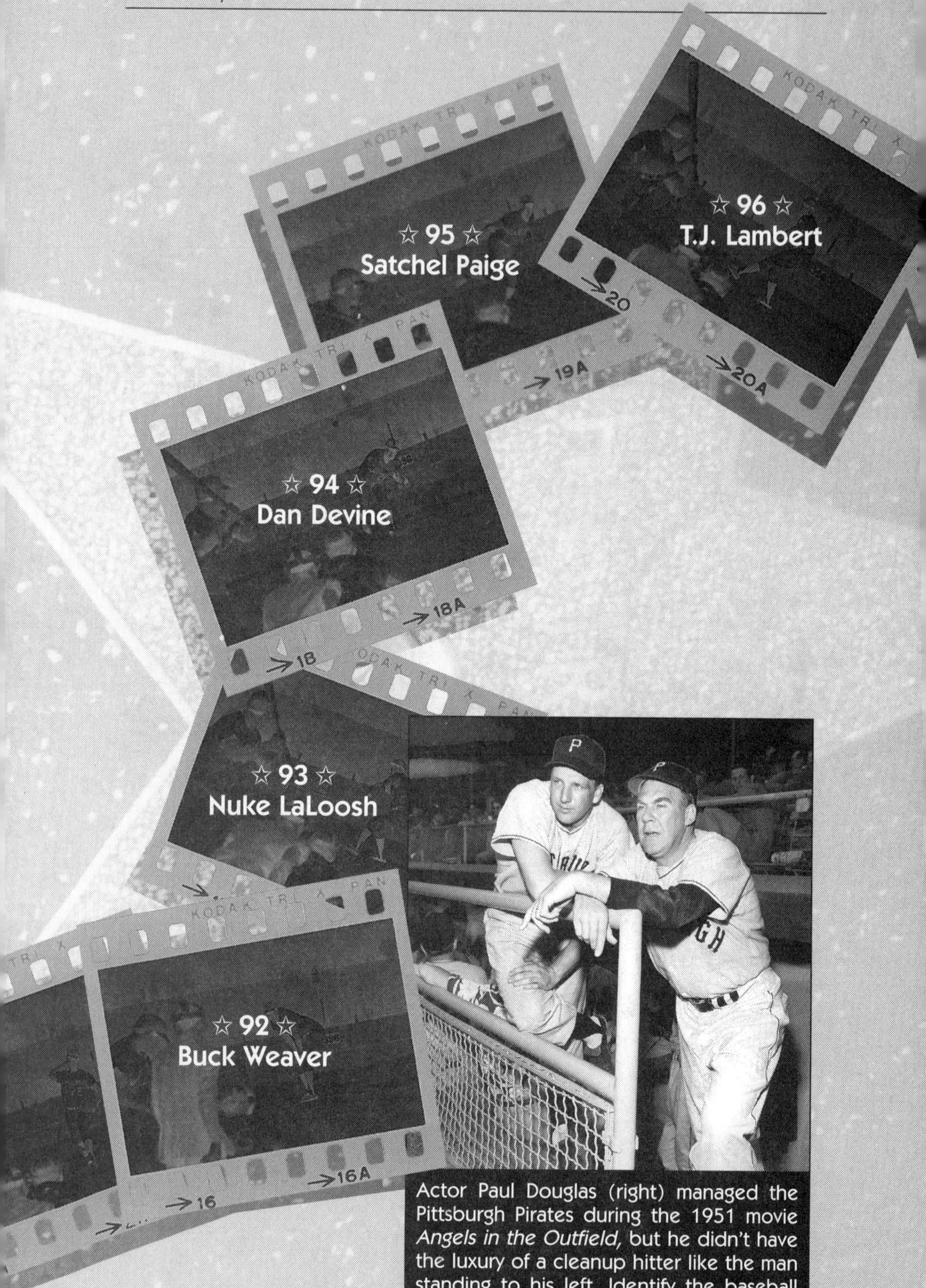

☆ 96 ☆
T.J. Lambert

☆ 95 ☆
Satchel Paige

☆ 94 ☆
Dan Devine

☆ 93 ☆
Nuke LaLoosh

☆ 92 ☆
Buck Weaver

Actor Paul Douglas (right) managed the Pittsburgh Pirates during the 1951 movie *Angels in the Outfield*, but he didn't have the luxury of a cleanup hitter like the man standing to his left. Identify the baseball star in the photo.

☆ 97 ☆
lly Leak

☆ 98 ☆
Coach
Sam Winters

→ 21

→ 17

☆ 99 ☆
Samson

→ 18

→ 18A

☆ 100 ☆
Spike Nolan

→ 19

→ 19A

☆ 101 ☆
Darren McCord

→ 20

→ 20A

Kevin Costner (left), Gaby Hoffmann (held by Costner) and Burt Lancaster teamed up in the 1989 hit movie *Field of Dreams*. What was the post-baseball career profession of Lancaster's "Moonlighting" character?

Jimmy Stewart (right) took on the role of baseball player Monty Stratton in the 1949 film *The Stratton Story*. Identify the similarly clad person on Stewart's left.

☆ 106 ☆
Junior Jackson

☆ 105 ☆
Jack Hanson

☆ 102 ☆
Jack Dundee

☆ 103 ☆
Jeff Hanson

☆ 104 ☆
Steve Hanson

☆ **107** ☆
Dean
ngblood

☆ **108** ☆
Henry Wiggen

☆ **109** ☆
Harry Doyle

☆ **110** ☆
Butch

☆ **111** ☆
Pete Maravich

☆ **112** ☆
Bobby Rayburn

Name the major league player, standing to the right of actor Jimmy Stewart, who played himself in a cameo for the movie *The Stratton Story*.

Chapter 6 answers begin on page 297.

Mystery Guest

Can you guess the athlete and sport? Answer, page 286.

1. Nobody could stop me during my three-sport high school days. But what the heck, Orrville, nobody can stop me now, either. Yeah, you could say I was a rambunctious kid with a mean streak—just don't say it to my face. No court where I live would convict me if I bounced you off the wall.

2. College was humbling, but I did develop a sixth sense about my future. While delivering in the

clutch, I studied and planned out my best career moves. Everything worked out fine. Professor Fred made us shoot for the stars—and we scored big.

3. Army life was good. I guess you could even call me an Army brat. My sergeant made me jump through hoops during basic training, but I turned the tables after a few years. The military life shaped my vision and prepared me for combat—and I am pretty good at it.

4. So you think you've got what it takes to be a champion? Come on over to my house and find out. But don't expect a tea party or a candlelit dinner. I might throw you a nasty stare or a chair if you promise to sit down and shut up. Like Patton and MacArthur, I think defensively and never consort with the enemy.

5. Some people call me a basket case. Others have wanted to put me in jail. But, believe it or not, I am a pretty popular guy and I do apologize when I'm wrong. I have a big family and my boys will do anything I ask. Sometimes I have to give them a little tough love, but the net results have been positive.

6. Hey, I know what I'm doing. I've got plenty of trophies to prove it. I've also got a gold medal and the respect of my peers. Well, most of them anyway. Dale might not like me, but that's probably because he's jealous.

7. There are more than 700 reasons for my success. But there are three really good ones. Do the numbers 76, 81 and 87 ring a bell? One was perfect. I'm sure Thomas and Smart Guy remember the others. Really, how could anybody forget?

8. OK, I admit it: I'm a real Hoosier. But don't hold that against me because I'm really a pretty classy guy. I might yell and scream a lot, but most of my boys will remember me fondly. And all that really counts is the final score.

The Great Ones

Warming up

1. Wayne Gretzky began his NHL career with the Edmonton Oilers, a former World Hockey Association team that entered the league in 1979. For what WHA team did Gretzky make his eight-game professional debut before going to the Oilers?

2. From 1980 through 1989, Gretzky won the Hart Trophy as the NHL's Most Valuable Player in every season but one. Who won the trophy in 1988?

3. During the 1983-84 season, Gretzky set an incredible NHL record for scoring points in consecutive games. How high did the streak go before the Great One was stopped?

4. On February 24, 1982, Gretzky scored his record-breaking 77th goal of the 1981-82 season against Buffalo goalie Don Edwards. What was his final goal total in that unprecedented season?

5. In 1985-86, Gretzky collected a record 163 assists en route to the highest single-season point total in NHL history. What was his record-setting point total?

6. The 50-goals-in-50-games milestone has been achieved only by a select few players. But Gretzky has done it three times. What is Gretzky's NHL record for most goals in the first 50 games of a season, a mark he achieved in 1981-82 and matched in 1983-84?

7. Most goal scorers are judged by their 50-goal seasons. How many times has Gretzky scored 70 or more goals in one campaign?

8. When the Edmonton Oilers shocked the hockey world by trading Gretzky to the Los Angeles Kings in 1988, much of the blame was placed on Gretzky's desire to relocate to the Hollywood area to accommodate his actress wife. Name her.

9. How many Stanley Cup championship rings does Gretzky possess?

10. On the list of 100-assist scorers in NHL history, Gretzky's name appears 11 times. Name the only other two players who have penetrated that select circle—once each.

> ### Did You Know
>
> That Andy Hebenton, a former member of the New York Rangers and Boston Bruins, played in all 70 of his teams' games for nine consecutive seasons—but never played a single game in any other campaign? His 630 consecutive games stood as an NHL record until Garry Unger broke it.

Chapter 7 answers begin on page 299.

Wayne Gretzky commands his own section in the NHL record book.

Gretzky is not the game's only Great One. We give you a former NHL great and the team he is most associated with. You provide the last club he played for:

1. Bobby Orr, Boston Bruins.
2. Phil Esposito, Boston Bruins.
3. Gordie Howe, Detroit Red Wings.
4. Guy Lafleur, Montreal Canadiens.
5. Ed Giacomin, New York Rangers.
6. Ted Lindsay, Detroit Red Wings.
7. Jacques Plante, Montreal Canadiens.
8. Garry Unger, Detroit Red Wings and St. Louis Blues.
9. Terry Sawchuk, Detroit Red Wings.
10. Bobby Hull, Chicago Blackhawks.
11. Marcel Dionne, Los Angeles Kings.
12. Brad Park, New York Rangers.

Boston's Bobby Orr

Net Worth

Warming up

1. Name the only goaltender to score a goal in both the regular season and the Stanley Cup playoffs.

2. Playing for a high-scoring team in the 1983-84 season, this goalie got into the act by scoring an NHL-record 14 points. Name him.

3. Name the Calgary Flames goalie who set an NHL record in 1993 by recording three assists in a 13-1 victory over San Jose.

4. Name the only two goalies in the last 20 years to record season goals-against averages under 2.00.

5. This goaltender complemented his 1.89 goals-against average in 1973-74 with an NHL-record 47 victories. Name him.

6. This Hall of Famer and six-time Vezina Trophy winner for Montreal was ambidextrous and wore catching gloves on both hands. Name him.

7. This goaltender got his name on the Stanley Cup as a member of the 1968-69 champion Montreal Canadiens. A year later, as a member of another team, he led the league with 38 victories and 15 shutouts to claim the Calder Trophy as the top NHL rookie.

Did You Know

That Howie Morenz, the legendary Montreal Canadiens star, died in 1937 of a heart attack while recovering at a hospital from a broken leg? Morenz, who broke his leg in a game against Chicago, suffered a nervous breakdown while hospitalized and died from the heart attack a month and a half after the accident at age 34.

8. Name the Hall of Fame goaltender who died tragically in 1970 as the result of injuries sustained in an off-ice fight with a teammate on his front lawn.

9. This goaltender is remembered in Stanley Cup lore for leading the Chicago Blackhawks to the championship two months before dying of a brain tumor. Name him.

10. One year after opposing each other in the 1964 Stanley Cup finals, these future Hall of Fame goalies became the first teammates to share a Vezina Trophy. Name them.

Getting serious

We provide the year and three of the top players from a Stanley Cup champion. You provide the goaltender who backstopped his team through the Cup finals:

1. 1975: Bobby Clarke, Rick MacLeish, Dave Schultz.
2. 1971: Peter Mahovlich, Yvan Cournoyer, Henri Richard.
3. 1990: Mark Messier, Glenn Anderson, Jari Kurri.
4. 1961: Bobby Hull, Stan Mikita, Murray Balfour.
5. 1989: Theo Fleury, Al MacInnis, Lanny McDonald.
6. 1969: Jacques Lemaire, Jean Beliveau, Dick Duff.
7. 1985: Wayne Gretzky, Paul Coffey, Jari Kurri.
8. 1955: Gordie Howe, Ted Lindsay, Alex Delvecchio.
9. 1940: Bryan Hextall, Neil Colville, Phil Watson.
10. 1992: Mario Lemieux, Jaromir Jagr, Rick Tocchet.
11. 1970: John Bucyk, Bobby Orr, Derek Sanderson.
12. 1986: Mats Naslund, Larry Robinson, Guy Carbonneau.

Expanding Horizons

Warming up

1. The NHL's 1967 expansion doubled the size of the league from six teams to 12. Name the two teams that were admitted to the NHL in 1967 but no longer operate out of the same city.

2. Name the future Hall of Fame goaltender who was the first overall selection of the 1967 expansion draft by the Los Angeles Kings.

3. In 1970, the NHL expanded from 12 to 14 teams with the addition of franchises in Buffalo and Vancouver. What East Division team moved to the West Division so that both expansion teams could compete in the East?

4. Name the 1974-75 first-year team that finished with an 8-67-5 record, the worst ever by an expansion newcomer.

5. The Florida Panthers finished with a 33-34-17 record in their 1993-94 expansion season, matching the 1-under-.500 feat

This former Hall of Fame goalie was the first overall pick of the 1967 expansion draft.

of an expansion team from an earlier era. Name the 1967-68 expansion team that finished 31-32-11.

6. The first all-expansion Stanley Cup finals, featuring teams formed after 1967, took place in 1975. Name the participants.

7. Name the only players to win the Hart Trophy (MVP) in the NHL and Most Valuable Player honors in the World Hockey Association.

8. What team captured championships in three of the WHA's seven seasons before merging into the NHL?

9. This goaltender became one of the first big-name stars to sign with the WHA in 1972, but contract problems forced him to return to the NHL before ever playing a WHA game. He went on to win two Conn Smythe trophies as a playoff MVP. Name him.

10. Name the only man to coach teams in the WHA championship finals and the Stanley Cup finals.

Getting serious

We provide the cities, you provide the nicknames of the following World Hockey Association franchises, each of which played at least 75 WHA games:

1. Birmingham.

2. Calgary.

3. Chicago.

4. Cincinnati.

5. Cleveland.

6. Houston.

7. Indianapolis.

8. Los Angeles.

9. Philadelphia.

10. San Diego.

The 50-500 Club

Warming up

1. Name the NHL's only father-son combination to notch 50-goal seasons and score 500 career goals.

2. Name the former 50-goal scorer who, like his Hall of Fame father-in-law Howie Morenz, starred for the Montreal Canadiens.

3. Wayne Gretzky and Mario Lemieux accomplished this feat three times, Brett Hull did it twice and Mike Bossy, Jari Kurri, Alexander Mogilny, Cam Neely and Rocket Richard did it once. Identify the requirement for membership in this exclusive club.

4. Name the Pittsburgh teammates who combined for an NHL first when they scored their 50th goals of the 1993 season in the same game against Edmonton.

5. Another NHL first: Name the St. Louis and Dallas players who scored their 50th goals of the 1994 season in the same game.

6. This high-scoring Edmonton trio set a record in 1983-84 when they each topped 50 goals. As if to prove that was no fluke, they duplicated that feat two seasons later. Name the players.

7. After starting the 1987-88 season with Pittsburgh, this player was traded to Edmonton and went on to become the first player in NHL history to score 50 goals while playing for two different teams. Name this 56-goal scorer.

8. In 1992-93, this member of the 500-goal club became the first NHL player to score at least 25 goals for two different teams in the same season. Name him.

9. Bobby Hull is one of two players to enjoy 50-goal seasons in both the NHL and WHA. The other player did it for Cincinnati of the WHA and Hartford of the NHL. Name him.

10. In 1996-97, this winger became the first U.S.-born player to reach the 500-goal plateau. Name him.

Bobby Hull was a 50-goal threat in any league.

By the Numbers

Players who have scored six or more goals in a game:

7—Joe Malone, Quebec, 1920.
6—Newsy Lalonde, Montreal, 1920.
   Joe Malone, Quebec, 1920.
   Corb Denneny, Toronto, 1921.
   Cy Denneny, Ottawa, 1921.
   Syd Howe, Detroit, 1944.
   Red Berenson, St. Louis, 1968.
   Darryl Sittler, Toronto, 1976.

Darryl Sittler

Getting serious

We provide the year in which a player notched his 500th career goal and the teams he (has) played for during that career. You name the player. Note: The team in italic was the one he was playing for when he reached the milestone:

1. 1962: *Detroit,* Hartford.
2. 1983: *Montreal,* N.Y. Rangers, Quebec.
3. 1970: *Chicago,* Winnipeg, Hartford.
4. 1990: *N.Y. Islanders,* Pittsburgh.
5. 1992: Edmonton, *Los Angeles,* N.Y. Rangers.
6. 1982: Detroit, *Los Angeles,* N.Y. Rangers.
7. 1974: Chicago, *Boston,* N.Y. Rangers.
8. 1986: *Edmonton,* Los Angeles, St. Louis, N.Y. Rangers.
9. 1973: Toronto, Detroit, *Montreal.*
10. 1996: Winnipeg, Buffalo, *St. Louis,* Philadelphia.

He Shoots, He Scores

Warming up

1. In 1968-69, this player became the first 100-point scorer in NHL history. Since that breakthrough, at least one player has collected 100 or more points in every season except the strike-shortened 1994-95 campaign. Name the 126-point scorer of 1968-69.

2. Who was the first defenseman to reach the 1,000-point plateau?

3. Name the former Toronto player who scored an NHL-record 10 points (six goals, four assists) in a 1976 game.

4. This team produced the top five NHL assist leaders and top four point men in one record-breaking season. Name the team and the year.

5. Name the Tampa Bay center who set an NHL first-year expansion team record (excluding WHA-NHL merger clubs) by scoring 86 points in the 1992-93 season.

6. Winnipeg's Doug Smail (1981), the Islanders' Bryan Trottier (1984) and Buffalo's Alexander Mogilny (1991) share the record for fastest goal from the start of a game. How many seconds did it take these three players to claim their distinction?

7. Name the Chicago Blackhawks player who scored three goals in a 21-second span of a 1952 game.

8. Boston's Bill Cowley set a record in 1940-41 when his assist total of 45 exceeded the scoring runnerup's point total. Cowley's feat has been matched only by Wayne Gretzky. How many times has the Great One's season assist total either matched or topped everybody else's point total?

Islanders star Bryan Trottier struck quickly in a 1984 game.

9. In a 1977 game, this Toronto player became the first defenseman to score five goals in a game. Name him.

10. This Hall of Famer scored seven goals for the Quebec Nordiques in a 1920 game against Toronto—a record that never has been matched. Name the player.

11. This player holds the WHA record for career goals with 316—13 more than Bobby Hull. Name him.

12. What goal-scoring distinction is shared by Wayne Gretzky, Pat LaFontaine, Pierre Larouche, Alexander Mogilny and Teemu Selanne?

13. What distinction is shared by Billy Smith, Ron Hextall, Chris Osgood and Martin Brodeur?

14. In 1991-92, this Pittsburgh winger became the first NHL player to record 50 goals, 100 points and 200 penalty minutes in the same season. Name him.

15. Name the player who, after jumping directly from high school to the NHL in 1981-82, became the first U.S.-born player to score 50 goals in a season. He accomplished his feat for Washington in 1984-85.

Getting serious

We provide the names of 12 players, arranged in order of the games they needed (fewest to most) to score their 1,000th points. See if you can rearrange them chronologically from the date when they reached that milestone:

1. Wayne Gretzky
2. Mario Lemieux.
3. Mike Bossy.
4. Peter Stastny.
5. Steve Yzerman.
6. Paul Coffey.

7. Bernie Federko.
8. Bobby Clarke.
9. Gordie Howe.
10. Steve Larmer.
11. Rod Gilbert.
12. Henri Richard.

Rangers 1,000-point scorer Rod Gilbert

What's My Line

Warming up

Each of the following NHL franchises had at least one previous home. Identify the city name and nickname the team used immediately before its move to the city listed below:

1. Phoenix Coyotes.
2. Colorado Avalanche.
3. Dallas Stars.
4. New Jersey Devils.
5. Colorado Rockies.
6. Calgary Flames.
7. St. Louis Eagles.
8. Cleveland Barons.

Clark Gillies and Mike Bossy formed two-thirds of a famous line.

Getting serious

We provide the players who combined on some of the most famous lines in NHL history. You provide the line's colorful nickname:

1. Rick Martin-Gilbert Perreault-Rene Robert.
2. Ted Lindsay-Sid Abel-Gordie Howe.
3. Vic Hadfield-Jean Ratelle-Rod Gilbert.
4. Pit Martin-Jim Pappin-Dennis Hull.
5. Dave Taylor-Marcel Dionne-Charlie Simmer.
6. Bobby Hull-Bill Hay-Murray Balfour.
7. Reggie Leach-Bobby Clarke-Bill Barber.
8. Clark Gillies-Bryan Trottier-Mike Bossy.
9. Charlie Conacher-Joe Primeau-Busher Jackson.
10. John LeClair-Eric Lindros-Mikael Renberg.

Did You Know

That Brian Lawton and Mike Modano, the only U.S.-born players to be selected first overall in the NHL draft, were picked five years apart by the same team? Lawton was selected in 1983 and Modano in 1988 by Minnesota.

This Vezina-winning Philadelphia goaltender died in an automobile accident after 157 NHL games.

A Trophy Case

Warming up

1. Name the only player to win both the Hart (MVP) and Masterton (perseverance, sportsmanship and dedication) trophies in the same season.

2. This former Chicago star is the only player in history to win the Hart (MVP), Art Ross (scoring) and Lady Byng (sportsmanship) trophies in the same year—and he did it in consecutive seasons. Name him.

3. This current NHL general manager was the first player from a post-1967-68 expansion team to win a Hart Trophy (MVP) and he added two more in the next three years. Name him.

4. New York's Andy Bathgate (1961-62) and Edmonton's Wayne Gretzky (1979-80) were the first players to tie for the NHL scoring lead and not win the Art Ross Trophy—because ties are broken by most goals. Name the player who joined that exclusive club in the 1994-95 season.

5. The Bill Masterton Trophy is named for a player who died as the result of injuries suffered in a 1968 game. Name the team Masterton played for at the time of his death.

6. This Philadelphia goaltender became the first European player to win a Vezina Trophy in 1984-85, but his career ended after only 157 games when he died in an automobile accident. Name him.

7. Name the American-born goaltender who made the jump from high school to the Buffalo Sabres in 1983-84 and won the Calder (top rookie) and Vezina trophies in a startling debut.

8. Name the goaltender who won the Conn Smythe Trophy as the Stanley Cup playoffs MVP a year BEFORE he won the Calder Memorial Trophy as rookie of the year.

9. Name the Chicago goaltender who won the Hart Memorial Trophy (MVP) in 1954, even though his 3.23 goals-against average was the worst in the league among regular goalies and his Blackhawks finished the season with a 12-51-7 record.

10. These goaltending teammates for Montreal shared the Vezina Trophy for three consecutive seasons, 1976-77 to 1978-79. Name the stingy tandem.

Any discussion of hockey trophies includes the name Gordie Howe.

Getting serious

We provide a category and the initials of players who fit into it. You provide the names:

1. Players who have won the Art Ross Trophy (given to the annual scoring leader) four or more times: W.G., G.H., M.L., P.E., S.M.

2. Players who have won the Hart (MVP) and Conn Smythe (playoff MVP) trophies in the same season: B.O., G.L., W.G.

3. The only players to win a Conn Smythe Trophy while playing for a team that did not win the Stanley Cup: R.C., G.H., R.L., R.H.

Did You Know

That the Rangers had another New York competitor before World War II? The New York Americans ceased operations in 1942.

4. The last teammates to finish first and second in voting for the Calder Memorial Trophy (rookie of the year): B.T., G.R.

5. Goaltenders who have won or shared the Vezina Trophy four or more times: J.P., B.D., K.D., B.L., T.S., T.T.

By the Numbers

The first five players to reach the NHL's 500-goal milestone:

1. Rocket Richard.
2. Gordie Howe.
3. Bobby Hull.
4. Jean Beliveau.
5. Frank Mahovlich.

Rocket Richard

6. Players who have won Hart (MVP) and Lady Byng (sportsmanship) trophies in the same season: B.O., B.H., S.M., W.G.

7. Defensemen who have won the James Norris Memorial Trophy five or more times: B.O., D.H., R.B.

8. Overall No. 1 draft picks who went on to win the Calder Memorial Trophy as rookie of the year: G.P., D.P., B.S., D.H., M.L., B.B.

9. Players who have won the Hart Trophy (MVP) three or more times: W.G., G.H., E.S., B.C., M.L., H.M., B.O.

10. Players who won the Art Ross Trophy (scoring) and Conn Smythe Trophy (playoff MVP) in the same season: B.O., G.L., W.G., M.L.

Good Lord, Stanley

Warming up

1. Name the last team to sweep the Stanley Cup finals in consecutive years.

2. Name the last year in which no Canadian team qualified for the Stanley Cup playoffs.

3. Name the only player to win an Olympic gold medal and Stanley Cup championship in the same season. Hint: He was a New York Islanders defenseman.

4. The 1919 Stanley Cup finals between the Montreal Canadiens and Seattle of the Pacific Coast Hockey Association ended prematurely with the series knotted at 2-2-1. Why was it called off?

5. After a 10-game, one-goal 1985-86 regular season, this Montreal winger exploded for 10 playoff goals, including a Game 4 winner in the finals against Calgary. Name the surprise hero.

6. Name the only player to take two penalty shots in Stanley Cup playoff history. He did it for Detroit in 1988 and Edmonton in 1990.

7. Name the only goaltender to face more than one penalty shot in Stanley Cup finals play—and he did it two days apart in 1985.

8. This Toronto player scored the winning goal in sudden-death overtime to clinch the 1951 Stanley Cup championship. A few months later, he died in a plane crash. Name him.

9. What "Original Six" team endured four consecutive sweeps and a playoff-record 16-game losing streak before finally winning a game in 1980?

10. This New York Islanders rookie scored the fastest two goals at the beginning of a period in a Stanley Cup playoff game—at 13 and 35 seconds of the third stanza—against the Edmonton Oilers in 1984. Name him.

Did You Know

That the 1987-88 Edmonton Oilers swept their
Stanley Cup finals series against Boston—in five games?
The fourth game was halted at 3-3 late in the second
period when Boston Garden went dark because of
an electrical malfunction.

Getting serious

Identify the franchises to which the following statements about the
Stanley Cup finals apply:

1. 23-for-32.

2. 36-year Cup drought through 1996-97 season.

3. 0-12 in three appearances.

4. 2-for-3 before folding in 1938.

5. 4 total championships, won in consecutive years.

6. 30-year Cup finals drought through 1996-97.

7. Appeared in 10 consecutive Cup finals, 1951-60.

8. Losers in last five Cup finals appearances.

9. 5 victories, 1 loss in eight-year span.

10. Perfection! Undefeated in only two Cup appearances.

Behind the Bench

Warming up

1. This long-time coach is one of three to win four consecutive Stanley
Cup titles and the only man ever to watch his team get swept in three
straight finals. Name him.

2. Name the only coach to win back-to-back Stanley Cup championships
with different teams. He won with Chicago in 1934 and the Montreal
Maroons in 1935.

3. After losing in the finals of the 1954 and 1955 Stanley Cup playoffs, this
coach reeled off a record string of five consecutive championships. Name
him.

4. Name the coach who died of brain cancer six months after leading his
team to the Stanley Cup championship.

5. After guiding the Chicago Blackhawks in their inaugural 1926-27 season
and getting fired, this outraged coach put a hex on the franchise. Name him.

6. When his only goaltender was injured midway through Game 2 of the
1928 Stanley Cup finals, this 44-year-old New York Rangers coach put on the
pads and backstopped his team to a 2-1 overtime victory. Name the gray-
beard coach/goaltender.

Did You Know

That Warren Young, a journeyman left winger who scored only 72 career goals, notched 40 of them as the Pittsburgh linemate of Mario Lemieux during Lemieux's Calder-winning rookie season of 1984-85?

7. After finishing the 1948-49 regular season with a 22-25-13 record, the Toronto Maple Leafs rolled through the playoffs, swept Detroit in the finals and joined the 1937-38 Chicago Blackhawks as the only teams to win the Stanley Cup championship with a sub-.500 record. Name the coach who guided the Leafs to a third straight title.

8. Name the Montreal Canadiens player who was hired as coach for the 1939-40 season, only to drown in the summer before getting his first chance behind the bench.

9. In 1937-38, this rookie Chicago boss became the first U.S.-born coach to guide his team to a Stanley Cup championship. Before his only full season as coach, he was an NHL referee. After the championship season, he became a prominent baseball umpire in the National League. Name him.

10. Name the gold medal-winning 1980 U.S. Olympic hockey coach who later guided the New York Rangers and Minnesota North Stars.

Getting serious

So you think you know your coaches? The top 20 in NHL career victories were used to compose the following groups of three. Name the team the coaches in each group have in common:

1. Jacques Demers-Mike Keenan-Scotty Bowman.
2. Emile Francis-Mike Keenan-Fred Shero.
3. Dick Irvin-Bob Pulford-Sid Abel.
4. Scotty Bowman-Bob Berry-Dick Irvin.
5. Jack Adams-Jacques Demers-Bryan Murray.
6. Punch Imlach-Roger Neilson-Billy Reay.
7. Mike Keenan-Pat Quinn-Fred Shero.
8. Scotty Bowman-Punch Imlach-Roger Neilson.
9. Bob Berry-Bob Pulford-Pat Quinn.
10. Sid Abel-Al Arbour-Bob Berry.

Montreal legend Toe Blake coached the Canadiens to eight Stanley Cup championships.

Chapter 7 answers begin on page 299.

Mystery Guest

Can you guess the athlete and sport? Answer, page 286.

1. My father was a real Buckeroo, so it was only natural for me to follow in his footsteps. All I've ever wanted to do is take my best shot and I've been fortunate to get the opportunities. Dad got me started in the business, but I have thrived through hard work and determination—qualities that I did not possess in the early years.

2. Size, power and speed—I guess you could say I had superstar written all over me. And I have a mean streak, to boot. I never get mad at anybody, I just get even. Blockers see me coming and cringe. But rush-hour in my business is the best time of day. That's when I do my best work.

3. Speed—that's an important part of my life. My first teammates were Racers and my hobby is fast cars. Early in my career, I also spent my social life in the fast lane. But since those youthful years, I have settled down and become very goal-oriented.

4. Life as I know it today began at the tender age of 18, when I autographed a sheet of paper that said I had entered the big time. I quickly began bouncing checks and increasing my net worth. It was nice because I fit right in with the crowd. My friends were all young, talented and not quite ready for prime time. But we would be soon.

5. Before long, we were scoring big points with our fans and ripping the heart out of our enemies. We were like a well-oiled machine and opposing defenders cringed when they saw us coming. One team had our number and called us names, but sticks and stones did not break our bones and we finally swallowed the Big Apple.

6. What a run! We lived the good life for most of a decade and received ringing endorsements for our efforts. But like all good things, our fun finally ended and we became victims of the Peter Principle. Great ones come and go, but when ours went, nothing was really the same again.

7. When I finally left home, I even changed countries. And my new friends welcomed me with open arms. Like an esteemed predecessor in my new city, I became the straw that stirred the icy drink and my team emptied the Cup after going thirsty for many years.

8. I'm really happy again. I have been reunited with my best friend and we are recreating the magic of our early years. I used to live in Wayne's World, but now I share space with him and that's kind of nice. The age-old question applies here: To retire or not to retire? The question will have to be answered soon.

8 Celebrities in Sports

Facing Facts

The following pages are filled with photographs of athletes who went on to make their mark in a different profession. Some found success by simply switching sports; others made career changes that vaulted them into a different kind of spotlight. Look closely at the faces, read the clues and see if you can identify the celebrity/athletes:

1. From the Ivy League to Hollywood.

2. His college career was no laughing matter.

3. From Illinois to Cleveland to the Hall of Fame.

4. Everybody's favorite daytime doctor.

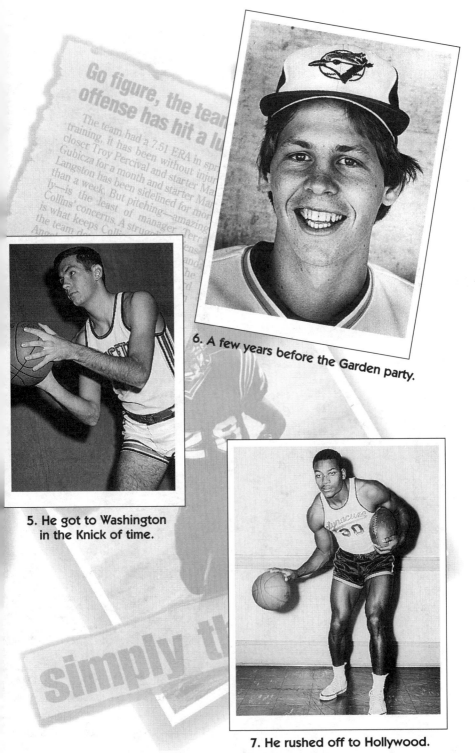

Go figure, the tea[m]
offense has hit a lu[ll]

The team had a 7.51 ERA in sp[ring]
training, it has been without inju[red]
closer Troy Percival and starter Ma[tt]
Gubicza for a month and starter Ma[rk]
Langston has been sidelined for mo[re]
than a week. But pitching—amazing[-]
ly—is the least of manager Terr[y]
Collins' concerns. A strug[gling]
is what keeps Coll[ins]
the team d[...]
Ang[...]

6. A few years before the Garden party.

5. He got to Washington
in the Knick of time.

7. He rushed off to Hollywood.

8. Preparing for a Rocky Mountain High.

9. "I love you, man."

10. It's funny how much some people change.

11. Garden gunner to a sodbuster.

13. "Works for me!"

12. A Minnesota Yankee in King George's court.

14. Fo-o-o-o-ore! He can be dangerous when he drives.

15. The ironman gets his shot.

16. A round ball and an oval office.

17. A driving force
in a different sport.

19. A First Family affair.

18. He hit his stride in another sport.

20. The Bear necessities.

21. A rebel without a cause.

22. A Semi-Tough route to the top.

23. A diamond in the rough steals The Show.

24. A big stick and red socks.

25. From the football stadium to the political arena.

26. "Mongo like candy."

27. A six-million-dollar face.

28. He gave his fans the Blues.

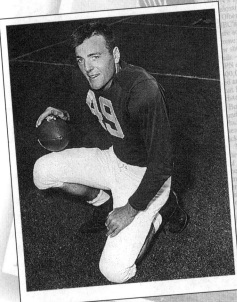

29. An Olympic golden boy.

30. Rocky follow-up to a professional football career.

A White House in a nice neighborhood.

32. A little house for a big man.

33. A Bandit in football clothing.

34. Act 1, scene 1.

35. He helped change the color scheme of a nation.

36. "You rang?"

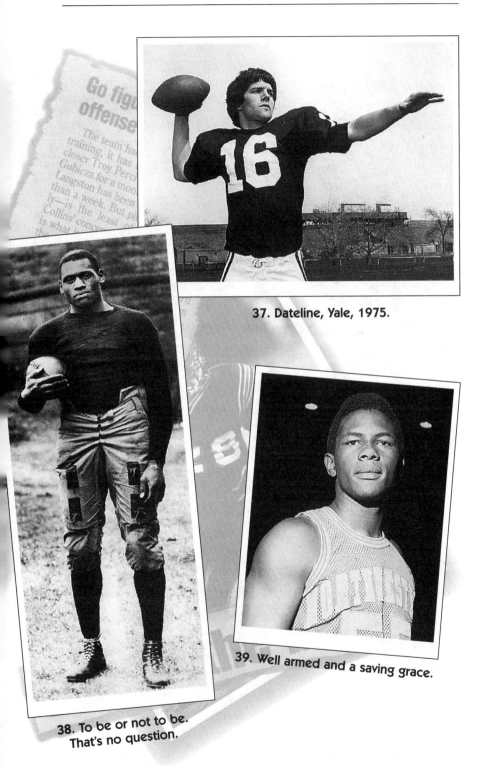

Go fig
offense

The team ha
training, it has
closer Troy Perci
Gubicza for a mon
Langston has been
than a week. But p
ly—is the least
Collins' concer
is what

37. Dateline, Yale, 1975.

39. Well armed and a saving grace.

38. To be or not to be.
That's no question.

40. He called 'em like he saw 'em.

41. From the winner's circle to The Hill.

42. Like father, like son—kind of.

Chapter 8 answers begin on page 301.

43. You don't have to be a detective to spot his star power.

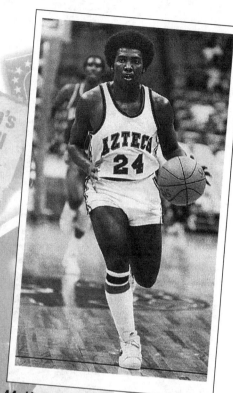

44. He saved his best shots for later.

45. From Southern Cal to Rio.

Mystery Guest

Can you guess the athlete and sport? Answer, page 286.

1. I guess you could say I did well for a Chicago ghetto kid. My eight older siblings taught me how to survive and I taught them a thing or two about hard work and determination. I discovered that the games people play were right up my alley and I got better than passing grades in my All-America high school career.

2. I attacked college with characteristic enthusiasm and it didn't go unnoticed. When I finally caught the eye of the professionals, they brought me in out of the draft and I took my best shot. I gained the reputation as something of a swinger, but I also could chase down air balls and cut down runners.

3. I was never accused of sticking my neck out too far. But that didn't keep my teammates and fans from loving me. When I think back on my incredible popularity, it makes me smile. But what the heck, everything makes me smile.

4. Let me get something off my chest: You should never judge a book by its cover. Some people judged me by my cover and they lost out. When I finally got my opportunity in the spotlight, I was a big hit. And when I ran home, I never looked back.

5. I could have been cast as the Single Guy. I also was known to double and triple my pleasure frequently. But I was not just your average guy. When I did my deep thinking, I usually had a blast. I never walked softly, but I always carried a big stick.

6. Like Michael Jackson, I flashed a pretty mean glove. It came in handy when others took their best shot. Sometimes everybody would think it was over, but I would pull it back. My field of dreams was other players' worst nightmare. But how can they complain: At least they had a roof over their heads?

7. Some people play entire careers without a family atmosphere. Me, I was blessed because I had Twins. I also had batting titles, All-Star Games and even a couple of World Series championships to add dimension to my accomplishments. It was a wild ride.

8. The only thing I didn't have in the end was a clear vision. When I retired, I did so with a deep sense of regret. My team and the fans were nice enough to give me a "34" sendoff, a party I'll always remember. They told me they would always remember me, too.

9 College Football

One Fine Day

Warming up

We provide descriptions for some of the best single-game performances in Division I-A football history. You identify the player:

1. This senior running back claimed one of college football's biggest prizes when he rushed for an NCAA-record 396 yards, 240 in the second half, in a game against Missouri.

   The player was: Marshall Faulk   Anthony Thompson
   Tony Sands   Rueben Mayes

2. This quarterback threw for a record 11 touchdowns in a game against Eastern Washington and for a record 716 yards later that season in a game against Arizona State.

   The player was: Ty Detmer   David Klingler
   Steve Young   Robbie Bosco

3. This receiver caught a record 23 passes in a game against Idaho, good for 363 yards.

   The player was: Randy Gatewood   Terance Mathis
   Howard Twilley   Chris Penn

4. This running back scored a record 48 points on a record eight touchdown runs (5, 51, 7, 41, 5, 18, 5 and 3 yards) in a game against Southern Illinois.

   The player was: Ed Marinaro   Marshall Faulk
   Howard Griffith   Steve Owens

5. This quarterback completed a record 55 passes, 41 in the second half, in a game against Duke.

   The player was: Rusty LaRue   Scott Milanovich
   Matt Vogler   Sandy Schwab

Did You Know

That a Mississippi running back with the appropriate name of Showboat Boykin once held the major-college record for single-game touchdowns? Boykin scored on runs of 85, 21, 14, 12, 14, 1 and 5 yards in a 49-7 victory over Mississippi State in a 1951 contest.

Showboat Boykin

---

6. This legendary running back, in a game against unbeaten Michigan, ran back the opening kickoff 95 yards for a touchdown, scored on runs of 67, 56, 44 and 13 yards and threw a 20-yard TD pass. He finished with 402 total yards—212 on 15 carries, 126 on three kickoff returns and 64 on six pass completions. And, oh yes, he also intercepted a pass.

The player was: Ernie Nevers Red Grange
Jim Thorpe Showboat Boykin

7. Playing in the final regular-season game of an outstanding college career, this running back scored six rushing touchdowns and converted seven conversion kicks in a then-record 43-point performance against Colgate.

The player was: Jim Taylor Steve Owens
Jim Brown Mike Rozier

8. This running back destroyed Notre Dame with a six-touchdown performance that included kickoff returns of 97 and 96 yards and TD runs of 1, 5, 4 and 8 yards.

The player was: Tony Dorsett Earl Campbell
Joe Washington Anthony Davis

9. This kicker blasted field goals of 64 and 65 yards in a game against Baylor. Before that game, only one kicker had made two 60-yarders—in a career.

The player was: Tony Franklin Dave Lawson
Carlos Huerta Kevin Butler

10. A former safety making his first start at quarterback, this player ran for a then-QB record 294 yards on 28 carries in a game against Oregon State.

The player was: Steve Young Jack Mildren
Nolan Cromwell Fred Solomon

Rueben Mayes

Getting serious

We provide a name, a yardage total and a year for the top 10 single-game rushing performances in Division I-A history. The yardage totals and the years are correct, but the names are out of order. Re-arrange the names with the correct yardage and years:

1. Rueben Mayes, 396, 1991.
2. Anthony Thompson, 386, 1991.
3. Scott Harley, 378, 1996.
4. Tony Sands, 377, 1989.
5. Marshall Faulk, 357, 1989.
6. Eric Allen, 357, 1984.
7. Eddie Lee Ivery, 356, 1994.
8. Troy Davis, 356, 1978.
9. Mike Pringle, 351, 1996.
10. Brian Pruitt, 350, 1971.

San Diego State's Marshall Faulk made a run for the record.

Scenarios

We provide the general scenarios for some of the most famous regular-season games in college football history. You provide the schools involved in the contests:

1. Coach John Heisman's team had 32 possessions in this 1916 game and scored on each of them. It scored 19 rushing touchdowns, five on interception returns, five on punt runbacks, two on fumble recoveries and one on a kickoff return. Final score: 222-0.

2. The coach of the underdog team, facing a scoreless tie at halftime, implored his players to "Win one for the Gipper," fulfilling the deathbed wish of a former player. Inspired by the speech, his team pulled off a 12-6 upset, ruining the opponent's hopes for a perfect 1928 season.

3. In a 1950 game played during a driving snowstorm, the winner earned a Rose Bowl berth by recording a 9-3 victory, even though it did not record a first down. The winner did not complete a pass and rushed for only 27 yards—scoring a touchdown and safety on blocked punts. The loser managed three first downs.

4. Dick Lynch's three-yard fourth-quarter run produced the only score in this 1957 contest, which ended the longest winning streak in college football history at 47 games. The underdog prevailed, 7-0.

5. No. 1 against No. 3 in 1959. Both undefeated. No. 1, trailing 3-0 with 10 minutes remaining, staves off defeat when Billy Cannon fields a bouncing punt, fights through traffic and returns it 89 yards for the winning touchdown. Final score: 7-3.

Billy Cannon breaks free on his game-deciding 89-yard punt return.

6. The nation's No. 1-ranked team, 9-0 and trying to wrap up an unbeaten 1964 season, built a 17-0 halftime lead and appeared to be in full control against an opponent that had lost three times. But the underdog rallied in the third and fourth quarters for a shocking 20-17 upset victory, which was sweet, but not sweet enough to earn a Rose Bowl berth.

7. A 1966 showdown. No. 1 vs. No. 2. The No. 1 team turns conservative and runs out the clock, preserving a 10-10 tie and its top ranking.

8. With a Rose Bowl berth at stake in a 1967 conference battle, a future Heisman Trophy winner decided the outcome with a fourth-quarter 64-yard sweep around left end that wiped out a 20-14 deficit and set the stage for his team's 21-20 victory over the nation's No. 1-ranked team.

9. Two Ivy League schools, both undefeated entering The Game in 1968, battled to a dramatic 29-29 tie. Dramatic because one school trailed, 29-13, with less than a minute remaining.

10. Team A led Team B 24-6 early in the third quarter of a 1968 game, but Team A suddenly turned offensive and scored 76 second-half points—four touchdowns in the third quarter and seven more in the fourth. Final score: 100-6.

11. The nation's No. 2-ranked team held a 14-0 lead over No. 1 entering the fourth quarter of a 1969 showdown that would decide the Southwest Conference title and a Cotton Bowl berth. But No. 1 rallied behind the clutch play of quarterback James Street for a 15-14 victory.

12. The so-called "Game of the Century" took place on Thanksgiving Day 1971 and lived up to expectations. No. 1 prevailed, 35-31, when running back Jeff Kinney scored on a two-yard run with 1:38 remaining—his fourth touchdown of the day.

13. Trailing 24-0 with less than a minute remaining in the first half of a 1974 game, Team A began an incredible surge that would net 55

Did You Know

That Nebraska is the only school to produce Heisman Trophy and Outland Trophy winners in the same season twice? Johnny Rodgers won the Heisman and Rich Glover won the Outland in 1972. Running back Mike Rozier and offensive lineman Dean Steinkuhler matched that feat in 1983.

Johnny Rodgers

Rich Glover

Laugh-In

If Cher married defenseman Bill Houlder her name would be Cher Houlder.

consecutive points in a 17-minute span. Anthony Davis scored four touchdowns and ran for a two-point conversion.

14. This incredible ending to a 1982 game required a lot of teamwork—and luck. Trailing 20-19 with four seconds remaining, the trailing team fielded a kickoff and began advancing downfield, using five laterals to keep the play alive. The amazing sequence ended when Kevin Moen grabbed a lateral, used the marching band that already had moved into the end zone as a shield and scored the winning touchdown, knocking down a trombone player in the process.

15. Gerald Phelan latched onto a final-play Hail Mary pass that gave his team a shocking 47-45 victory on a rainy, windy 1984 day that provided an incredible quarterback duel. One completed 34 of 46 passes for 472 yards and three touchdowns, including the winner to Phelan. The other connected on 25 of 38 passes for 447 yards and two TDs.

Statue of Liberty

Warming up

1. Ed Smith, a former New York University backfield star, never won a Heisman Trophy. But he had more than a passing interest in the award. What was Smith's Heisman connection?

2. Despite the "Heisman as in Theismann" campaign waged on behalf of Notre Dame quarterback Joe Theismann in 1970, he could do no better than a second-place finish. Name the future Super Bowl-winning quarterback who beat Theismann by more than 800 votes.

3. Name the former Mississippi quarterback who finished third in the 1960 Heisman voting before embarking on a 538-game career as a catcher for the New York Yankees.

Did You Know

That Texas-El Paso quarterback Brooks Dawson passed for touchdowns on his first six completions of a 1967 game against New Mexico? Dawson completed only three more passes in UTEP's 75-12 victory.

Laugh-In

If Picabo Street made a major donation to the intensive care wing of a major hospital it could be called the Picabo ICU.

University of Chicago running back Jay Berwanger holds a special place in Heisman Trophy lore.

4. What a finish! I won the 1962 Heisman Trophy, scored on a 99-yard run in the Liberty Bowl, was selected No. 1 overall in the NFL draft and played in an NCAA basketball Final Four—all in the same school year. Who am I?

5. Cornell running back Ed Marinaro, who would go on to greater fame as an actor, was the sentimental Heisman choice in 1971. Name the Auburn quarterback who edged him by a narrow 152 votes.

6. What Ivy League school was the first to produce Heisman Trophy winners in consecutive years?

7. Name the 1985 and 1993 Heisman winners who pursued professional careers in sports other than football.

By the Numbers

The five winningest major-college football teams in the 1960s:

1.	Alabama	85
2.	Arkansas	80
	Texas	80
4.	Penn State	73
	Southern Cal	73
6.	Arizona State	72
	Mississippi	72
	Missouri	72
	Nebraska	72
10.	Bowling Green	71

8. For an 11-year period from 1973 to 1983, running backs won every Heisman Trophy. Name the flanker and the quarterback who won before and after that string.

9. Name the 1991 Heisman Trophy-winning wide receiver who struggled through most of his professional career before finally emerging as an outstanding kick returner for the 1996 Green Bay Packers and winning the Super Bowl MVP award.

10. Name the last Heisman Trophy winner at a position other than running back or quarterback.

Getting serious

The following players hold or share a Heisman Trophy distinction. Identify what it is:

1. Jay Berwanger.
2. Archie Griffin.
3. Ernie Davis.
4. Paul Hornung.
5. Larry Kelley, Leon Hart.
6. Doc Blanchard, Glenn Davis, Pete Dawkins, Joe Bellino, Roger Staubach.
7. Davey O'Brien.
8. Doc Blanchard.
9. Hugh Green.
10. Jay Berwanger, Larry Kelley, Clint Frank, Nile Kinnick, Doc Blanchard, Dick Kazmaier, Pete Dawkins, Ernie Davis, Charlie Ward.

School Spirit

Warming up

We provide a conference, the initials of a Pro Football Hall of Famer and the school for which he competed. You provide the name.

1. Big Ten: D.B, Illinois; L.D., Purdue; O.G., Northwestern; B.G., Purdue; P.W., Ohio State.
2. Southeastern: G.B., Kentucky; J.N., Alabama; F.T., Georgia; J.T., LSU; B.S., Alabama; D.A., Tennessee.
3. Pacific 10: D.F., Oregon; F.G., USC; E.N., Stanford; N.V.B., Oregon; O.J.S., USC.
4. Southwestern: L.A., Arkansas; B.L., TCU; D.W., SMU; S.B., TCU; E.C., Texas.
5. Big Eight: J.R., Kansas; K.W., Missouri; G.S., Kansas.
6. Atlantic Coast: S.J., Duke; R.W., Maryland; H.J., Virginia.
7. Independents: F.H., Penn State; J.U., Louisville; P.H., Notre Dame; F.B., Florida State; M.D., Pittsburgh; J.O., Miami.

Getting serious

Several Pro Football Hall of Famers played collegiately at schools not known as football factories. We provide the name of a school, the final year in which a Hall of Famer played there and the pro team for which he later excelled. You identify the athlete:

1. Louisiana Tech, 1969, Pittsburgh Steelers.
2. Morgan State, 1966, Kansas City Chiefs.
3. Navy, 1964, Dallas Cowboys.
4. Jackson State, 1974, Chicago Bears.

By the Numbers

The longest Division I-A losing streaks:

1. Northwestern, 34, 1979-82, defeated Northern Illinois.
2. Kansas State, 28, 1944-48, defeated Arkansas State.
   Virginia, 28, 1958-61, defeated William & Mary.
4. Eastern Michigan, 27, 1980-82, defeated Kent.
   New Mexico State, 27, 1988-90, defeated Cal State Fullerton.
6. Colorado State, 26, 1960-63, defeated Pacific.
7. Kent, 21, 1981-83, defeated Eastern Michigan.
   New Mexico, 21, 1967-69, defeated Kansas.
9. Florida State, 20, 1972-74, defeated Miami (Fla.).
   Texas Christian, 20, 1974-75, defeated Rice.

Did You Know

That former LSU wide receiver Carlos Carson scored touchdowns on each of his first six college receptions? Carson caught five TD passes in his 1977 collegiate debut against Rice and one the next week against Florida.

Carlos Carson

5. Maryland State-Eastern Shore, 1967, Oakland/Los Angeles Raiders.
6. Mississippi Vocational, 1960, Los Angeles Rams.
7. North Texas State, 1968, Pittsburgh Steelers.
8. Bethune-Cookman, 1966, Miami Dolphins.
9. Prairie View A&M, 1966, Houston Oilers and Washington Redskins.
10. Southern University, 1969, Pittsburgh Steelers.

Whistle Blowers

Warming up

We provide the record (through the 1996 season) and colleges at which some of the 25 winningest coaches in Division I-A history have worked. You provide the name:

1. 234-65-8, Miami (Ohio) and Michigan.
2. 216-95-7, William & Mary, North Carolina State, Arkansas, Minnesota, Notre Dame.
3. 323-85-17, Maryland, Kentucky, Texas A&M, Alabama.
4. 238-72-10, Denison, Miami (Ohio), Ohio State.
5. 270-82-4, Samford, West Virginia, Florida State.
6. 314-199-35, Springfield, Chicago, Pacific.
7. 222-165-10, SMU, North Texas, Iowa.
8. 200-154-4, Montana State, Washington State, Fresno State.
9. 319-106-32, Georgia, Cornell, Carlisle, Pittsburgh, Stanford, Temple.
10. 184-60-5, Mississippi State, Washington, Texas.

Did You Know

That Big Eight schools Nebraska, Oklahoma and Colorado ranked 1-2-3 in the Associated Press' final poll of the 1971 season, which was published after the January 1, 1972, bowl games?

Getting serious

We provide the name of a current or former coach. You provide the name of the school and the legendary coach he succeeded:

1. Ray Perkins.
2. John Robinson.
3. Fred Akers.
4. Gomer Jones.
5. Gary Moeller.
6. Dale Hall.

7. Earle Bruce.
8. Phillip Fulmer.
9. Hunk Anderson.
10. Ray Goff.
11. Hootie Ingram.
12. Bob Toledo.

Fred Akers had a tough coaching act to follow.

The Match Game

Warming up

1. What Pacific-10 Conference teams meet annually in the "Big Game?"

2. What Big Ten rivals compete annually for the "Old Oaken Bucket?"

3. Name the two Ivy League schools that get together each season for "The Game."

4. Name the Division I-AA teams that had played a record 132 times through the 1996 season. Hint: Neither team competes in the Ivy League.

5. What prize goes annually to the winner of the Michigan-Minnesota Big Ten game?

6. Name the November 9, 1946, matchup that featured four past and future Heisman Trophy winners.

The Old Oaken Bucket

7. Of UCLA-USC, Alabama-Auburn and Michigan-Michigan State, which is the oldest rivalry?

8. Illinois vs. UCLA: This 1947 matchup was a significant first for college football. What was the significance?

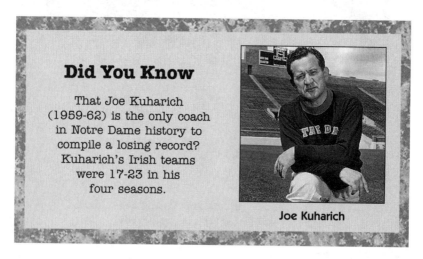

Did You Know

That Joe Kuharich (1959-62) is the only coach in Notre Dame history to compile a losing record? Kuharich's Irish teams were 17-23 in his four seasons.

Joe Kuharich

9. Tulane defeated Temple and Bucknell defeated Miami (Fla.). These two games, played on the same day in 1935, also were significant firsts. Identify the significance.

10. The oldest Ivy League rivalry has been renewed 119 times. Name the teams.

Getting serious

We provide the criteria for a Division I-A matchup. You provide the teams. Note: All records are through the 1996 season.

1. The team with the most Rose Bowl victories vs. the team with the most Orange Bowl wins.

2. The winningest teams in the 1980s.

3. The two Big Ten teams with the nation's longest-running rivalry.

4. The winningest teams in college football history.

5. The team with the most Cotton Bowl victories vs. the team with the most Sugar Bowl wins.

6. The two Big 12 teams with the nation's second-longest-running rivalry.

7. The winningest teams in the 1970s.

8. The teams with the most No. 1 rankings in the final Associated Press polls.

9. Teams that compiled the longest winning streaks in college history.

10. The winningest teams in the 1990s.

Bucknell (white uniforms) battled Miami in a significant 1935 first.

Let's Go Bowling

Warming up

1. Of the long-time "Major" bowl foursome of Rose, Orange, Sugar and Cotton, which one is the oldest?

2. Alabama, Georgia Tech, Notre Dame, Penn State and Georgia are the only schools to win all of the Big Four (Rose, Orange, Sugar and Cotton) bowls. Which one of the five has won each of the Big Four at least twice?

3. What is the Rose Bowl connection between the cities of Pasadena, Calif., and Durham, N.C.?

4. Which of the following schools did not win a Big Four bowl inaugural: Michigan, Bucknell, Alabama, Tulane, Texas Christian?

5. What Pac-10 team took unbeaten records into the 1949, 1950 and 1951 Rose Bowls—and lost every game? Hint: It was not USC or UCLA.

6. Name the only member of the Big Ten and Pacific-10 conferences (through 1996) that has never played in a Rose Bowl?

7. Name the last Big Eight/12 team (through 1996) other than Nebraska, Colorado or Oklahoma to play in an Orange Bowl.

8. What school played in each of the first seven Holiday Bowls?

9. What team, appropriately, holds the record (through 1996) for Gator Bowl victories with six?

10. Name the two charter members of the Southeastern Conference that have never played in the Sugar Bowl.

Woody Hayes

Getting serious

College bowl games often are memorable because of a single play or unusual occurrence. We provide a name or a descriptive phrase and a date. You provide the bowl to which they apply.

1. Woody Hayes, December 29, 1978.

2. Roy Riegels, January 1, 1929.

3. 12 defenders on the field, January 1, 1969.

4. Dan Marino to John Brown, January 1, 1982.

5. Scott Bentley kicks a 21-yard field goal with 22 seconds remaining; Byron Bennett misses from 47 as time expires, January 1, 1994.

The Sooner Schooner went bowling in 1985 and the referees took exception.

6. Tommy Lewis tackles Dicky Moegle, January 1, 1954.

7. Pete Giftopoulos intercepts Vinny Testaverde with 18 seconds remaining, January 2, 1987.

8. The Sooner Schooner, January 1, 1985.

9. Cotton Speyrer saves the day, January 1, 1970.

10. Robbie Bosco connects with Kelly Smith, December 21, 1984.

11. Ken Calhoun tips Turner Gill's end zone pass away from Jeff Smith, January 2, 1984.

12. Bob Apisa KOs Bob Stiles, but can't score the tying TD conversion, January 1, 1966.

Sites and Sounds

Warming up

We provide the field, you identify the team that plays there:

1. Husky Stadium.

2. Neyland Stadium.

3. Kinnick Stadium.

4. Folsom Field.

5. Doak Campbell Stadium.

6. Jordan-Hare Stadium.

7. Kyle Field.

8. Dowdy-Ficklen Stadium.

9. Beaver Stadium.

10. Faurot Field.

11. Dyche Stadium.

12. Commonwealth Stadium.

When Ralphie heads for the end zone, everybody moves out of the way.

Getting serious

1. Which of the stadiums/fields in the "Warming up" section is the largest?
2. Which is the smallest?
3. Which was named after a former Heisman Trophy winner?
4. Which was named after the coach who created the split-T offense in 1941?
5. Which is the oldest?
6. Which is the newest?
7. Which became the first in the country to be named after an active coach (in 1973)?
8. Which is the home to a real, live buffalo named "Ralphie?"
9. Which serves as the home to the winningest team in the 1990s (through 1996)?
10. Which is home of the "Twelfth Man" tradition, which demands that its fans stand throughout the game, ready to go in if needed?
11. Which has the fourth largest seating capacity in the nation but only the second largest in its own conference?
12. Which is home to the resurgent 1995 team that earned its first bowl appearance—major or minor—since 1949?

Conference Calls

Warming up

1. The oldest conference traces its roots to 1896 when it began play as the Intercollegiate Conference of Faculty Representatives. Name the midwestern organization.

2. From 1959-1968, this major conference was known as the Athletic Association of Western Universities. Name the conference that traces its roots to 1916.

3. Name the school, coached for 41 years by Amos Alonzo Stagg, that dropped football following the 1939 season, after 44 years as a charter member of what now is the Big Ten Conference.

4. What Division I-A conference, which boasted seven teams when it began play in 1969, now has a six-school roster—none of which were charter members?

5. Name two of the three Division I-A conferences that have more than doubled their membership since their inaugural seasons.

6. Name the Pacific-10 Conference school, not a charter member, that has more than doubled its nearest rival in league championships.

7. Name the Division I-AA conference that officially began play in 1956 and exists today with the same eight charter schools.

8. Name the non-Texas-based school that won the most championships in the now-extinct Southwest Conference.

9. Which one of the following schools was a Big Ten charter member: Ohio State, Indiana, Purdue, Michigan State?

10. Which of the following was not a Big 12 original: Nebraska, Colorado, Kansas, Missouri?

Getting serious

The following schools were charter members of one conference but now play in another. Identify the before-and-after conferences:

1. Oklahoma.

2. Georgia Tech.

3. South Carolina.

4. Arkansas.

5. Oklahoma State.

6. Arizona State.

7. Texas.

8. Fresno State.

9. Iowa.

10. Rice.

Chapter 9 answers begin on page 303.

Mystery Guest

Can you guess the athlete and sport? Answer, page 286.

1. I was a poor Southern kid who made it big because of Northern exposure. Ever hear of Manhasset? If you have, it's probably because of me. I never met a sport I didn't like and I earned 13 letters in my last three years of high school. If I had the time, the number could have been a lot higher.

2. College life was hectic. Coach, coach, everywhere a coach—they just wouldn't leave me alone. Basketball, football, track, lacrosse and sports too numerous to mention. I even had to fend off some determined baseball scouts. I tried to accommodate everybody, but I told them my priority and stuck to it. I ran with a fast crowd and never looked back.

3. Some say I could have been a Jim Thorpe-caliber Olympic decathlete at Melbourne, but that would have interfered with my career plan. My stubborn tunnel vision turned some of my coaches orange with envy. But before I was through, all America knew who I was and I have the press clippings to prove it.

4. Nobody said it was going to be easy, but everybody said I made it look that way. Raw power, speed, desire, determination—I had it all. I always figured that the shortest distance between two points is a straight line and I carried that philosophy with me everywhere I went. And I was known to travel great distances over the course of a season.

5. Call me sentimental, but my favorite colors have always been orange and brown. My favorite numbers are 32, 44, 100, 200 and 1,000. I'm not one to brag, but I was so efficient at my craft that my enemies were obsessed with bringing me down. Sometimes they did, but I won my share of battles and I always knew the score.

6. When I finally experienced that championship feeling, it didn't last long. Two years later, I was caught in the act and moved on to a different career. Nobody ever accused me of being camera shy and that became painfully obvious when me and 11 of my friends fought a war that everybody watched with a lot of interest.

7. When I gave up sports, I went out on top. I could have played a lot longer and not many athletes can make that claim. But that doesn't mean I faded from the public eye—not by a longshot. If anything, I became more visible and nobody could blame me for the way I acted.

8. 12,312. For years, that number stood the test of time and some incredible athletes. When Walter and Eric finally caught me, it was considered a major feat. First I lost my legacy, then my old fans lost their team. Let's just call it a Brownout that can never be fixed.

Facing Facts

What do you get when you cross a third baseman with a wide receiver? A third receiver? Or maybe a wide baseman? Well, find out for yourself as you take a photo-morphing journey through the world of sports. The game is simple: We have combined the last name of one sports star or celebrity with the first name of another to form one name (i.e. John Franco Harris) and then morphed their faces into one combined photo. Your challenge is to provide the combined name for the morphed photographs that follow. The first one is easy because we provide the answer. Look at the photograph below and see if you can see former major league pitcher Jim "Mudcat" Grant and current NBA star Grant Hill, which you combine for Jim "Mudcat" Grant Hill.

1.

2.

3.

4.

5.

6.

7.

8.

9.

10.

11.

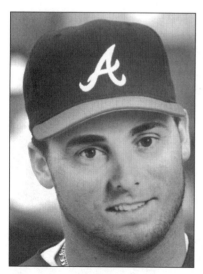

12.

13.

14.

15.

16.

17.

Chapter 10 answers begin on page 306.

Mystery Guest

Can you guess the athlete and sport? Answer, page 286.

1. I wasn't like most kids when I was growing up. By age 12, I knew exactly what I wanted out of life and how to get it. By the time I finished high school, I was a multi-sport athlete on a mission. So I rode the Chattanooga Choo Choo to fame, fortune and success on two different kinds of fields.

2. College was a drag—for my opponents. All America noticed my exploits and, like E.F. Hutton, when I spoke, everybody listened. And well they should—I had a lot of good lines. My junior and senior seasons were a real blur, kind of a rush.

3. Everybody accused me of being a showboat. I guess in retrospect I was. But that was only temporary. I'm really a pretty nice guy and I have plenty of supporters.

4. I wasn't an Eagle scout, but I've earned plenty of merit badges in my career. I don't care all that much for the spotlight. I actually prefer working in the trenches. The biggest thing in my life is consistency and I always try to practice what I preach.

5. I tackle any challenge with enthusiasm. But sometimes my work leaves me vulnerable to cheap shots. Oh well, I'm a big man; I can take it. But I do subscribe to the philosophy that it's better to give than to receive.

6. My lifestyle requires some serious sack time. And a fair amount of soul-searching. On one day, I run with a Pack that shows no mercy. On the others, I show mercy to everyone I meet. I'm always asked to justify the contradictions in my life, but I don't think that's necessary.

7. Yeah, I've developed into a Superman. And I've got a ring to prove it. But those who think that winning is the only focus in my life are badly mistaken. All I have to do is give the word and somebody's life could change forever.

8. Professional sports is my pulpit and I intend to take full advantage of my opportunities. You can find me on Sundays, either speaking the gospel truth or delivering a different kind of word to my enemies. Well, they're not exactly my enemies. But they would like to knock me off my pedestal.

First and Foremost

Warming up

1. The National Invitation Tournament preceded the NCAA Tournament by one year and was the more prestigious of the postseason classics for a number of years. What eastern power won the inaugural NIT in 1938?

2. Name the Southeastern Conference coach who is the only man to direct teams to a junior college national championship, an NIT championship and an NCAA Tournament championship.

3. Only two coaches have played for and coached national championship teams. Both are members of the 700-victory club. Name them.

4. Hank Luisetti is credited with introducing the one-handed set shot to an amazed New York audience during a game against Long Island University at Madison Square Garden. Name Luisetti's West Coast school, which snapped LIU's 43-game winning streak that day.

5. Fourteen teams played in both the NCAA Tournament and NIT from 1940-52. One scored a double victory. Name the only school to pull off the prestigious basketball sweep.

6. Name the team that ranked No. 1 on the all-time victory list through the 1996-97 season.

7. This team won more games (240) than any other team in the 1950s, but it couldn't win an NCAA Tournament or NIT championship until 1974. Name the school.

By the Numbers

Undefeated NCAA Tournament champions:

Team	Year	Record	Coach
North Carolina	1957	32-0	Frank McGuire
Indiana	1976	32-0	Bob Knight
UCLA	1964	30-0	John Wooden
UCLA	1967	30-0	John Wooden
UCLA	1972	30-0	John Wooden
UCLA	1973	30-0	John Wooden
San Francisco	1956	29-0	Phil Woolpert

8. Name the team that dominated the 1960s and '70s, compiling an amazing 507-79 record that averaged out to a 25-4 annual record over a 20-year period.

9. What team won 281 times and averaged 28.1 victories per season in the 1980s?

10. Although this team has failed to win an NCAA title in the 1990s, it has won 230 games, nine more than second-place Kentucky. Name the team.

Name the player who was responsible for the big regular-season performance or play described below:

1. 81 points: Playing for Portland State vs. Rocky Mountain in a 1978 game.

2. 69 points: Playing for LSU vs. Alabama in a 1970 game.

3. 22 assists: Playing for Syracuse vs. Providence in a 1989 game.

4. 14 blocked shots: Playing for Brigham Young vs. Eastern Kentucky in a 1990 regular-season game.

5. 21-of-21 free throws: Playing for Santa Clara vs. St. Mary's (Cal.) in a 1995 game.

6. 13 steals: Playing for Oklahoma vs. Loyola Marymount in a 1988 game.

7. 51 rebounds: Playing for William & Mary vs. Virginia in a 1953 game.

8. 68 points: Playing for Niagara vs. Syracuse in a 1968 game.

9. 14 3-point shots: Playing for Kansas State vs. Fresno State in a 1994 game.

10. 15-of-15 field goals: Playing for Louisville vs. Eastern Kentucky in a 1993 game.

Magic Numbers

Warming up

1. During the 1973-74 season in which North Carolina State ended UCLA's seven-year run as national champion, the Wolfpack lost one game. Name the team that defeated them.

2. Magic Johnson went on to fame and fortune wearing No. 32 for the Los Angeles Lakers after his college career at Michigan State. But what number was he wearing when the Spartans defeated Indiana State for the

1979 NCAA Tournament championship?

3. Name the fast-shooting LSU guard who set a freshman scoring record in 1988-89 by averaging 30.2 points.

4. This man, one of basketball's original 7-footers, led Oklahoma A&M to consecutive NCAA Tournament championships in 1945 and '46. Name him.

5. Name the only coach to lead teams to the Final Four in four different decades.

6. Name the Furman sharpshooter who scored an NCAA single-game record 100 points in a 1954 game against Newberry.

7. On January 31, 1989, Loyola Marymount defeated U.S. International in the highest scoring game in college basketball history. Within 20 points, what was the combined point totals of the two teams?

8. In a similar matchup two years later between the same schools, a U.S. International sharpshooter set a single-game scoring record against a Division I opponent. Name the player who erupted for 72 points.

9. Name the only man to play for an NBA championship team and coach an NCAA Tournament champion.

This 'Cowboy' was a big man in Oklahoma A&M's NCAA double.

10. What team, trailing LSU by 31 points with 15:34 remaining in a 1994 game, stormed back for a 99-95 victory, matching the biggest second-half comeback in major college history?

Getting serious

Identify the significance of each number or the common links between each series of numbers:

1. 1948, 1949, 1951, 1958, 1978, 1996.

2. 43.8, 44.2, 44.5.

3. 50-50.

4. 30-0, 29-1, 29-1, 28-2, 29-1, 30-0, 30-0.

5. 88.

6. 21-of-22

7. 32-0.

8. 122.4.

9. 879-254.

10. 1940, 1953, 1976, 1981, 1987.

As Easy as U-C-L-A

Warming up

1. Name the team that recorded an 89-82 victory over UCLA in 1971—the last loss the Bruins would suffer before beginning their incredible 88-game winning streak.

2. UCLA broke San Francisco's record for consecutive victories in 1973 when it won its 61st straight game. What team did the Bruins beat, 82-63?

3. Name the team that handed UCLA a dramatic 71-70 loss midway through the 1973-74 season, ending the Bruins' winning streak at 88.

4. Name the player who connected on a corner jump shot with 21 seconds remaining to give his No. 2-ranked team the victory that ended UCLA's 88-game streak and hand the Walton Gang its first-ever loss.

5. UCLA also owns the third-longest winning streak in Division I history. Name the team that halted the Bruins' 47-game run in a memorable 1968 game.

6. Name the opponent who scored 39 points, grabbed 15 rebounds and blocked four shots in his team's 71-69 streak-ending 1968 victory over the Lew Alcindor-led Bruins.

7. The combined record of the Lew Alcindor and Bill Walton-led teams sounds like something out of a coach's fantasy. Their combined record was: 158-12   174-6   182-4   164-9

8. Separating the Alcindor and Walton eras was the lesser-discussed Steve Patterson era. What was UCLA's record in the 1970 and 1971 seasons behind Patterson?

9. After sitting out the Final Four in 1977, '78 and '79, the Bruins returned to the college basketball spotlight when they lost to Louisville in the 1980 NCAA Tournament championship game. Name the coach and leading scorer for the 1979-80 Bruins.

10. En route to their record 11th NCAA championship in 1995, the Bruins needed a life-saving 4.5-second, full-court dash and basket by point guard Tyus Edney in a second-round West Regional game. Name the upset-minded team Edney deflated with his Mad Dash.

UCLA's Steve Patterson era wasn't too shabby, either.

Did You Know

That as late as 1950 the New York-based NIT boasted a larger field than the NCAA Tournament? The 1950 NIT had 12 teams, the NCAA 8.

The following players were starting centers for UCLA championship teams: Fred Slaughter, Doug McIntosh, Lew Alcindor, Steve Patterson, Bill Walton and Richard Washington. Match the player combinations below to the center for their team:

1. Keith Wilkes-Greg Lee.
2. Mike Warren-Lucius Allen.
3. Keith Erickson-Fred Goss.
4. Dave Meyers-Marques Johnson.
5. Terry Schofield-Sidney Wicks.
6. Curtis Rowe-Lynn Shackelford.
7. Walt Hazzard-Gail Goodrich.
8. Dave Meyers-Larry Farmer.
9. Henry Bibby-John Vallely.
10. Ken Heitz-Sidney Wicks.

Follow the Leaders

Warming up

We provide a school and the career statistical categories in which he is the leader. You identify the player.

1. Kansas: Points scored, rebounds.
   The leader is: Wilt Chamberlain   Dave Robisch
   Danny Manning   Darnell Valentine
2. Kentucky: Points scored, rebounds.
   The leader is: Dan Issel   Jack Givens
   Kevin Grevey   Sam Bowie
3. UCLA: Points scored, free throws made.
   The leader is: Lew Alcindor   Don MacLean
   Bill Walton   Reggie Miller
4. Indiana: Points scored.
   The leader is: Steve Alford   Calbert Cheaney
   Kent Benson   Alan Henderson
5. Louisville: Points scored, steals.
   The leader is: Pervis Ellison   Wes Unseld
   LaBradford Smith   Darrell Griffith
6. North Carolina: Points scored.
   The leader is: Sam Perkins   Phil Ford
   Charlie Scott   Michael Jordan
7. Duke: Points scored.
   The leader is: Johnny Dawkins   Christian Laettner
   Danny Ferry   Grant Hill
8. Michigan: Points scored.
   The leader is: Cazzie Russell   Gary Grant
   Jalen Rose   Glen Rice

Cazzie Russell scored big for Michigan, but did somebody else score more often?

9. Syracuse: Points scored.
    The leader is: Derrick Coleman   John Wallace
                       Lawrence Moten   Sherman Douglas
10. Arizona: Points scored, free throws made.
    The leader is: Chris Mills   Sean Elliott
                       Steve Kerr   Damon Stoudamire

Getting serious

We provide a name and a position. You provide the school and the superstar player he succeeded:

1. Steve Patterson, center.
2. Olden Polynice, center.
3. Travis Best, point guard.
4. Greg "Cadillac" Anderson, center.
5. Terry Donnelly, point guard.
6. Richard Washington, center.
7. Dirk Minniefield, point guard.
8. Tony Brown, point guard.
9. Ralph Dalton, center.
10. Dave Colescott, point guard.

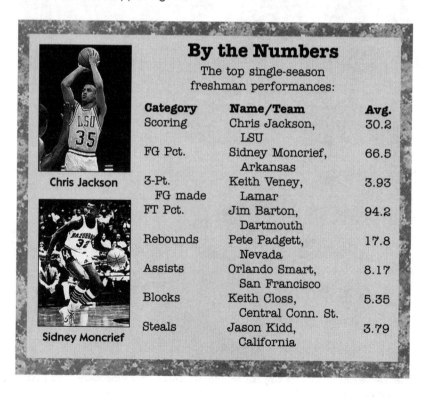

By the Numbers

The top single-season freshman performances:

Category	Name/Team	Avg.
Scoring	Chris Jackson, LSU	30.2
FG Pct.	Sidney Moncrief, Arkansas	66.5
3-Pt. FG made	Keith Veney, Lamar	3.93
FT Pct.	Jim Barton, Dartmouth	94.2
Rebounds	Pete Padgett, Nevada	17.8
Assists	Orlando Smart, San Francisco	8.17
Blocks	Keith Closs, Central Conn. St.	5.35
Steals	Jason Kidd, California	3.79

Chris Jackson

Sidney Moncrief

Who's In Charge?

Warming up

The following items and descriptive phrases create instant images of well-known college coaches. Identify the coach:

1. A towel draped over his shoulder.
2. A brown suit.
3. A rolled-up program.
4. Black and white turtlenecks.
5. A chewed-up towel.
6. A plaid sportcoat.
7. A red and white polka-dot crying towel.
8. Loud, colorful sweaters.
9. A red towel.
10. An oversized bowtie.

For Jud Heathcote, there was life before Michigan State.

Getting serious

The following coaching trios have a common track history at major colleges. Name the schools where all three served as head coach:

1. Tates Locke, Bob Knight, Mike Krzyzewski.
2. Fred Taylor, Eldon Miller, Gary Williams.
3. Bernie Bierman, Jud Heathcote, Mike Montgomery.
4. John Bach, Digger Phelps, Tom Penders.
5. John Kundla, Bill Fitch, Bill Musselman.
6. Tex Winter, Cotton Fitzsimmons, Lon Kruger.
7. Jack Ramsay, Jack McKinney, Jim Lynam.
8. Lute Olson, Ralph Miller, George Raveling.
9. John Wooden, Bill Hodges, Tates Locke.
10. Eddie Sutton, Willis Reed, Tony Barone.

Did You Know

That Indiana coach Bob Knight is the only man to direct champions in the NCAA Tournament, NIT, Pan American Games and the Olympic Games?

Bob Knight

Tournament Talk

Warming up

The following players were named Most Outstanding Player of the NCAA Tournament, even though they did not play for the championship team. We provide the year and name, you provide the team:

1. 1953, B.H. Born.
2. 1956, Hal Lear.
3. 1957, Wilt Chamberlain.
4. 1958, Elgin Baylor.
5. 1959, Jerry West.
6. 1961, Jerry Lucas.
7. 1963, Art Heyman.
8. 1965, Bill Bradley.
9. 1966, Jerry Chambers.
10. 1971, Howard Porter.
11. 1983, Akeem Olajuwon.

Getting serious

Name the player who was responsible for the big NCAA Tournament performance or play described below:

1. 61 points: Playing for Notre Dame vs. Ohio in a 1970 first-round game.
2. 49 points, 27 rebounds: Playing for Houston vs. Loyola (Ill.) in a 1968 first-round game.
3. 58 points: Playing for Princeton vs. Wichita State in a 1965 Final Four third-place game.
4. 11 3-point field goals: Playing for Loyola Marymount vs. Michigan in a 1990 second-round game.

Did You Know

That the record 88-game winning streak the Bill Walton-led UCLA teams compiled from 1971-74 was almost topped by an earlier UCLA run? From 1966-69 behind Lew Alcindor, UCLA won 88 of 89 games, with only a loss to Houston separating winning streaks of 47 and 41.

Bill Walton

5. 30 rebounds: Playing for Ohio State vs. Kentucky in a 1961 regional final game.

6. A game-winning halfcourt shot: Playing for Arkansas vs. Louisville in a 1981 second-round game.

7. 50 points: Playing for Navy vs. Michigan in a 1987 first-round game.

8. 11 blocked shots: Playing for LSU vs. BYU in a 1992 first-round game.

9. A turnaround, top-of-the-key, game-winning jump shot: Playing for Duke vs. Kentucky in a 1992 regional final game.

10. 56 points: Playing for Cincinnati vs. Arkansas in a 1958 regional third-place game.

Finally, Four

Warming up

1. The NCAA Tournament's first championship winner came from the West Coast and has never won another basketball title. Name the Pacific-10 Conference school.

2. The NCAA's first championship game was played at an Illinois city that has never served as a championship game or Final Four host since. Name the city.

Notre Dame coach Johnny Dee and his Top Gun in 1970.

3. The concept of a "Final Four" originated in 1952 when teams from Kansas, St. John's, Illinois and Santa Clara gathered at the same site to determine an NCAA champion. Name the Northwest city that played host to the first real Final Four playoff.

4. In 1985, three teams from the same conference reached the Final Four—an NCAA Tournament first. Identify the teams.

5. Since the NCAA Tournament expanded to 64 teams in 1985, how many No. 1 seeds have lost to No. 16s in first-round matchups?

6. Name the team that needed a Final Four-record six overtimes in two days to get past Michigan State and Kansas en route to the 1957 NCAA Tournament championship.

7. Name the Pacific-10 Conference school that ended Duke's streak of five straight Final Four appearances with a second-round Midwest Regional upset in 1993.

8. Before 1988, this major conference went 30 seasons without winning a Final Four game. Name the conference that broke the streak with three 1988 victories.

9. Name the only two schools to win national championships in four different decades.

10. Name the coach who took two different teams to a national championship game in the 1980s.

Name the teams that answer the following questions about the Final Four (through the 1997 NCAA Tournament):

1. The two teams that have combined for 17 championships.

2. The team that has lost the championship game a record five times.

3. The team that holds the record for most Final Four appearances (5) without winning a championship.

4. The two teams that have combined for 28 Final Four appearances.

5. Two of the first Final Four participants in 1939.

Identify what the following team combinations have in common:

6. Oklahoma A&M, Texas Western.

7. UCLA, Oklahoma A&M, Kentucky, San Francisco, Cincinnati, Duke.

8. Oregon, Wisconsin, Stanford, Wyoming, Loyola of Chicago, Texas Western.

9. Texas Western, North Carolina State.

10. UCLA, Kentucky, Indiana, North Carolina.

En-Titled

Warming up

We provide the year and a name. You provide the team and what the player did to help decide an NCAA championship game:

1. 1982: Michael Jordan.
2. 1978: Jack Givens.
3. 1983: Lorenzo Charles.
4. 1993: Chris Webber.
5. 1987: Keith Smart.
6. 1959: Darrall Imhoff.
7. 1989: Rumeal Robinson.
8. 1965: Gail Goodrich.
9. 1985: Dwayne McClain and Gary McLain.
10. 1963: Vic Rouse.

Jack Givens was a shooting star for Kentucky in 1978.

We provide the year and the four coaches who gathered their teams for the Final Four. You provide the NCAA championship and runnerup teams:

1. 1977: Jerry Tarkanian, Dean Smith, Lee Rose, Al McGuire.
2. 1974: Ted Owens, Al McGuire, Norm Sloan, John Wooden.
3. 1986: Dale Brown, Mike Krzyzewski, Denny Crum, Larry Brown.
4. 1966: Adolph Rupp, Jack Gardner, Don Haskins, Vic Bubas.
5. 1982: John Thompson, Denny Crum, Guy Lewis, Dean Smith.
6. 1961: Fred Taylor, Jack Ramsay, Jack Gardner, Ed Jucker.
7. 1991: Jerry Tarkanian, Roy Williams, Mike Krzyzewski, Dean Smith.
8. 1978: Joe B. Hall, Eddie Sutton, Digger Phelps, Bill Foster.
9. 1963: Vic Bubas, George Ireland, Slats Gill, Ed Jucker.
10. 1972: Dean Smith, Hugh Durham, John Wooden, Denny Crum.

Matching Up

We provide the year and four-fifths of a national championship team's starting lineup. You provide the team and the missing fifth name:

1. 1970: Sidney Wicks, John Vallely, Curtis Rowe, Steve Patterson.
2. 1982: James Worthy, Michael Jordan, Matt Doherty, Jimmy Black.
3. 1974: David Thompson, Tom Burleson, Moe Rivers, Tim Stoddard.
4. 1977: Bo Ellis, Jerome Whitehead, Gary Rosenberger, Jim Boylan.
5. 1960: Jerry Lucas, Larry Siegfried, Mel Nowell, Joe Roberts.
6. 1968: Lew Alcindor, Mike Warren, Lynn Shackelford, Mike Lynn.
7. 1985: Dwayne McClain, Harold Pressley, Gary McLain, Dwight Wilbur.
8. 1978: Jack Givens, Kyle Macy, Mike Phillips, Truman Claytor.
9. 1955: Bill Russell, Hal Perry, Jerry Mullen, Stan Buchanan.
10. 1983: Dereck Whittenburg, Sidney Lowe, Lorenzo Charles, Cozell McQueen.
11. 1948: Ralph Beard, Wallace Jones, Ken Rollins, Cliff Barker.
12. 1990: Larry Johnson, Stacey Augmon, Greg Anthony, George Ackles.
13. 1979: Greg Kelser, Magic Johnson, Ron Charles, Terry Donnelly.
14. 1972: Bill Walton, Henry Bibby, Larry Farmer, Greg Lee.

Greg Kelser (32) was the inside force for Michigan State's 1979 champions.

Did You Know

That Oklahoma State's Eddie Sutton is the only coach in NCAA history to lead four different schools into the NCAA Tournament? Sutton has guided Creighton, Arkansas, Kentucky and the Cowboys in the postseason classic.

Eddie Sutton

15. 1992: Antonio Lang, Christian Laettner, Bobby Hurley, Thomas Hill.
16. 1964: Gail Goodrich, Jack Hirsch, Keith Erickson, Fred Slaughter.
17. 1976: Kent Benson, Scott May, Ted Abernethy, Bobby Wilkerson.
18. 1986: Milt Wagner, Pervis Ellison, Herbert Crook, Jeff Hall.

Home Sweet Home

Warming up

We provide the name of a college basketball facility. You provide the name of the team that plays there:

1. Cameron Indoor Stadium.
2. USAir Arena.
3. Lloyd Noble Center.
4. Bud Walton Arena.
5. Mackey Arena.
6. McGonigle Hall.
7. St. John Arena.
8. Hearnes Center.
9. Littlejohn Coliseum.
10. The Pyramid.
11. Maravich Assembly Center.
12. Freedom Hall.

Getting serious

We provide two former college players. You identify the arena where they played their home games:

1. Kent Benson, Steve Alford.
2. Keith Erickson, Larry Farmer.
3. Lawrence Moten, Sherman Douglas.

Did You Know

That Wilt Chamberlain, who would one day lead the NBA with a 50.4 scoring average, averaged 29.6 and 30.1 in his two collegiate seasons at Kansas? And Chamberlain's Jayhawks did not win a national championship.

Wilt Chamberlain

4. Kyle Macy, Jack Givens.
5. Larry Micheaux, Clyde Drexler.
6. Jo Jo White, Darnell Valentine.
7. Eric Montross, Jerry Stackhouse.
8. Austin Carr, Kelly Tripucka.
9. Larry Johnson, Anderson Hunt.
10. John Lucas, Len Bias.

Chapter 11 answers begin on page 309.

Mystery Guest

Can you guess the athlete and sport? Answer, page 286.

1. I guess you could say I was a prodigy, although my brothers and sisters never noticed. I think my dad did, though, because he used to be a pretty fair athlete himself. I was 12 when professional scouts first noticed me and by age 14, I was under contract.

2. Wanna play a little one-on-one? Back off, hotshot, you wouldn't stand a chance. Speed was my game and nobody needed a radar gun to see that. When I started moving, all hell usually broke loose and the net result was pure excitement.

3. When I hit the big time, nobody threw me a tea party and I received a lot of icy stares. But most of those came from enemies and stodgy critics who didn't appreciate my flamboyant style. Fortunately, I never heard any complaints from my bosses. I was effective—and I was pretty. What a nice combination!

4. I was especially hard to follow during rush hour. I got an assist from some pretty amazing friends and I helped them a lot, too. I guess you could say we always made our point.

5. I don't know that I revolutionized anything, but I do know that nobody had ever seen a player quite like me. I shot down many of the barriers that had kept my sport in the dark ages and I did it with conviction. I was not what you would call a carouser, but I seldom stayed at home.

6. My crowning achievement? There were many highlights—scoring titles, championship rings, trophies. My first century season plays in my mind like a broken record. But more than anything else, it was the impact I had. I can honestly say I moved the game into fast-forward and handled a sticky stiuation with poise and grace. I'll always be No. 4 on everybody's list.

7. I tried to be a Hawk, but that didn't last very long. I fought the battle of Wounded Knee—and lost. I celebrated the American Bicentennial on crutches and my later comeback attempts were hopeless. Oh well, you can't have everything. I reached all my goals and made some lasting impressions.

8. I'm all business now. I watch the game and I see a lot of players in my mold. That's gratifying. It's also nice to see the wide-open offensive style I helped inspire. That's not too shabby considering I played defense, man.

Go Figure

Numbers provide the foundation for sports and there are plenty on the following pages for both the avid and casual fan. Unlike the previous chapters, this collection of trivial graffiti is meant merely to entertain and amuse, not to test knowledge. Pay close attention and you might learn something. But we can't guarantee you'll ever put what you learn to good use.

Former Boston Braves pitcher Bill Voiselle was from the town of Ninety Six, S.C.—and he didn't mind letting everyone know.

The allowable height a regulation tennis ball can bounce when dropped 100 inches onto a concrete base is 58 inches.

The maximum length of a baseball bat is 42 inches.

WILT CHAMBERLAIN reached a record 50.4 pts in 1962.

The 1901 Michigan football team outscored its opponents, 501-0.

A baseball team could get a maximum of 54 hits in a major league game without scoring.

THE MAXIMUM WEIGHT OF A PGA-SANCTIONED GOLF BALL IS 1.62 OUNCES

Eddie Gaedel, the midget who batted for the St. Louis Browns in a 1951 promotional stunt, wore the uniform number 1/8.

5,000 Mudville fans ("10,000 eyes") watched Mighty Casey strike out.

There are 336 dimples in a golf ball.

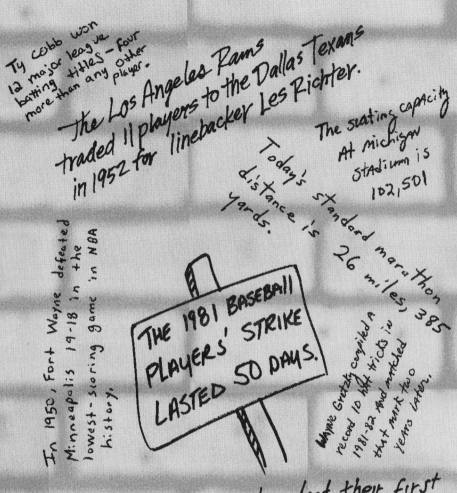

Ty Cobb won 12 major league batting titles—four more than any other player.

The Los Angeles Rams traded 11 players to the Dallas Texans in 1952 for linebacker Les Richter.

Today's standard marathon distance is 26 miles, 385 yards.

The seating capacity At michigan stadium is 102,501

In 1950, Fort Wayne defeated Minneapolis 19-18 in the lowest-scoring game in NBA history.

THE 1981 BASEBALL PLAYERS' STRIKE LASTED 50 DAYS.

Wayne Gretzky compiled a record 10 hat tricks in 1981-82 and matched that mark two years later.

The Baltimore Orioles lost their first 21 games of the 1988 baseball season.

5 Delahanty brothers played major league baseball and 6 Sutter brothers competed in the National Hockey League.

Dave Williams, A veteran of five NHL teams in A 14-year career, spent A record 3,966 minutes in the penalty box.

The regulation height of the basketball hoop and the football uprights crossbar is 10 feet.

Winnipeg's Teemu Selänne scored A rookie-record 76 goals and 132 points in the 1992-93 season.

There are 220 yards in a furlong.

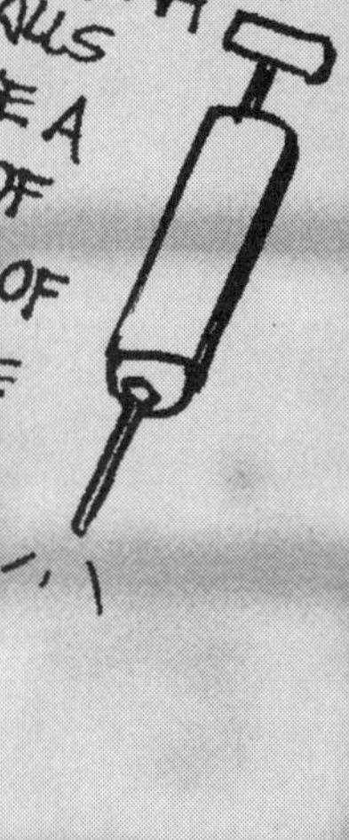

Bob Beamon long jumped 29 feet, 2½ inches in the 1968 Mexico City Olympics — a record that stood for 24 years.

NFL and NCAA footballs must have a minimum of 12½ pounds of air pressure and a maximum of 13½.

Doc Blanchard and Glenn Davis, Army's Mr. Inside and Mr. Outside, combined for 97 collegiate touchdowns.

England's Roger Bannister broke the magical 4-minute mile barrier on May 6, 1954, with a time of 3:59.4.

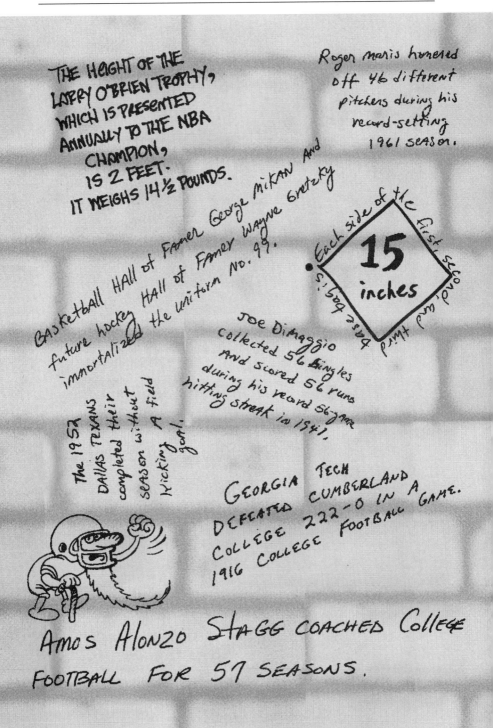

THE HEIGHT OF THE LARRY O'BRIEN TROPHY, WHICH IS PRESENTED ANNUALLY TO THE NBA CHAMPION, IS 2 FEET. IT WEIGHS 14½ POUNDS.

Roger Maris homered off 46 different pitchers during his record-setting 1961 season.

Basketball Hall of Famer George Mikan and future hockey Hall of Famer Wayne Gretzky immortalized the uniform No. 99.

Each side of the first, second, and third base bags is 15 inches.

Joe DiMaggio collected 56 singles and scored 56 runs during his record 56-game hitting streak in 1941.

The 1952 Dallas Texans completed their season without kicking a field goal.

GEORGIA TECH DEFEATED CUMBERLAND COLLEGE 222–0 IN A 1916 COLLEGE FOOTBALL GAME.

Amos Alonzo Stagg coached college football for 57 seasons.

THERE ARE 108 DOUBLE STITCHES IN A REGULATION BASEBALL.

Hank Aaron hit his record-breaking home run at 9:07 p.m. at Atlanta Stadium.

The width of a football field is 53⅓ yards.

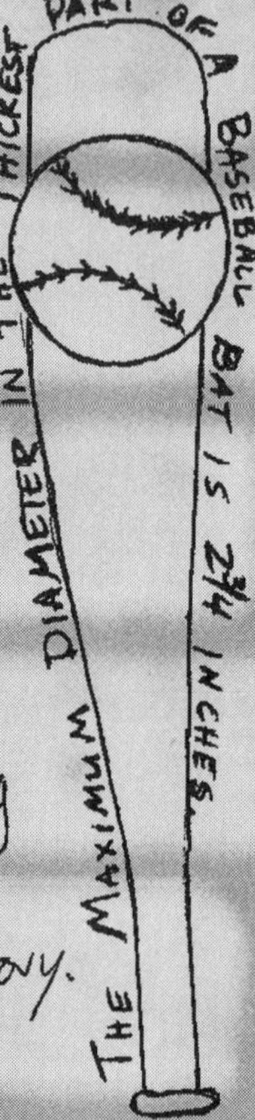

In a forfeited major league game, the winning team is credited with a 9-0 victory.

The Orioles and Yankees made a 1954 trade that involved 17 players.

PART OF A BASEBALL BAT IS 2¾ INCHES.

THE MAXIMUM DIAMETER IN THE THICKEST

The expansion Dallas Cowboys compiled an 0-11-1 first-year record in 1960.

CANADIAN BEN JOHNSON LOST HIS GOLD MEDAL AND 9.79-SECOND WORLD-RECORD CLOCKING WHEN HE TESTED POSITIVE FOR STEROIDS AT THE 1988 SEOUL SUMMER OLYMPIC GAMES.

THE YANKEES HAVE PULLED OFF WORLD SERIES SWEEPS 6 TIMES.

FENWAY PARK'S LEFT-FIELD FENCE, ALIAS THE GREEN MONSTER, IS 37 FEET HIGH.

Chicago Bears running back GALE SAYERS scored 6 touchdowns in a December 12, 1965, game against San Francisco.

Home plate is 18 inches wide!

The Heisman Trophy weighs 25 pounds.

Clown prince Max Patkin's uniform number was "?."

Canadian Football League teams get only 3 downs instead of 4 to cover 10 yards.

American swimmer Mark Spitz won an incredible 7 gold medals in the 1972 Olympic Games at Munich.

BOXING GLOVES HAVE TO WEIGH AT LEAST 8 OUNCES

The width & depth of an NBA backboard is 6 feet by 3 1/2 feet.

Indiana completed its 1976 championship basketball season with a 32-0 record — the last unblemished mark in NCAA history

A golf hole is 4¼ inches in diameter, includes deep

DON LARSEN THREW 97 PITCHES IN HIS 1956 WORLD SERIES PERFECT GAME.

The maximum pressure in an NBA regulation ball is 8½ pounds.

THERE HAVE BEEN 11 TRIPLE CROWN WINNERS IN HORSE RACING HISTORY.

There are: **8** equally spaced laces on footballs used in NCAA play

The official score of a forfeited football game is 1-0

Nolan Ryan struck out a major league career-record 5,714 batters.

NOTRE DAME ENDED UCLA's RECORD 88-GAME COLLEGE BASKETBALL WINNING STREAK IN 1974 WITH A 71-70 VICTORY.

EDDIE GAEDEL, baseball's only MIDGET PLAYER, stood 43 INCHES tall AND WEIGHED 65 POUNDS.

When the Russians ended the U.S. Olympic basketball dominance in 1972, the final score of the controversial game was 51-50.

A tennis ball weighs between 2 and 2 1/16 ounces.

The distance between NCAA goalpost uprights is 23 feet, 4 inches.

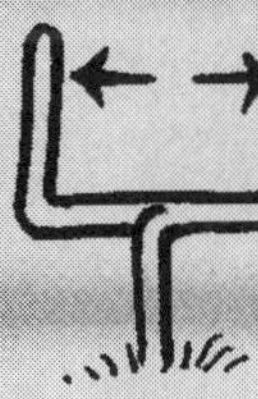

Edwin Moses recorded 122 consecutive victories in the 400-meter hurdles before finally losing in 1987.

The length and width of a tennis court is 78 feet by 27 feet.

The Vince Lombardi Trophy, presented annually to the winner of the Super Bowl, weighs 7 pounds.

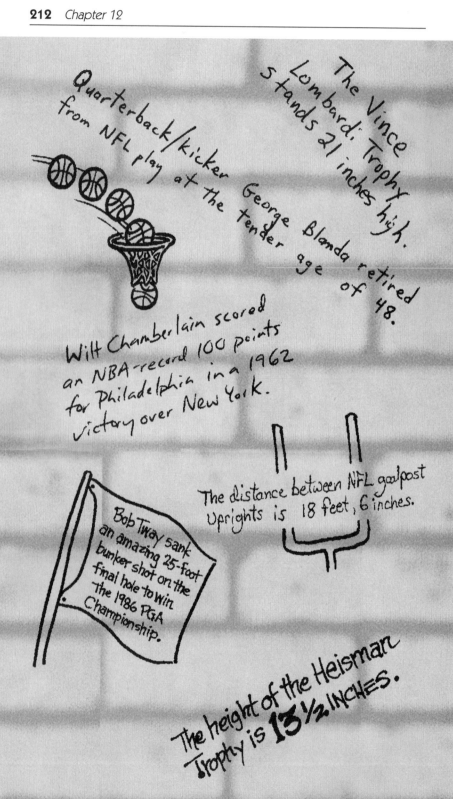

The Vince Lombardi Trophy stands 21 inches high.

Quarterback/kicker George Blanda retired from NFL play at the tender age of 48.

Wilt Chamberlain scored an NBA-record 100 points for Philadelphia in a 1962 victory over New York.

The distance between NFL goalpost uprights is 18 feet, 6 inches.

Bob Tway sank an amazing 25-foot bunker shot on the final hole to win the 1986 PGA Championship.

The height of the Heisman Trophy is **13 ½ INCHES**.

The New York Yankees paid Boston owner Harry Frazee $125,000 for Babe Ruth's contract in 1920.

THE 1982 NFL PLAYERS' STRIKE LASTED 57 DAYS AND WIPED OUT 112 GAMES.

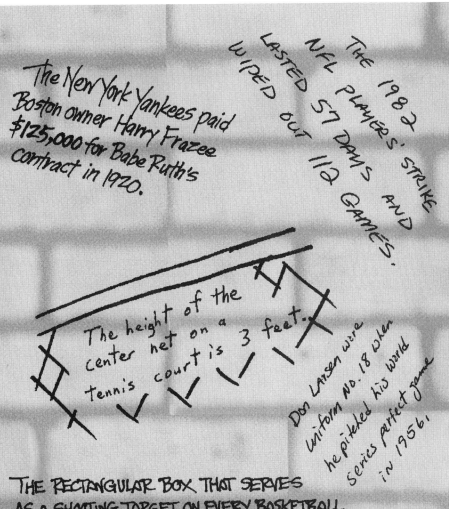

The height of the center net on a tennis court is 3 feet.

Don Larsen wore uniform No. 18 when he pitched his world series perfect game in 1956.

THE RECTANGULAR BOX THAT SERVES AS A SHOOTING TARGET ON EVERY BASKETBALL BACKBOARD IS 24 INCHES BY 18 INCHES.

The average margin of victory for the undefeated 1944 Army football team was 52.1 points.

NBA
6 HOST TEAMS ARE REQUIRED TO MAKE
WARMUP BALLS AVAILABLE TO THE VISITING TEAM.

Southern Cal blitzed Notre Dame with 55 points in a 17-minute span during a 1974 college football game.

16

The America's Cup weighs 16 pounds.

GOLFER BYRON NELSON WON A RECORD 18 TOURNAMENTS ON THE 1945 PGA TOUR.

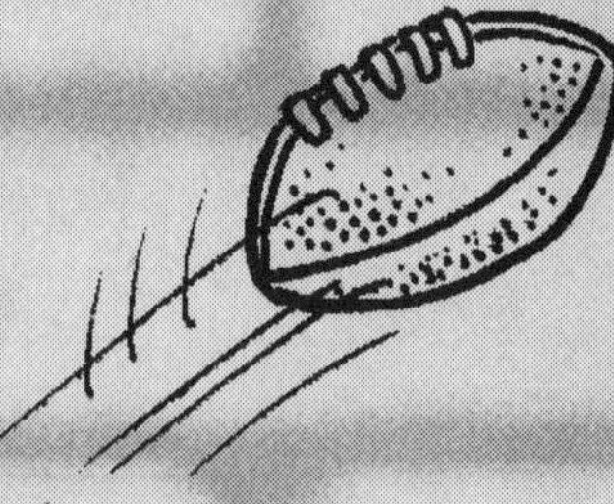

New York Jets punter Steve O'Neal booted an NFL-record 98-yarder in 1969.

The longest field goal in NFL history, a 63-yarder, was kicked by New Orleans' Tom Dempsey in 1970.

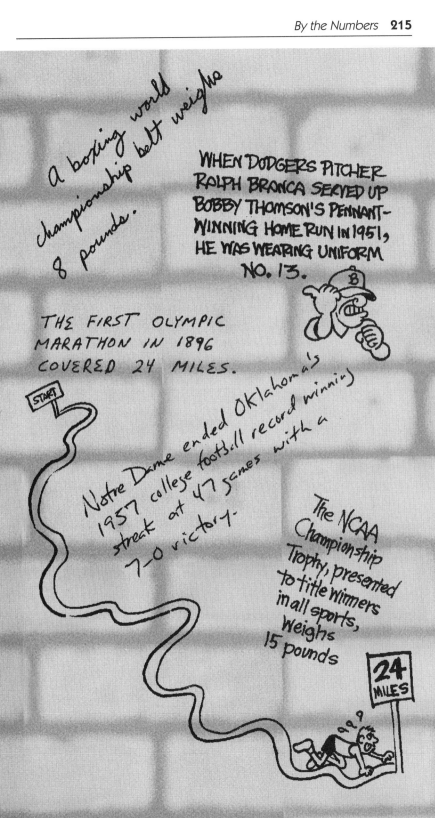

A boxing world championship belt weighs 8 pounds.

WHEN DODGERS PITCHER RALPH BRANCA SERVED UP BOBBY THOMSON'S PENNANT-WINNING HOME RUN IN 1951, HE WAS WEARING UNIFORM NO. 13.

THE FIRST OLYMPIC MARATHON IN 1896 COVERED 24 MILES.

START

Notre Dame ended Oklahoma's 1957 college football record winning streak at 47 games with a 7-0 victory.

The NCAA Championship Trophy, presented to title winners in all sports, weighs 15 pounds

24 MILES

One-armed St. Louis Browns outfielder Pete Gray wore uniform No. 14 in 1945, his only major league season.

AL GEIBERGER NEEDED 59 STROKES TO COMPLETE HIS RECORD-BREAKING SECOND ROUND IN THE 1977 MEMPHIS GOLF CLASSIC.

The winning quarterback in Super Bowls VI through XIV wore the uniform No. 12.

The distance to the deepest point in center field at New York's Polo Grounds was 483 feet.

The 1975 University of California football team rushed for 2,522 yards and passed for the EXACT SAME TOTAL.

Lew Worsham won the World Championship of Golf tournament in 1953 by sinking a 140-yard approach shot on the 18th hole of the final round.

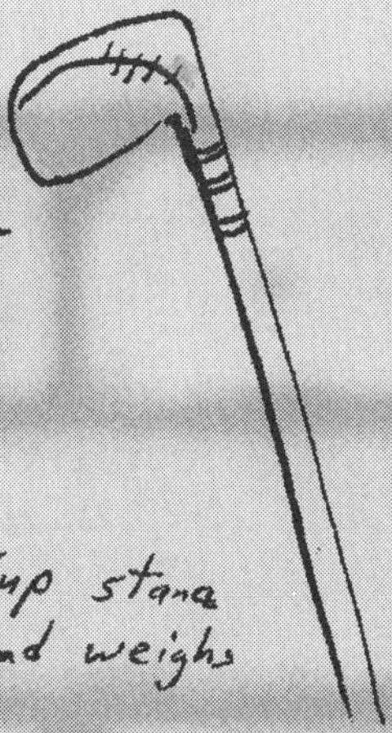

Hockey's Stanley Cup stand 35½ inches tall and weighs 32 pounds.

THE FIRST TELEVISED BASEBALL GAME WAS VIEWED BY A NEW YORK AUDIENCE ON STATION W2XBS.

New York Giants outfielder Bobby Thomson hit his pennant-winning home run at 4:11 p.m. October 3, 1951.

AMOS ALONZO STAGG's University of Chicago football team ended Michigan's 56-game unbeaten streak in 1905 by the unlikely score of 2-0.

When Atlanta's Hank Aaron connected for his record 715th home run in 1974, off Dodgers pitcher Al Downing, both were wearing uniform No. 44.

Bill Shoemaker rode 8,833 winners in his legendary horse racing career.

AN OLYMPIC GOLD MEDAL MUST CONTAIN A MINIMUM OF 6 GRAMS OF PURE GOLD.

Mystery Guest

Can you guess the athlete and sport? Answer, page 286.

1. I think things have worked out pretty well considering my mom wanted me to be a swimmer and my dad preferred another sport. I threw them both a curve and trust me, I never look back.

2. I never liked being a Junior. I appreciated what my predecessors accomplished, but I wanted to carve out my own identity. After a brief period living in their shadow, everything worked out fine. I must admit, growing up to play for my childhood team was a real kick.

3. I walk softly and carry a big stick. My defense is impeccable. I have never won a Gold Glove, but that's really not my fault. I have won other awards and, like some circuses, I have three rings.

4. Go ahead and take your best shot. I can take it. But just remember, if you get too close to me I'll wipe that smile off your face and put a permanent crease in the back of your head. I get a little surly when I don't get a little help from my friends.

5. Like most other players at my position, I need ice during the game and I have trouble walking. The job can be painful, but I get paid big money and my net worth has increased dramatically. I guess you could say I'm at the cutting edge of my career.

6. I can never be accused of padding my statistics. I'm no Lone Ranger; my work is right out there in front of me. Trust me: I'm a target for every would-be Top Gun in my sport.

7. I'm not from the home of the brave, but I live there now. That's because my former bosses got mad at me and sent me away. Oh well, that might have saved my career. Now that I've completed the transition to my new team, I don't believe I have any more mountains to climb.

8. I look forward every year to the end of the season and an opportunity to see my friend Stanley. Sometimes we get together, sometimes it doesn't work out. Some of my buddies have never even met him, and that's a real shame.

Title Towners

Warming up

We provide the champions, you provide the year. Note: Each grouping reflects the year in which pro football's champion played its regular season, not the date of the Super Bowl game:

1. Cincinnati Reds, Pittsburgh Steelers, Golden State Warriors, Philadelphia Flyers.

2. St. Louis Cardinals, Green Bay Packers, Philadelphia 76ers, Toronto Maple Leafs.

3. Los Angeles Dodgers, San Francisco 49ers, Boston Celtics, New York Islanders.

4. Baltimore Orioles, Baltimore Colts, New York Knicks, Boston Bruins.

5. Los Angeles Dodgers, San Francisco 49ers, Los Angeles Lakers, Edmonton Oilers.

6. New York Yankees, Pittsburgh Steelers, Washington Bullets, Montreal Canadiens.

7. New York Yankees, New York Giants, Philadelphia Warriors, Montreal Canadiens.

8. Detroit Tigers, San Francisco 49ers, Boston Celtics, Edmonton Oilers.

9. Pittsburgh Pirates, Philadelphia Eagles, Houston Oilers, Boston Celtics, Montreal Canadiens.

10. Oakland Athletics, Miami Dolphins, New York Knicks, Montreal Canadiens.

We provide the championship seasons, you provide the team. Note: Each grouping reflects the year in which pro football's champion played its regular season, not the date of the Super Bowl game:

1. 1970, 1973.

2. 1926, 1931, 1934, 1942, 1944, 1946, 1964, 1967, 1982.

3. 1981, 1984, 1988, 1989, 1994.

4. 1929, 1939, 1941, 1970, 1972.

5. 1966, 1970, 1983.

6. 1984, 1985, 1987, 1988, 1990.

7. 1977.

8. 1949, 1950, 1952, 1953, 1954, 1972, 1980, 1982, 1985, 1987, 1988.

9. 1971, 1977, 1992, 1993, 1995.

10. 1935, 1945, 1968, 1984.

11. 1909, 1925, 1960, 1971, 1979.

12. 1974, 1975, 1978, 1979.

Chapter 13 answers begin on page 311.

Common Knowledge

Warming up

1. The Los Angeles Lakers won an NBA-record 33 consecutive games in 1972 and the New York Giants won a baseball-record 26 straight games in 1916. Name the teams that hold the NHL and NFL records for consecutive wins with 17.

2. 23 (MLB), 12 (NFL), 16 (NBA), 23 (NHL): Name the teams that hold the record in each sport for championships won.

3. Name the teams that hold the single-season record for victories in the American and National leagues. One won 116 games in 1906 and the other won 111 in 1954.

4. The 1976-77 Montreal Canadiens compiled the best winning percentage in NHL history, but their record for single-season victories (60) was broken in the 1995-96 campaign. Identify the record-setting team and its victory total.

5. Through the 1997 NBA and NHL seasons, how many different cities had celebrated Big Four sports championships in the 1990s?

6. Within four, how many different cities celebrated Big Four sports championships in the 1980s?

7. What city was championship central during the 1980s with eight Big Four titles? What city was second with six?

8. Through the 1997 NBA and NHL seasons, how many different Canadian-based teams had won Big Four sports championships since 1980?

9. In the 20 NHL seasons from 1960 through 1979, only three American-based teams won championships. Name the three teams that accounted for five titles.

10. Who was the last player/coach to lead his team to a Big Four championship?

Getting serious

The players, teams and numbers in the following lists tie the Big Four sports together. Identify what the items in each list have in common:

1. Bo Jackson, Charlie Ward, Tim Stoddard, Bob Hayes, Dave Winfield.

2. New York Yankees, Boston Celtics, Montreal Canadiens, New York Islanders.

3. Jimmie Foxx, Bobby Orr, Bob Cousy, Ted Williams, Bill Russell, Dave Cowens, Eddie Shore, Larry Bird, Phil Esposito, Carl Yastrzemski, Roger Clemens.

4. Spud Webb, Luis Aparicio, Nolan Smith, Albie Pearson, Theo Fleury, Eric Metcalf.

5. 72-10, 116-36, 14-0, 60-8-12.

6. St. Louis Browns, Syracuse Nationals, Quebec Nordiques, Buffalo Braves, Cleveland Browns, Cincinnati Royals, Winnipeg Jets.

7. Philadelphia, New York, Detroit, Chicago, Denver, Dallas, Miami, Boston, Phoenix.

8. Kevin McHale, Dave Winfield, Neal Broten, Karl Mecklenburg, Lou Hudson.

9. New York Jets, Kansas City Royals, Washington Bullets, Philadelphia Phillies, Calgary Flames, Seattle SuperSonics.

10. California Angels, New Orleans Saints, Los Angeles Clippers, St. Louis Blues, Tampa Bay Buccaneers, Texas Rangers, Utah Jazz.

Tim Stoddard (left) found baseball success in New York and other cities. Eddie Shore performed hockey magic in Boston.

Honors Roll

Warming up

1. Michael Jordan has won a record nine NBA scoring titles and Wilt Chamberlain ranks second with seven. Who ranks No. 3 on the list with four?

2. Name the only player to win MVP awards in both the American Basketball Association and the National Basketball Association.

3. Name the only two players to win MVP awards in both the World Hockey Association and the National Hockey League.

4. Name the only man to win election to both the Baseball Hall of Fame and the Pro Football Hall of Fame.

5. Name the only baseball player to win MVP honors in both the American and National leagues.

6. The number "500" is magic for professional baseball and hockey stars. Who were the first players in each profession to reach 500 home runs and 500 goals?

7. NBA scorers tune into 20,000 points as a major career achievement while NFL running backs set their sights on 10,000 yards. Name the first two players to reach these milestones.

8. Name the Hall of Famer who holds the distinction as the only player to record a triple-double in his first NBA game.

9. When Boston's Fred Lynn became baseball's first rookie MVP in 1975, a fellow rookie finished third in the A.L. MVP voting and second to Lynn in Rookie of the Year voting. Who was he?

10. When the Chicago Bulls compiled their all-time best 72-10 regular-season record in 1996, they lost to only one team twice. Name the team.

Getting serious

We provide the categories and initials, you provide the names:

1. Winners of four or more MVP awards: W.G., K. A., G.H., B.R., W.C., M.J., E.S.

Fred Lynn was a rookie wonder for Boston in 1975.

2. Men who have coached or managed two different teams to championships: W.E., B.M., B.H., S.A., A.H., S.B., T.G., D.I.

3. Heisman Trophy winners in the Pro Football Hall of Fame: D.W., P.H., R.S., O.J.S., E.C., T.D.

4. The all-time winningest managers and coaches in each sport: D.S., C.M., S.B., L.W.

5. 1996 All-Star Game MVPs: M.P., J.R., M.J., R.B.

6. The first husband and wife elected to their respective sport's Hall of Fame: A.M., D.D.

7. The only three brother combinations in the Baseball, Pro Football and Basketball Hall of Fames: L.W.-P.W., G.W.-H.W., A.M.-D.M.

8. The three most prominent brother combinations in the players' section of the Hockey Hall of Fame: T.E.-P.E., B.C.-B.C., H.R.-M.R.

9. Players who performed for the most championship teams: B.R., H.R., Y.B., S.J., J. B., Y.C., J.D, C.P.

10. MVPs in the 1996 World Series, Super Bowl, NBA Finals and Stanley Cup Finals: J.W., L.B., M.J., J.S.

Double Jeopardy

Warming up

1. Name the two Heisman Trophy winners who went on to double professional careers in baseball and football.

2. This Pro Football Hall of Famer, who holds the NFL's single-game scoring record with 40 points, surrendered two of Babe Ruth's 60 home runs in 1927 while pitching for the St. Louis Browns. Name him.

3. In 1973, this former University of Minnesota star was selected by the San Diego Padres as the fourth overall pick of baseball's free-agent draft, the Atlanta Hawks in the fifth round of the NBA draft, the Utah Stars in the sixth round of the ABA draft and the Minnesota Vikings in the 17th round of the NFL draft. Identify him.

Did You Know

That from 1918, the first season of the National Hockey League, through 1926, the Stanley Cup winner was decided in a playoff between the Pacific Coast Hockey Association and NHL champions, with the Western Canada Hockey League champ joining a three-way playoff in 1923 and '24? The NHL playoff system began in 1927.

Gene Conley had illustrious teammates, no matter what sport he played.

4. Name the only player to appear in both a Super Bowl and a World Series.

5. Name the two big relief pitchers who played in separate World Series and against each other in the 1958-59 NBA championship series. One played for the New York Yankees and Minneapolis Lakers; the other for the Milwaukee Braves and Boston Celtics.

6. I played one major league game for Brooklyn in 1949 and 66 for the Chicago Cubs two years later. I also played two seasons from 1946-48 for the Boston Celtics. But I am much more famous for what I did after giving up my sports career. Go ahead, take your best shot—but you better be fast.

7. Name the 6-foot-7 righthander who spent 13 years as a major league relief pitcher after playing a prominent role in North Carolina State's 1974 NCAA basketball championship.

8. Name the 1993 Florida State Heisman Trophy winner who went on to a professional career in the National Basketball Association.

9. This former "World's Fastest Human", a two-time gold medalist at the 1964 Tokyo Summer Olympics, went on to carve out a productive career as a wide receiver for the Dallas Cowboys. Name him.

10. Name the only player to be selected in the first round of both the NBA and Major League Baseball drafts. He currently plays for the NBA's Golden State Warriors.

Getting serious

Name the current or former two-sport stars who could claim the following players as teammates. The names become harder as you move down the list.

1. Greg Maddux and Emmitt Smith.
2. George Brett and Marcus Allen.
3. Lloyd Moseby and Larry Bird.
4. Ozzie Smith and Brett Favre.
5. Luis Aparicio and Walt Frazier.
6. Mike Schmidt and Dave Bing.
7. Hank Aaron and Bill Russell.
8. Mickey Mantle and Elgin Baylor.
9. Bob Gibson and Larry Foust.
10. Red Grange and Wally Pipp.
11. Joe Guyon and Christy Mathewson.
12. Ted Williams and Y.A. Tittle.

Elgin Baylor

Mickey Mantle

Joe (left), Dominic (center) and Vince: All in the family.

Family Ties

Warming up

We provide the first names of these brother acts, you provide the last names and sports:

1. Brian, Darryl, Duane, Rich, Ron, Brent.

2. Clete, Ken, Cloyd.

3. Ed, Frank, Tom, Jim, Joe.

4. Major, Caldwell, Wil, Charles.

5. Joe, Vince, Dominic.

6. Aaron, Neal, Paul.

7. Pascual, Melido, Carlos, Vladimir, Dario, Valerio.

8. Barclay, Bob, Billy.

9. Jon, Brent, Drew.

10. Kevin, Gord, Peter.

Getting serious

1. What do these former players-turned-managers/head coaches have in common: Felipe Alou, Hal McRae, Cal Ripken Sr., Bill Dineen?

2. What do these former players and family men have in common: Ken Griffey Sr., Gordie Howe?

3. What do these four brother combinations have in common: Rich and Ron Sutter, Jose and Ozzie Canseco, Horace and Harvey Grant, Tom and Dick Van Arsdale.

4. Father was an outstanding running back for the Dallas Cowboys; son is an all-star performer in the NBA; mother was a college roommate of First Lady Hillary Clinton. Identify this family.

5. This brother-sister act would be tough to beat in any 2-on-2 game. Both enjoyed outstanding careers at UCLA and brother went on to an NBA career with the Milwaukee Bucks while sister got an NBA tryout with the Indiana Pacers before starring in women's professional basketball. Who are they?

6. Name the baseball brother combinations that compiled the most career hits (5,611) and the most career pitching victories (539).

7. Father and son are both 500-goal NHL scorers and a brother/uncle notched a not-too-shabby 303 career goals. Provide the first and last names of this famous family.

8. This football clan spans five decades and brings almost 800 pounds of beef to family reunions. Father was an end for the San Francisco 49ers in the 1950s. One son is an offensive guard/center and the other is a linebacker. Both sons have enjoyed long, successful careers. Who are they?

Boom Boom Geoffrion: Did he or didn't he?

9. This NBA Hall of Famer could star in his own version of "My Three Sons." All the sons, like their father, are guards and they play for three different NBA teams. Identify this family.

10. When their teams meet on the field, one brother, a defensive back, is likely to try to cover the other brother, a wide receiver. Identify these still-active brothers, who do not share the same last name.

11. Name the only family duo in which both men hit 30 home runs and stole 30 bases in a season.

12. One brother is a 500-goal scorer and the top American-born point producer in NHL history. The other produced 260 goals over an 11-year career that ended in 1993. Identify the family.

The Leader Board

Warming up

From each of the following lists, select the player who has never led his sports league in one of these major statistical categories—batting, home runs, RBIs, stolen bases in baseball; passing, rushing and receiving yards, receptions in football; scoring, rebounding, assists in basketball; scoring, goals, assists in hockey:

1. Ed Mathews, Herschel Walker, Elgin Baylor, Jaromir Jagr.

2. Frank Thomas, Eric Dickerson, Charles Barkley, Guy Lafleur.

3. Tony Oliva, Craig Morton, Moses Malone, Boom Boom Geoffrion.

4. Johnny Bench, Gale Sayers, Larry Bird, Stan Mikita.

5. Bill Madlock, Floyd Little, Hakeem Olajuwon, Steve Yzerman.

6. Ron LeFlore, Jim Kelly, Karl Malone, Marcel Dionne.

7. Thurman Munson, Steve Van Buren, Adrian Dantley, Mike Bossy.

8. Bill Bruton, Franco Harris, Dave Bing, Jean Beliveau.

9. Andre Dawson, Warren Moon, Patrick Ewing, Pavel Bure.

10. Fred McGriff, Dwight Clark, Elvin Hayes, Mark Messier.

Getting serious

We provide leaders in key statistical categories from the four professional sports. You provide the season:

1. Vince Coleman 107 stolen bases; Dan Marino 4,746 passing yards; Dominique Wilkins 30.3 scoring average; Wayne Gretzky 215 points.

2. Tommy Davis 153 RBIs; Jim Taylor 1,474 rushing yards; Wilt Chamberlain 50.4 scoring average; Bobby Hull 50 goals.

3. Pete Rose .338 average; O.J. Simpson 2,003 rushing yards; Nate Archibald 34.0-point and 11.4-assist averages; Phil Esposito 130 points.

4. Kirby Puckett .339 average; Christian Okoye 1,480 rushing yards; Michael Jordan 32.5 scoring average; Mario Lemieux 199 points.

5. Dick Groat .325 average; Paul Hornung 176 points; Bob Cousy 715 assists; Bobby Hull 81 points.

Jim Taylor (left) and Paul Hornung were Green Bay leading men.

6. George Brett .390 average; Earl Campbell 1,934 rushing yards; Swen Nater 15.0 rebounding average; Danny Gare, Charlie Simmer and Blaine Stoughton 56 goals.

7. Bobby Avila .341 average; Norm Van Brocklin 2,637 passing yards; Neil Johnston 24.4 scoring average; Rocket Richard 37 goals.

8. Julio Franco .341 average; Haywood Jeffires 100 receptions; David Robinson 13.0 rebounding average; Brett Hull 86 goals.

9. Rickey Henderson 130 steals; Freeman McNeil 786 rushing yards; George Gervin 32.3 scoring average; Wayne Gretzky 212 points.

10. Joe Torre .363 average; Bob Griese 2,089 passing yards; Lew Alcindor 31.7 scoring average; Phil Esposito 152 points.

City Slickers

Warming up

We provide the city, a retired uniform number shared by two players and the sports in which they competed. You provide the names.

1. Los Angeles: 32, baseball and basketball.

2. Chicago: 9, baseball and hockey.

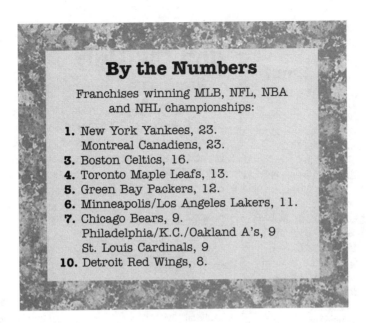

By the Numbers

Franchises winning MLB, NFL, NBA
and NHL championships:

1. New York Yankees, 23.
   Montreal Canadiens, 23.
3. Boston Celtics, 16.
4. Toronto Maple Leafs, 13.
5. Green Bay Packers, 12.
6. Minneapolis/Los Angeles Lakers, 11.
7. Chicago Bears, 9.
   Philadelphia/K.C./Oakland A's, 9
   St. Louis Cardinals, 9
10. Detroit Red Wings, 8.

3. New York: 22, basketball and hockey.
4. Boston: 9, baseball and hockey.
5. Philadelphia: 32, baseball and basketball.
6. Montreal: 10, baseball and hockey.
7. Denver: 44, football and basketball.
8. New York: 7, baseball and hockey.
9. Philadelphia: 1, baseball and hockey.
10. St. Louis: 9, baseball and basketball.
11. Cleveland: 14, baseball and football.
12. Chicago: 4, baseball and basketball.

Getting serious

We provide the year and the records of a city's four major sports teams. You identify the city. Notes: All records are listed in order of baseball, football, basketball and hockey and the team preceded by an asterisk captured its sport's championship.

1. 1980: *91-71, 12-4, 59-23, 48-12-20.
2. 1991: 87-75, 11-5, *61-21, 49-23-8.
3. 1976: 83-79, 11-3, *54-28, 48-15-17.
4. 1981: 59-48, 9-7, 50-32, *48-18-14.
5. 1996: 83-79, 8-8, 35-47, *47-25-10.
6. 1984: *104-58, 4-11-1, 49-33, 31-42-7.
7. 1972: 85-70, 6-7-1, *69-13, 20-49-9.
8. 1995: 74-70, *12-4, 36-46, 17-23-8.
9. 1986: *108-54, *14-2, 23-59, 39-29-12.
10. 1983: 90-72, 5-11-0, *65-17, 49-23-8.

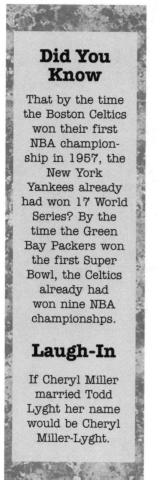

The Good, the Bad, and the Ugly

Warming up

1. The 1962 expansion New York Mets lost a modern-record 120 games and provided living proof that bad teams still can be fun. Name the first baseman who personified the inept, bumbling Mets on the field and later rose to fame in television commercials.

2. Two basketball Hall of Famers spent their entire NBA careers coming up second best to the Boston Celtics. One was part of a team that lost seven times to Boston from 1959 to 1969 and the other played on six of those losers. Name the two players.

3. Name the controversial baseball and football owners who battled players, man- agers, coaches and league officials while building championship teams in Oakland, Los Angeles and New York.

4. Name the New York Mets righthander who made baseball history by losing 27 con- secutive games over two seasons before finally winning in July 1993.

5. The Mets hold the modern baseball record for losses in a season with 120. Name the teams that hold the NBA and NHL records for single-season losses with 73 and 71, respectively.

6. The 0-4 Super Bowl frustration of the Vikings, Broncos and Bills has been well documented, but 10 of the current NFL teams have never played in pro football's ultimate game. Name the longest-tenured franchise that has never qualified for a Super Bowl.

7. Things were so bad for frustrated New Orleans football fans in 1980 that many began wearing bags over their heads while attending games to avoid the embarrassment of being identified as a Saints supporter. What was the creative name adopted by these low-profile fans in a 1-15 season?

8. Name the former Chicago coach who turned locker-room criticism, bickering and controversy into an artform while leading the 1991-92 Blackhawks all the way to the Stanley Cup finals.

9. Name the 1968 and 1985 record-setters who followed outstanding baseball careers by serving time in jail.

10. Name the former baseball bad boy who was fined several times for spitting at fans and missed several MVP opportunities because of a long-standing feud with writers.

Ugly is in the eye of the beholder. The following three-somes were members of teams that were "ugly" for different reasons. Identify the teams and the source of their ugliness:

1. Dave Schultz, Don Saleski, Bob Kelly.
2. Roger Craig, Al Jackson, Ed Kranepool.
3. Greg Luzinski, Ron Kittle, LaMarr Hoyt.
4. Bill Laimbeer, Rick Mahorn, Dennis Rodman.
5. John Matuszak, Jack Tatum, Ken Stabler.
6. Fred Carter, Leroy Ellis, Manny Leaks.
7. Felipe Lira, Greg Gohr, Brian Williams.
8. Claude Lemieux, Scott Stevens, Stephane Richer.
9. Reggie Jackson, Sparky Lyle, Thurman Munson.
10. Joe Medwick, Dizzy Dean, Frank Frisch.

John Matuszak

Getting serious

The Name Game

Warming up

1. What was the rather obscure nickname adopted by Miami Dolphins defenders during their perfect 1972 season?

2. What was the Spanish nickname of the 1967 and '68 St. Louis Cardinals, a tribute to team leader Orlando Cepeda?

3. The Pittsburgh Steelers, boasting a defense featuring Mean Joe Greene, L.C. Greenwood, Jack Ham, Jack Lambert and Mel Blount, captured four Super Bowls in the 1970s. What was the appropriate nickname of this powerful unit?

4. What is the long-running nickname that focuses on the trademark speed and nationality preference of the Montreal Canadiens?

5. What's the one-word description that captured the flashy, run-and-gun style of the 1980s Los Angeles Lakers?

6. What was the colorful nickname of Denver's 1977 defense, which was good enough to get the Broncos to their first Super Bowl?

Orlando Cepeda was an inspiration for the 1967 and '68 Cardinals.

Did You Know

That NHL star Wayne Gretzky is a nine-time winner of the Hart Memorial Trophy, awarded annually to the league's most valuable player? Gretzky has three more MVPs than hockey's Gordie Howe and the NBA's Kareem Abdul-Jabbar.

Wayne Gretzky

7. With "Pops" Stargell serving as the spiritual and physical leader, the 1979 Pittsburgh Pirates captured the World Series under the ultimate team concept. What was their nickname?

8. In the late 1930s and early 1940s, the Boston Bruins featured a line of German-born stars. What was the appropriate name given to this high-scoring unit?

9. When the Chicago Bears pounded the Washington Redskins, 73-0, in the 1940 NFL championship game, they reaffirmed a nickname that reflected their early domination of the league. What were the big, bad Bears frequently called?

10. After sitting in last place in mid-July, Boston raced to an incredible 68 victories in 87 games, won the National League pennant by 10½ games and swept the powerful Philadelphia Athletics in the 1914 World Series. What nickname was assigned to this surprising team?

Getting serious

Provide the colorful nicknames associated with the following groups of players:

1. Ricky Nattiel, Mark Jackson, Vance Johnson.

2. Eric Lindros, John LeClair, Mikael Renberg.

3. Ralph Sampson, Hakeem Olajuwon.

4. Joe Jacoby, George Starke, Russ Grimm, Fred Dean, Jeff Bostic.

5. Michael Jordan, Larry Bird, Magic Johnson, Charles Barkley, Karl Malone, David Robinson, Patrick Ewing, Scottie Pippen, Clyde Drexler, Chris Mullin, John Stockton, Christian Laettner.

6. Gorman Thomas, Ben Oglivie, Cecil Cooper, Robin Yount, Paul Molitor, et al.

7. Toe Blake, Elmer Lach, Rocket Richard.

8. Deacon Jones, Merlin Olsen, Rosie Grier, Lamar Lundy.

9. Babe Ruth, Lou Gehrig, Bob Meusel, Tony Lazzeri.

10. Alvin Garrett, Charlie Brown.

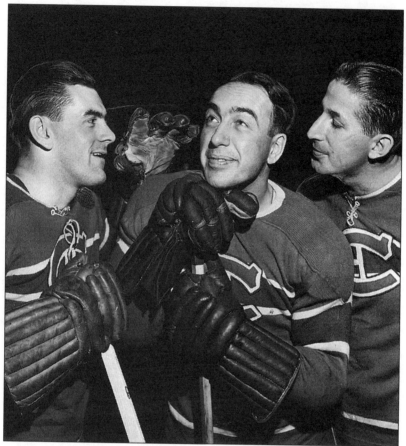

Rocket Richard, Toe Blake, Elmer Lach: What's my line?

11. Mickey Mantle, Roger Maris.
12. Tony Perez, Joe Morgan, Dave Concepcion, Pete Rose, Johnny Bench, George Foster, Ken Griffey, Cesar Geronimo, et al.

Roots

Warming up

Many of today's major professional sports franchises underwent difficult growing pains in the formative and expansion periods of their leagues. Match these previously used nicknames with teams that now play under a different monicker:

1. St. Pats.
2. Nationals.

3. Staleys.
4. Highlanders.
5. Zephyrs.
6. Pilots.
7. Rockies.
8. Spartans.
9. Nordiques.
10. Titans.

Getting serious

The following teams were members of rival leagues that challenged MLB, the NFL, the NBA and the NHL at various periods of their existence. Identify the league in which they competed:

1. Dallas Chaparrals.
2. Houston Aeros.
3. Los Angeles Dons.
4. Anaheim Amigos.
5. Birmingham Americans.
6. Chicago Whales.
7. Indianapolis Racers.
8. Houston Gamblers.
9. Kansas City Packers.
10. Minnesota Muskies.

Seasonal Offerings

The following events and performances all occurred in the same year. Identify the year:

1. ◆ Bill Masterton, a Minnesota North Stars center, died of a massive internal brain injury at a Bloomington hospital 30 hours after he cracked his head on the ice during a game against the Oakland Seals.

◆ Boston's Carl Yastrzemski, the American League's only .300 hitter, won the A.L. batting title with the lowest winning mark in baseball history—.3005.

◆ National Football League owners averted cancellation of regular season and preseason games when they reached agreement with striking players, clearing the way for the opening of training camps.

◆ Montreal coach Toe Blake watched his Canadiens sweep St. Louis for their eighth Stanley Cup title in 13 years and then announced his retirement.

◆ St. Louis center Red Berenson exploded for six goals in an 8-0 victory over Philadelphia—the best single-game effort in 24 years.

The year was: 1967 1968 1970

Norm Van Lier's desperation produced a miracle.

Did You Know

That the 1949-50 Minneapolis Lakers were the first true
"NBA" champions? The league was known as the
Basketball Association of America in its first three seasons
before merging with the National Basketball League and
adopting its current name.

2. ◆ Philadelphia's Julius Erving dazzled fans and fellow players with an
aerial wizardry that produced 30 points, 12 rebounds and an MVP
award in his first NBA All-Star Game.

◆ Gordie Howe, playing for the World Hockey Association's New
England Whalers, scored his 1,000th professional goal.

◆ The Los Angeles Dodgers finished the season with four 30-homer
men: Steve Garvey (33), Reggie Smith (32), Ron Cey (30) and Dusty
Baker (30).

◆ Chicago guard Norm Van Lier connected on a desperation 84-foot
hook shot in an NBA game against San Antonio—his only basket of
the contest.

◆ St. Louis speedster Lou Brock swiped two bases in a game against
San Diego and supplanted Hall of Famer Ty Cobb as baseball's
modern all-time leading basestealer with 894.

The year was: 1974   1976   1977

3. ◆ The 12,315 fans who attended a Boston-Minneapolis matchup at
Boston Garden watched the Celtics roll to a 173-139 victory in a game
that produced the most combined points in NBA history.

◆ A young San Francisco Giants prospect named Willie McCovey collected four hits, including a pair of triples, in his major league
debut—a 7-2 victory over Philadelphia.

◆ Montreal's Jacques Plante, tired of putting his life on the line every
time he stepped onto the ice, began wearing a specially designed
goalie mask on a regular basis.

◆ Pittsburgh relief ace Elroy Face watched his 22-game winning streak
end when he surrendered two ninth-inning runs in a 5-4 loss to the
Los Angeles Dodgers.

◆ The Baltimore Colts captured their second straight NFL championship
with a 31-16 title-game victory over the New York Giants.

The year was: 1956   1958   1959

4. ◆ San Diego first baseman Steve Garvey played in his 1,118th consecutive game, breaking the National League ironman record held by
former Chicago star Billy Williams.

- Chicago Blitz defensive back Luther Bradley intercepted six passes in a 42-3 USFL victory over the Tampa Bay Bandits.
- Edmonton's Great One, Wayne Gretzky, stretched his scoring streak to an NHL-record 31 games, but the Oilers still dropped an 8-5 decision to the New York Islanders.
- Los Angeles center Kareem Abdul-Jabbar joined Wilt Chamberlain as the only NBA players to reach the magic 30,000-point plateau.
- George "Papa Bear" Halas, founder of the NFL's Chicago Bears and the team's owner and coach for more than half a century, died at age 88.
  The year was: 1983   1984   1986

5. - Slick-fielding Chicago Cubs second baseman Ken Hubbs, a 22-year-old former Rookie of the Year, died when the plane he was flying crashed on a frozen lake near Provo, Utah.
   - Houston righthander Ken Johnson became the first major league pitcher to lose a nine-inning no-hitter when Cincinnati defeated the Colt .45s, 1-0.
   - The Buffalo Bills captured their first American Football League championship with a 20-7 victory over San Diego.
   - The Toronto Maple Leafs earned their third consecutive Stanley Cup championship with a seven-game finals triumph over the Detroit Red Wings.
   - Kansas City shortstop Bert Campaneris became only the second player since 1900 to hit two home runs in his major league debut— a game against Minnesota.
   The year was: 1963 1964 1965

6. - Walter Payton, the NFL's all-time leading rusher, played his final game when his Chicago Bears dropped a 21-17 playoff decision to Washington.
   - 40-year-old former basketball great Pete Maravich died of a heart attack while playing in a pickup game at Pasadena, Calif.
   - The Baltimore Orioles set a baseball record for frustration when they opened their season with 21 consecutive losses before finally beating the Chicago White Sox, 9-0.
   - Seattle wide receiver Steve Largent broke the all-time record for reception yards when he reached 12,167 in a game against San Diego.
   - Cincinnati manager Pete Rose was suspended for 30 days after shoving umpire Dave Pallone during an argument.
   The year was: 1985 1986 1988

Did You Know

That no city has ever boasted more than two Big Four championship teams in the same season?

7. ◆ The World Hockey Association's Houston Aeros pulled off a publicity coup when it signed former NHL great Gordie Howe to play on the same team with sons Marty and Mark.
   ◆ Mets center fielder Willie Mays hit the 660th and final home run of his career off Cincinnati lefthander Don Gullett.
   ◆ Veteran Los Angeles Lakers center Wilt Chamberlain signed a three-year contract to coach the ABA's San Diego Conquistadors.
   ◆ The NHL announced expansion to 20 teams and a split into a four-division format.
   ◆ California fireballer Nolan Ryan struck out 17 Detroit Tigers while pitching his second no-hitter of the season, a 6-0 decision at Tiger Stadium.
   The year was: 1972 1973 1975
8. ◆ With Jack Brickhouse at the microphone, WGN aired the first baseball telecast in Chicago history—an exhibition game between the Cubs and White Sox.
   ◆ A fractured ankle ended the playing career of Montreal left winger Toe Blake and broke up the Canadiens' high-scoring Punch Line featuring Blake, Rocket Richard and Elmer Lach.
   ◆ The great Babe Ruth died of throat cancer, sending the baseball world into mourning.
   ◆ The Cleveland Browns capped a 15-0 season by defeating Buffalo 49-7 in the All-American Football Conference championship game.
   ◆ The upstart Baltimore Bullets needed six games to defeat Philadelphia and claim the Basketball Association of America's second championship.
   The year was: 1948 1949 1950
9. ◆ The Minnesota North Stars defeated Philadelphia, 7-1, and halted the Flyers' NHL-record 35-game unbeaten streak.
   ◆ When Chicago White Sox first baseman Mike Squires caught the final inning of an 11-1 loss to Milwaukee, he became the first lefthanded catcher in the major leagues since Dale Long in 1958.
   ◆ The Dallas Mavericks paid their $12 million admission price and were accepted as the NBA's 23rd franchise.
   ◆ Houston ace J.R. Richard suffered a stroke during a workout at the Astrodome and underwent surgery for a blocked artery in his neck, ending his short but successful career.
   ◆ Hartford's 51-year-old Gordie Howe scored his record 800th regular-season NHL goal during the Whalers' 3-0 victory over St. Louis.
   The year was: 1979 1980 1982

Laugh-In

If Chris Evert married Jeff Cross her name would be Chris Cross.

Jack Brickhouse provided the voice for a Chicago baseball first.

10. ◆ When NHL president Clarence Campbell suspended volatile Canadiens winger Rocket Richard for the remainder of the season after a
stick-swinging melee, Montreal fans rioted, vandalizing and looting
stores in a violent demonstration that lasted for several hours.

◆ The Chicago White Sox belted seven home runs and pounded the
helpless Kansas City Athletics, 29-6.

◆ The Green Bay Packers took a big step in their championship devel-
opment when they selected Alabama quarterback Bart Starr in the
NFL draft—in the 17th round.

◆ Detroit's Al Kaline became the youngest batting champion in major
league history when he topped the A.L. with a .340 average.

◆ The NBA unveiled its 24-second shot clock as Rochester defeated
Boston, 98-95.

The year was: 1952 1954 1955

The Rookies

Warming up

1. When Cincinnati lefthander Tom Browning won 20 games in 1985, he
became the first rookie to reach that single-season plateau in 31 years. Name
the New York Yankees righthander who finished 20-6 in his 1954 rookie campaign.

2. Midway through the 1980-81 NHL season, these two brothers both
broke the rookie single-game record for points—in the same game. Name
the brother teammates who incredibly collected eight points apiece in their
team's 11-7 victory over Washington.

3. When this former Chicago running back set the NFL's rookie record for
touchdowns in a season in 1965, he did it creatively—14 rushing, 6 receiving,
1 on a punt return and 1 on a kickoff return. Name the versatile youngster.

4. Wilt Chamberlain holds the NBA rookie records for points and
rebounds in a season. Another center ranks second in both categories.
Name the unsung Hall of Famer who averaged 31.6 points and 19.0
rebounds in his 1961-62 rookie season with the Chicago Packers.

5. When Oakland first baseman Mark McGwire hit 49 home runs in his
1987 debut season, he broke a 57-year-old rookie record. Name the two
National Leaguers who set and tied the rookie home run record in 1930 and
1956.

6. In 1992-93, this Boston Bruins rookie piled up 70 assists, tying Peter
Stastny's first-year record. His 102 points rank fourth on the all-time rookie
scoring list. Who is he?

7. This running back gained 1,605 yards in his rookie 1979 season and
tied the rookie record with nine 100-yard games. Although he enjoyed five
1,000-yard seasons with the St. Louis Cardinals, he is better known as the
MVP of Super Bowl XXV. Identify him.

Willis Reed set the precedent for triple award excellence.

8. Six NBA players have tripled their pleasure by winning Rookie of the Year, regular-season MVP and NBA Finals MVP awards. Willis Reed was the first to complete the triple and Michael Jordan was the last. Name the four who fall between Reed and Jordan.

9. Name the San Diego Padres catcher who compiled a rookie-record 34-game hitting streak in 1987.

10. When this former NHL player compiled 100 points in his 1984-85 debut, he ranked third on the all-time single-season rookie scoring list. Name the Pittsburgh star who has since dropped to fifth on the list.

Getting serious

Identify the players who put together these big rookie performances:

1. 1964: A league-leading .323 average, 217 hits, 109 runs, 32 home runs, 94 RBIs.

2. 1983: An NFL-leading 1,808 rushing yards, 4.6-yard average, 20 touchdowns, 51 catches for 404 yards.

3. 1992-93: An NHL-leading 76 goals, 56 assists, 132 points.

4. 1959-60: NBA-leading totals in scoring average (37.6), points (2,707), rebounding average (27.0) and rebounds (1,941).

5. 1976: A 19-9 record, 2.34 ERA, 250 innings pitched.

6. 1983: 2,210 passing yards in 11 games, 20 touchdown passes, a .585 completion percentage.

Casey Stengel was anything but a buffoon during 12 Yankee seasons.

7. 1981-82: 45 goals, 58 assists, 103 points.

8. 1960-61: A 30.5 scoring average, a 10.1 rebound average, an NBA-leading 9.7 assist average.

9. 1977-78: 53 goals, 38 assists, 91 points.

10. 1975: A .331 average, 47 doubles, 103 runs, 21 home runs, 105 RBIs.

11. 1981: An NFL-leading 1,674 rushing yards, 4.4-yard average, 13 touchdowns, 126 reception yards.

12. 1968-69: An NBA-leading 28.4 scoring average with 2,327 points and a 17.1 rebound average.

Who's the Boss?

1. Before and after his long, successful stint with the New York Yankees, Casey Stengel was considered something of a managerial buffoon. But there was nothing funny about what he accomplished for the Yankees. In his 12 Yankee seasons, how many pennants and World Series did Stengel win?

2. When Toe Blake retired after the 1968 NHL playoffs, he ended an incredible 13-year coaching reign with another Stanley Cup title. How many championships did the Canadiens win under Blake?

3. Red Auerbach coached the Boston Celtics for 16 seasons. But the first six were nothing more than a warmup for the final 10. How many NBA championships did the Celtics win in Auerbach's final decade as coach?

4. Vince Lombardi made the most of his nine seasons as coach of the Green Bay Packers. How many NFL championships did the Packers win under Lombardi?

5. Stengel, Blake and Auerbach hold the distinction of having directed teams to five consecutive championships. Name the other three coaches who have guided as many as four straight winners.

6. Name the only manager/coach who directed championship teams in four different decades.

7. Name the only baseball manager to guide teams to World Series championships in both the American and National leagues.

8. Buffalo coach Marv Levy and former Minnesota coach Bud Grant are much-publicized four-time Super Bowl losers. Name the only other coach who has lost in four Super Bowls.

9. Name the only coach to lead teams to an NCAA hockey championship and a Stanley Cup title.

10. Who is the only man to serve as the first coach for two NBA expansion teams?

Identify the seasons in which the following groups of managers/coaches directed championship winners. Note: Each grouping reflects the year in which pro football's champion played its regular season, not the date of the Super Bowl game:

1. Joe Altobelli, Tom Flores, Billy Cunningham, Al Arbour.
2. Earl Weaver, Don McCafferty, Red Holzman, Harry Sinden.
3. Leo Durocher, Paul Brown, John Kundla, Tommy Ivan.
4. Bob Lemon, Chuck Noll, Dick Motta, Scotty Bowman.
5. Hank Bauer, Vince Lombardi, Red Auerbach, Toe Blake.
6. Tommy Lasorda, Bill Walsh, Pat Riley, Glen Sather.
7. Bucky Harris, Jimmy Conzelman, Eddie Gottlieb, Hap Day.
8. Mayo Smith, Weeb Ewbank, Bill Russell, Toe Blake.
9. Sparky Anderson, John Madden, Tom Heinsohn, Scotty Bowman.
10. Fred Haney, George Wilson, Red Auerbach, Toe Blake.
11. Tom Kelly, Joe Gibbs, Phil Jackson, Bob Johnson.
12. Walter Alston, George Halas, Red Auerbach, Punch Imlach.

Getting serious

Chuck Noll guided the Pittsburgh Steelers into the NFL spotlight.

Chapter 13 answers begin on page 311.

Mystery Guest

Can you guess the athlete and sport? Answer, page 286.

1. I was born in Aliquippa, Pa., but I blossomed athletically in different parts of the country. I guess I developed my affinity for ballgames from my dad, who used to play professionally. Press clippings, stories, knowledge—dad had 'em all. I had a ball when I was just a tyke and I quickly developed an obsession to be the best.

2. Dad gave me a pistol when I was young and I became a trick-shot artist. I put that hand-eye coordination to good use during my high school years while moving from city to city with my folks. When I earned a scholarship and settled into college life, everyone began watching me closely and I put on a show.

3. I guess you could say I was a passing fancy. But that was only one of my talents. I always gave it my best shot and I worked my magic in ways nobody had ever seen. I was a product of the 1960s and my avant-garde look and style became my trademark. But nothing I did sat well with the traditionalists and purists.

4. Watching me work was very moving. My fans said I was dazzling; my enemies called me hotshot. I sure wasn't dull. I wasn't your typical athlete, but I was an average guy. Just look at the record books and see for yourself.

5. Speaking of records, I have a lot of them. If you have a few hours, I can play some for you. I was like an uncaged tiger on game days and I did everything I could to help us win. But, frankly, I didn't get much help from my friends.

6. Have gun, will travel. I guess you could say I was a hawk during the Vietnam years, although I don't remember those days with great satisfaction. Fans appreciated my efforts, but teammates often resented me and I became something of a loner. Whenever I went to court, I satisfied the only judge who counts—myself.

7. I jazzed up my game after Atlanta, and I even made my points better than anyone else one year. But I never recaptured my college form. And I never played for a winner. I thought I might when I was traded in my final season, but that hope was deep-sixered in the playoffs.

8. What did everybody expect from me, for Pete's sake? I did the best I could playing the game I loved. I even died the way my fans would appreciate: playing in a pickup game. Floppy hair, sagging socks—the image of my greatness will live forever.

Also Known As ...

What's in a name? If you're talking about athletes, plenty. Most of the better ones seldom escape their career without a nickname, often a term of endearment or one that suggests a physical or personality characteristic that adds color to their exploits. On the following pages, we provide nicknames of star-quality and Hall-of-Fame players and ask you to identify the real athletes:

Misters

1. Mr. Cub
2. Mr. October
3. Mr. Coffee
4. Mr. Goalie
5. Mr. Inside
6. Mr. Outside
7. Mr. Hockey

Chapter 14 answers begin on page 314.

Big and Little

1. Big Six
2. The Big Train
3. Big Poison
4. Little Poison
5. Tiny
6. The Little Colonel
7. Big Dog
8. The Big O
9. The Big E
10. Big Bird
11. Li'l Abner
12. The Big Unit

13.

16.

15.

17.

14.

Fierce Creatures

1. Kong
2. The Bull
3. The Human Eraser
4. Bruiser
5. The Galloping Ghost
6. Battleship
7. Bad News
8. Manimal
9. The Beast
10. Cujo
11. Snake

12.

13.

14.

15.

16.

12.

13.

1. The Cat
2. The Kitten
3. Moose
4. The Penguin
5. Ducky
6. The Bird
7. The Kangaroo Kid
8. The Rooster
9. Bear
10. The Horse
11. The Bald Eagle

14.

15.

Animals

16.

17.

18.

Colors

1. The Grey Eagle
2. The Greyhound
3. The Golden Brett
4. White Shoes
5. Le Grand Orange
6. The Black Babe Ruth

7.

8.

9.

11.

Authority Figures

1. Prince Hal
2. The Old Perfesser
3. Dr. J
4. The Wizard of Westwood
5. The Wizard of Oz
6. Pops
7. Pop
8. The Great One
9. The Mahatma
10. Preacher

12.

13.

14.

15.

1. Easy Ed
2. The Pearl
3. The Dream
4. The Flower
12. 5. Sunny Jim
6. The Georgia Peach
7. Slick
8. Bells
9. Bingo
13. 10. Twinkle Toes
11. Marvelous

16.

14.

15.

Sugar and Spice

Joes and Sams

7.

1. Shoeless Joe
2. Sad Sam
3. Marse Joe
4. Sudden Sam
5. Slingin' Sammy
6. Mean Joe

8.

9.

10.

"The" Men

1. The Human Highlight Film
2. The Roadrunner
3. The Hammer
4. The Rocket
5. The Barber
6. The Killer
7. The Dodger Killer
8. The Count
9. The Old Arbitrator
10. The Silver Fox
11. The Brat
12. The Express

44.

45.

47.

46.

13. The Throwin' Samoan
14. The Vulture
15. The Mad Bomber
16. The Boz
17. The Cobra
18. The Hawk
19. The Monster
20. The Answer
21. The Thrill
22. The Stork
23. The Tall Tactician
24. The Octopus

48.

49.

50.

25. The Old Fox
26. The Clown Prince of Baseball
27. The Rain Man
28. The Boy Wonder
29. The Iron Horse
30. The Glove
31. The Splendid Splinter
32. The Mailman
33. The Mechanical Man
34. The Jet

51.

52.

53.

35. The Fridge
36. The Round Mound of Rebound
37. The Glide
38. The Flying Dutchman
39. The Hick From French Lick
40. The Commerce Comet
41. The Fordham Flash
42. The Schnozz
43. The Human Rain Delay

54.

55.

One-Namers

58.

59.

61.

1. Pepper
2. Zeke
3. Doc
4. Goofy
5. Hurricane
6. Monbo
7. Ryno
8. Hondo
9. Slug
10. Quiz
11. Toothpick
12. Moonlight
13. Zorro
14. Koos
15. Campy
16. Yogi
17. Robby
18. Killer
19. Satch
20. Magic
21. Stonewall
22. Juice
23. Clyde
24. Shaq
25. Muggsy
26. Ace
27. Dizzy
28. Ironhead

57.

60.

62.

63.

64.

29. Hopalong
30. Gump
31. Smokey
32. Rajah

65.

  33. Sleepy
   34. Yaz
    35. Bullet
    36. Air
    37. Spud
    38. Espo
    39. Dugie
   40. Senor

66.

67.

  41. Luke
42. Slats
 43. Stretch
  44. Country
  45. Turk
  46. Irish
  47. Toe
48. Nails
49. Hoover

68.

69.

  50. Skoonj
   51. Suitcase
    52. Spaceman
   53. Maz
   54. Motormouth
   55. Wamby
   56. Superchief

70.

71.

Significant Others

1. Baby Doll
2. Ee-Yah
3. Reading Rifle
4. Big Country
5. Wild Thing
6. Dollar Bill
7. Tony O
8. Louisiana Lightning
9. Dr. Strangeglove
10. Candy Man

41.

40.

42.

11. Houdini of the Hardwood
12. Daddy Wags
13. Old Reliable
14. Tyler Rose
15. Mick the Quick
16. Vinegar Bend
17. Old Pete
18. Say Hey
19. Hot Rod
20. Rapid Robert

43.

39.

 **44.**

21. Russian Rocket
22. Touchdown Tony
23. Stan the Man
24. Super Mario
25. Sliding Billy
26. Three Finger
27. Finnish Flash
28. Fast Eddie
29. High Pockets
30. Home Run

45.

46.

47.

31. Pistol Pete
32. Uncle Robbie
33. Tom Terrific
34. Silent George
35. Double X
36. Bye-Bye
37. Panamanian Express
38. No-Neck

48.

49.

50.

Chapter 14 answers begin on page 314.

Mystery Guest

Can you guess the athlete and sport? Answer, page 286.

1. I guess you could say I stood out among my eight brothers and sisters and my high school graduating class of 14. The University of Arkansas noticed me, but I stayed closer to home. I wasn't what you would call an average guy, although I developed into one.

2. It got a little drafty for me in 1985 and I heeded the call. The timing was perfect because I was outgrowing my competition. As Horace Greeley once advised, I headed west and tested my skills in the Land of the Giants.

3. I became a big fish in a little pond. I suppose that was only fitting. My fans consider me the salt of the earth, but my enemies try to beat me into submission. That's all right, let them try. That's a pretty large task.

4. I have never received a pass I didn't like. And I've had some pretty good friends throwing them to me. I'm also known as somebody who can take your best shot. You might knock me down briefly, but I always rebound.

5. I had a dream—twice. And that should tell you where I rank among my contemporaries. People seem to count on me and I always deliver. I've built a career around performing well in the clutch.

6. Diddle diddle dumplin' my friend John. Say what you want, but I wouldn't have made it this far without him. He certainly gets passing grades. And believe me, I should know.

7. It has been a nice run, but there's still something missing. My team came close once, and that's no Bull. But close only counts in horseshoes and grenades. We'll keep trying, but time is running out.

8. I play in Michael's World, and there aren't enough MVPs to go around. But after all those 2,000-point seasons, I finally beat him at his own game. It was a nice feeling to finally win a battle from him, although he still won the war.

What's in a Name?

Warming up

On any football Saturday early in a season, you might find the big boys beating up on the little guys. The following nickname-inspired matchups would imply domination. Name the schools that go with the nicknames:

1. Sun Devils vs. Saints.
2. Fighting Irish vs. Quakers.
3. Gators vs. Ducks.
4. Cyclones vs. Rainbows.
5. Leathernecks vs. Gents.
6. Thundering Herd vs. Peacocks.
7. Beavers vs. Sycamores.
8. Nittany Lions vs. Horned Frogs.
9. Rattlers vs. Spiders.
10. Grizzlies vs. Gamecocks.

This holiday basketball tournament could be both colorful and exciting. Identify the schools that go with the nicknames:

1. Blue Devils vs. Blue Hens.
2. Red Storm vs. Red Foxes.
3. Scarlet Knights vs. Crimson Tide.
4. Black Bears vs. Blackbirds.
5. Golden Gophers vs. Golden Flashes.
6. Yellow Jackets vs. Orangemen.
7. Green Wave vs. Greyhounds.
8. Blue Demons vs. Bluejays.

Conference Calls

Warming up

1. What conference produced the winners of 14 football and basketball national championships in the 14-year period from 1962-75?

2. What Big Ten Conference school has appeared in eight Final Fours and won or shared six national football championships—all before 1971?

3. Name the two Big 12 Conference schools that have never won a national football championship or appeared in basketball's Final Four.

4. Name the only Big Ten Conference school that has never won a national football championship or appeared in a basketball Final Four.

5. Name the two Southeastern Conference schools that have never won a national football championship or appeared in a basketball Final Four.

6. Name the only Pacific-10 Conference school that has never won a national football championship or appeared in a basketball Final Four.

7. How many Atlantic Coast Conference schools have never won a national football championship or appeared in a basketball Final Four?

8. Name the two Big East Conference schools that have never won a national football championship or appeared in a basketball Final Four.

9. What conference has produced the most combined football and basketball champions (shared or outright) in the 1990s?

10. Six national football championships were claimed by teams with Independent status in the 1980s. Name the three schools that accounted for those six titles.

Getting serious

The college football and basketball champions for a school year have come from the same conference eight times since the NCAA Tournament started in 1939. We provide the school year and the conference, you provide the champions. Note: The football championships in the 1952-53, 1957-58, 1974-75 and 1990-91 school years were shared.

1. 1940-41, Big Ten.
2. 1952-53, Big Ten.
3. 1957-58, Southeastern.
4. 1967-68, Pacific-10.
5. 1972-73, Pacific-10.
6. 1974-75, Pacific-10.
7. 1981-82, Atlantic Coast.
8. 1990-91, Atlantic Coast.

Did You Know

Lew Alcindor

That only one school has produced the NCAA Tournament's Most Outstanding Player and college football's Heisman Trophy winner in the same school year? Those honors were claimed by UCLA basketball center Lew Alcindor and Bruins quarterback Gary Beban in 1967-68.

Gary Beban

The Winning Formula

Warming up

Four of the five players in each group played for a team that won or shared a national championship. Identify the player who did not:

1. O.J. Simpson, Danny Manning, Herschel Walker, Wilt Chamberlain, Joe Namath.

2. Kyle Macy, Billy Cannon, Pete Maravich, Ernie Davis, Patrick Ewing.

3. Archie Griffin, David Thompson, Angelo Bertelli, Butch Lee, Todd Blackledge.

4. John Havlicek, Anthony Davis, Phil Ford, Johnny Rodgers, Kent Benson.

5. Vinny Testaverde, Sam Perkins, Doc Blanchard, Isiah Thomas, Lee Roy Selmon.

6. Jerry Lucas, Tony Dorsett, K.C. Jones, Brian Bosworth, Oscar Robertson.

7. Bernie Kosar, Glen Rice, John Elway, Greg Kelser, Johnny Lujack.

8. Elgin Baylor, Charles White, Darrell Griffith, Robbie Bosco, Christian Laettner.

9. Eric Bieniemy, Rick Robey, Mike Rozier, Bob Kurland, Rex Kern.

10. Gail Goodrich, D.J. Dozier, Monty Towe, Steve Emtman, George Mikan.

11. Roger Staubach, Larry Johnson, Joe Washington, Bill Russell, Jerry Tagge.

12. Walt Hazzard, Ross Browner, Ed Pinckney, Steve Young, Steve Alford.

David Thompson

Ross Browner

Getting serious

The following descriptions are for schools that played in one of football's four major bowl games (Rose, Sugar, Orange, Cotton) and a Final Four in the same school year. Identify the school.

1. 1945-46: Won Sugar Bowl, won NCAA Tournament championship.

2. 1950-51: Won Sugar Bowl, won NCAA Tournament championship.

3. 1958-59: Lost Rose Bowl, won NCAA Tournament championship.

4. 1964-65: Won Rose Bowl, lost in NCAA Tournament championship game.

5. 1975-76: Won Rose Bowl, finished third in NCAA Tournament championship finals.

6. 1975-76: Lost Orange Bowl, lost in NCAA Tournament championship game.

7. 1977-78: Won Cotton Bowl, finished fourth in NCAA Tournament championship finals.

8. 1982-83: Lost Sugar Bowl, tied for third in NCAA Tournament championship finals.

9. 1987-88: Lost Orange Bowl, lost in NCAA Tournament championship game.

By the Numbers

Through the 1996-97 basketball season, the winningest coaches in Notre Dame basketball and football history:

	Name	Wins
1.	Digger Phelps, 1971-91	393
2.	George Keogan, 1923-43	327
3.	John Jordan, 1951-64	199
4.	Johnny Dee, 1964-71	116
5.	Knute Rockne, 1918-30	105
6.	Lou Holtz, 1986-96	100
8.	Edward Krause, 1943-44; 1946-51	98
9.	Ara Parseghian, 1964-74	95
10.	Frank Leahy, 1941-43; 1946-53	87

Digger Phelps

Knute Rockne

Ara Parseghian

10. 1988-89: Won Rose Bowl, won NCAA Tournament championship.

11. 1989-90: Lost Cotton Bowl, tied for third in NCAA Tournament championship finals.

12. 1991-92: Lost Rose Bowl, lost in NCAA Tournament championship game.

Crossing the Line

Warming up

1. Before Dr. James Naismith invented basketball in 1891, he played football for Springfield College in Massachusetts. Name Naismith's legendary football coach.

2. Name the Florida State star who completed his basketball career as the school's all-time leader in steals after quarterbacking the Seminoles football team to a national championship and winning the Heisman Trophy.

3. Name the former UCLA offensive lineman who enjoyed a solid career in the early 1970s while his brother was dominating college basketball for the same school.

4. Name the University of California star who doubled as a basketball power forward and a football tight end before being selected in the first round of the 1997 NFL draft by the Kansas City Chiefs.

5. Name the former Super Bowl quarterback who split his college time at California playing football and basketball.

6. What Big Ten team shared a national football championship with Alabama a few months after and a few months before losing in the NCAA Tournament championship game to Cincinnati?

Dr. James Naismith

7. This 1995-96 starter for the Wake Forest basketball team holds the NCAA Division I football record for most passes completed in a game—55. Name him.

8. Notre Dame has won or shared 13 national football championships since Knute Rockne's coaching debut in 1918, but the Fighting Irish have not fared so well in basketball. How many Final Fours have included Notre Dame teams?

9. Name the basketball Hall of Famer who, despite never having played college football, was drafted by the Cleveland Browns in the seventh round of the 1962 NFL draft.

10. Name the only school to win a national football championship and NIT championship in the same school year.

We provide categories and initials. You provide names. Warning: These lists include both football and basketball players.

Getting serious

1. UCLA retired numbers: L.A., B.W., K.E., K.W., G.B., J.R.
2. Kentucky coaches: P.B., F.C., B.C., A.R., J.H., E.S., R.P.
3. Notre Dame No. 1 overall draft picks: A.B., L.H., P.H., W.P., A.C.
4. Syracuse 40-point single-game scorers: J.B.
5. LSU Heisman Trophy/consensus Player of the Year winners: B.C., P.M., S.O.
6. Alabama 1987 first-round draft picks: C.B., D.M., J.F.
7. Michigan retired numbers: C.R., G.F., T.H., R.K.
8. Kansas players who went on to lead their pro leagues in scoring in the same 1965 season: G.S., W.C.
9. Georgia players who went on to lead their pro leagues in scoring in the same 1986 season: K.B., D.W.
10. Illinois coaches: G.M., M.W., J.M., G.B., L.H.

Did You Know

That both the basketball and football jerseys of Wallace "Wah Wah" Jones, a two-sport star at Kentucky in the late 1940s, were retired by the university? Jones was a two-time All-Southeastern Conference end for Bear Bryant's football teams from 1945-48. He was a starting forward for Kentucky's 1948 and 1949 national championship basketball teams and later played in the NBA.

Seasonal Offerings

1. ◆ Trailing 17-0 at halftime against undefeated Notre Dame, Southern Cal rallied for a stunning 20-17 victory that ruined the Fighting Irish's hopes for a national championship.

◆ Undefeated Alabama lost a 21-17 Orange Bowl thriller to Texas while undefeated Arkansas escaped the Cotton Bowl with a 10-7 victory over Nebraska.

◆ The AFL's New York Jets pulled off a major coup when they signed Alabama quarterback Joe Namath and Notre Dame Heisman Trophy-winning quarterback John Huarte one week apart.

◆ High-scoring Utah State forward Wayne Estes, who had scored 48 points in a game against Denver a few hours earlier, was electrocuted by a dangling high-voltage wire in a freak accident when he stopped at the scene of an automobile wreck.

◆ University of Miami guard Rick Barry completed the season with a national-best 37.4 scoring average.

The school year was: 1963-64   1964-65   1966-67

2. ◆ A 10-10 tie between No. 1-ranked Ohio State and No. 4 Michigan at Ann Arbor set up a Rose Bowl controversy and ruined the national-championship aspirations of both schools.

◆ Brigham Young's Jay Miller caught a major college-record 22 passes, good for 263 yards and three touchdowns, in a game against New Mexico.

◆ Tennessee 11, Temple 6. The 17-point basketball yawner at Knoxville was the lowest-scoring college game since 1938.

◆ Notre Dame, led by the passing of Tom Clements, claimed a share of the national championship with an exciting 24-23 Sugar Bowl victory over No. 1-ranked Alabama.

◆ North Carolina freshman Walter Davis connected on a 30-foot bank shot to force overtime and the Tar Heels, who were down by eight points with 17 seconds remaining in regulation, went on to post a regular-season-closing 96-92 victory over Duke.

The school year was:
1973-74   1974-75
1975-76

North Carolina's Walter Davis

By the Numbers

The top 10 programs in combined all-time basketball and football victories (regular season only):

School	Wins
1. North Carolina	2,246
2. Kentucky	2,179
3. Notre Dame	2,158
4. Kansas	2,125
5. Syracuse	2,058
6. Texas	1,992
7. Alabama	1,963
8. Ohio State	1,945
9. Washington	1,943
10. Duke	1,940

3. ◆ North Carolina tailback Kelvin Bryant rushed for 520 yards and 15 touchdowns in the Tar Heels' first three games—victories over East Carolina, Miami (Ohio) and Boston College.

   ◆ Alabama coach Bear Bryant won his record-setting 315th victory when he guided the Crimson Tide to a season-closing 28-17 win over Auburn and moved past Amos Alonzo Stagg on the all-time list.

   ◆ Cincinnati, despite David Thirdkill's 25 points, defeated Bradley, 75-73, in seven overtimes—the longest basketball game in NCAA history.

   ◆ Southern California's Marcus Allen completed a record-setting season with 2,342 rushing yards and eight 200-yard games.

   ◆ No. 2-ranked DePaul was shocked, 82-75, by Boston College in an NCAA Tournament second-round Midwest Regional upset.

   The school year was: 1979-80   1980-81   1981-82

4. ◆ University of Miami quarterback Vinny Testaverde connected on 21 of 28 passes for 261 yards and four touchdowns while engineering a 28-16 upset victory over top-ranked Oklahoma.

   ◆ Niagara's Gary Bossert, taking advantage of college basketball's new 3-point shot, connected on 11 straight in a game against Siena.

   ◆ The NCAA, citing SMU's "abysmal" record of rules violations, shut the school's football program down for a year and assessed numerous long-term penalties.

   ◆ Former Ohio State coaching great Woody Hayes died at his Columbus, Ohio, home at age 74.

   ◆ UCLA's Walt Hazzard became the first Final Four Most Outstanding Player to later coach his alma mater into the NCAA Tournament.

   The school year was: 1985-86   1986-87   1987-88

5. ◆ Florida quarterback John Reaves passed for 342 yards and five touchdowns in his varsity debut, helping the Gators post a 59-34 victory over Houston.

◆ Oklahoma running back Steve Owens outpolled Purdue quarterback Mike Phipps by a slim 144 points and won the Heisman Trophy.

◆ San Diego State quarterback Dennis Shaw fired an NCAA-record nine touchdown passes in a 70-21 victory over New Mexico State.

◆ LSU's Pete Maravich outscored Kentucky star Dan Issel 64-51, but the Wildcats posted a 121-105 victory at Baton Rouge.

◆ Oklahoma State's Hank Iba and Butler's Tony Hinkle retired after 41-year basketball coaching careers.

The school year was:
1966-67   1968-69   1969-70

6. ◆ LSU sophomore wide receiver Carlos Carson made a quick impact, scoring touchdowns on his first six collegiate receptions covering two games.

◆ A chartered DC-3 plane carrying the University of Evansville basketball team crashed shortly after takeoff in a dense fog at the Evansville airport, killing all 29 persons aboard.

◆ Texas running back Earl Campbell was awarded the Heisman Trophy.

◆ New Mexico went into Las Vegas and ended UNLV's 72-game homecourt winning streak with an 89-76 victory.

Did You Know

That the number 44 carries a special significance in Syracuse sports history? The number was worn by three of the greatest running backs in college football history—Jim Brown (1954-56), Ernie Davis (1959-61) and Floyd Little (1964-66). The "44" tradition also has been mirrored on the basketball court and the jerseys of such Orangemen stars as Dan Schayes, Derrick Coleman and John Wallace.

Ernie Davis

Derrick Coleman

Did You Know

That since 1966, when the NBA abolished its territorial draft, the No. 1 overall picks in the NFL and NBA drafts have come from the same conference three times? Southern California's O.J. Simpson and UCLA's Lew Alcindor were No. 1 overalls in 1969; Ohio State's Tom Cousineau and Michigan State's Magic Johnson were No. 1s in 1979, and Ohio State's Dan Wilkinson and Purdue's Glenn Robinson were first picks in 1994.

Houston's David Klingler

◆ Guard Bob Bender, who played on Indiana's 1976 NCAA Tournament championship team before transferring to Duke, became the only player in history to play for two different teams in the title game when the Blue Devils lost to Kentucky.

The school year was:
1977-78   1978-79   1979-80

7. ◆ Washington State running back Rueben Mayes ran for a Division I-record 357 yards in a wild 50-41 victory over Oregon.

◆ Doug Flutie's 48-yard final-play touchdown pass to Gerard Phelan gave Boston College an exciting 47-45 victory over Miami and quarterback Bernie Kosar in a game at the Orange Bowl.

◆ Indiana coach Bob Knight was ejected from a game against Purdue when he picked up a folding chair and hurled it across the court as the Boilermakers were shooting a technical foul.

◆ All eight members of the Atlantic Coast Conference were handed bids to postseason tournaments—five to the NCAA and three to the NIT.

◆ An NCAA Tournament first: The Big East Conference landed three teams in the Final Four.

The school year was: 1982-83   1983-84   1984-85

8. ◆ In an incredible passing duel, TCU's Matt Vogler threw for an NCAA-record 690 yards and Houston's David Klingler countered with 563 yards and seven touchdowns. Houston won, 56-35.

◆ U.S. International's Kevin Bradshaw set a single-game record for points against a Division I school when he connected for 72 in a contest against Loyola Marymount.

◆ UConn set an NCAA record by scoring the first 32 points in a basketball victory over New Hampshire.

◆ La Salle guards Randy Woods (46) and Doug Overton (45) combined for 91 points in a 133-118 victory over Loyola Marymount.

◆ Notre Dame Heisman Trophy runner-up Raghib Ismail spurned the NFL and signed the richest contract in Canadian Football League history—a four-year, $18.2 million deal with Toronto.

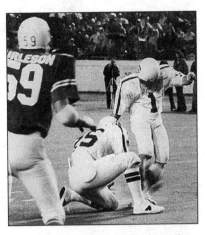

Texas A&M kicker Tony Franklin

The school year was: 1989-90   1990-91   1991-92

9. ◆ Texas-El Paso quarterback Brooks Dawson entered the NCAA record books when he passed for touchdowns on his first six completions in a victory over New Mexico.

◆ In a close vote, UCLA quarterback Gary Beban edged USC running back O.J. Simpson for the Heisman Trophy.

◆ Duke managed only two field goals and dropped a 12-10 decision to North Carolina State in the lowest-scoring basketball game in 26 years.

◆ LSU's Pistol Pete Maravich finished his sophomore season with an NCAA single-season-record 43.8 scoring average.

◆ UCLA, Houston and North Carolina all recorded Regional finals victories, marking the first time in history three teams had returned to the Final Four.

The school year was: 1966-67   1967-68   1968-69

10. ◆ Texas A&M kicker Tony Franklin connected on field goals of 64 and 65 yards in a record-setting performance against Baylor.

◆ Ohio State running back Archie Griffin made history when he became the first player to win two Heisman Trophies.

◆ Griffin and the No. 1-ranked Buckeyes saw their national-championship hopes dashed when UCLA rallied for three second-half touchdowns and a 23-10 Rose Bowl victory.

◆ Oregon shocked powerful UCLA, ending the Bruins' 98-game basketball homecourt winning streak.

◆ A young coach named Mike Krzyzewski ended his first campaign with an 11-14 record at Army.

The school year was: 1973-74   1974-75   1975-76

Chapter 15 answers begin on page 316.

Mystery Guest

Can you guess the athlete and sport? Answer, page 286.

1. I've always taken a ribbing about Hibbing, but I really don't consider that my home town. My father was a railroad man so we kind of made tracks. They made a movie recently about the city I consider home and, yaaaaaaaah, I'm well remembered around those parts for my athletic accomplishments.

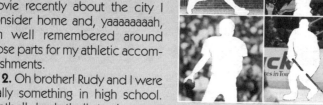

2. Oh brother! Rudy and I were really something in high school. Football, basketball, track ... you name it. And we weren't too shabby as the stars of a state-champion American Legion baseball program, either. Just follow the bouncing ball. We did, and one of us prospered as a result.

3. Bud tried to lure me to Oklahoma, but all things considered, I decided I would much rather be in Cleveland. So I signed my first autograph, got to work and quickly made an impression on my superiors. The impression apparently was not all good. They considered me a swinger with an attitude.

4. When I was sent away, everything was up to date in my life for a couple of years. Then I was sent away again and my life began to play like a broken record. I was an instant hit in my new digs, but I paid a big price for success. I was a Babe in the woods and it was not within my power to win a popularity contest.

5. I tried and I failed. The mantle of fame just didn't fit, but I did make it over some pretty big fences. My 60 minutes of fame were harrowing and disturbing, but the end justified the means—and I have the ring to prove it.

6. It's as simple as MVP—I guess you could say I was twice blessed. After that, I was never the same. I swallowed the big apple and endured five more unhappy seasons before entering my twilight zone. At least I was happy under the golden arch and I earned another championship ring to boot.

7. In retrospect, everything was kind of a haze. What should have been a good experience wasn't and I withdrew from the life to which I had devoted everything. I know it was kind of a Busch thing to do, but it worked out well.

8. You have to wonder if the wear and tear of New York might have contributed to my early death. You also have to wonder if my name will ever be included among all the greats in the Hall of Fame. If so, I have only one request: No asterisks, please.

Crosswords

Puzzling

So you like a more traditional trivia challenge? Have we got a solution for you—or 10 of them to be precise. Each of the following crossword puzzles are customized to a specific sport and each is a threat to trifle with the patience of even the veteran sports fanatic. Go ahead, have a ball—or a puck if the occasion warrants.

Baseball

ACROSS

1 Field covering
5 Ascent
10 —— Yankees
14 Nasty Nastase
15 Hitter's rope
16 Friend in France
17 Desire
18 Bobby was the last Indian to win an AL batting title when he hit .341 in 1954
19 Baseball card condition
20 Disney team
22 Peaches' pilot in *A League Of Their Own*
24 Stand up
26 Senior league playoffs
27 Team that set a major league attendance mark (4,483,350) in their first season
31 Creed in Rocky
35 Pick off base
36 Sailor's drink
38 Top minors
39 Justice
40 Sheriff's star
41 Give off
42 Had for lunch
43 Hurler Hershiser
44 Bowling mark
45 Suffered the "Curse of the Bambino"
48 Cardinals
50 Catcher's wear
52 Terry on the golf course
53 Dale relieved in AL record 13 consecutive games in 1986
57 "Knucksie"
61 Airline in Israel
62 Pepper Martin, "Wild Horse Of The ——"
64 Sulk
65 Happy tune
66 Rodeo cowboy
67 Super Bowl in '68
68 John Matuszak
69 Carbonic compounds
70 Desires

DOWN

1 Pueblo people
2 Trammell on the Tigers
3 Champion's jewelry
4 All-time hits leader (4,256)
5 Low minors
6 Actress Ullmann
7 Competitive
8 Fat pitch
9 Kansas State hoop coliseum
10 Garcia at 2B
11 Madman Idi
12 Cary Grant sat in the Yankees dugout in *That Touch Of ——*
13 Team in New York and New Jersey
21 Money in Italy
23 Handicap race (abbr.)
25 Mariner Martinez
27 Tree
28 Speak formally
29 Washed up
30 Batting lineup
32 1B-DH Johnson
33 Colt back Bruce led the AFC in kick returns as a rookie in '72
34 Johnny was co-Manager of the Year with Joe Torre in 1996
37 Leered at
40 Game summary in the paper
41 Grover Cleveland Alexander's malady
44 NFL championship game in 2017
46 1996 Cy Young Award winner
47 Row your boat
49 Small eateries on wheels
51 Bruce was 4-0 in postseason play 1971-85
53 Dissolve
54 Hodgepodge
55 Angel's wear
56 Bar for a guitar
58 Laker Bryant
59 Destroy
60 Base thief Nixon
63 Gaylord's goo

Pro Football

ACROSS

1 Sports info direc-
tors
5 Heavyweight
champ Max
9 Copycat
13 Football hero
14 Conference that
preceded the
Pac-10
15 Quarterback Kreig
16 King of Crete
18 Charlie the Dolphin
19 High point
20 Only three- time
Super Bowl MVP
22 Dallas QB named
Super Bowl MVP
24 —— of Liberty
play
25 Netter Minter
26 Dull sound
28 Pro grid union
33 First Viking to rush
for 1,000 yards in a
season (1975)
36 Lubricates
37 Trick play
38 Green Bay gridiron
41 Fit to ——
42 Ambassador's
building

43 Gridiron gains
45 Jet George was
AFC reception
leader in '67
46 Mr. Moreno
48 Desperation pass
play
53 Patriots' park in
the '60s
56 Fifteen-yarder
57 Backed up
Montana in
San Francisco &
Kansas City
58 Netter Lacoste
60 College World
Series site
61 Actor Alan
62 Flower
63 —— out a win
64 Cris Dishman
65 Dream Mile city
66 Blood fluids

DOWN

1 Super Bowl MVP
for the Giants
2 Fool
3 Caponi on the
course
4 T formation with a
slotback

5 Ali
6 Minors level
7 Coached Jets to
Super Bowl win
8 Nose tackle Carter
1975-86
9 "A.J." Duhe
10 "—— Bear" Halas
11 Tied up
12 Defensive back
Kern for the Colts
& Bills
17 Cup holder
21 Redskin Mike led
the NFL in kickoff
returns (29.7)
in 1981
23 Quarterback
Anderson or
O'Brien
25 Hoopster Meyers
27 United Arab
Emirates (abbr.)
29 Watch chains
30 Fibs
31 Quarterback's call
32 Sun Devils' univ.
33 Greek cheese
34 The Redskins' "——
The Hill Gang"
35 Andre or Larson
37 Guy in Oakland

38 Loyola's Lions
39 Bikila took the gold
twice in the
Olympic marathon
40 First NFL QB to
pass for 50,000
yards
42 Matador's prize
44 Razorback's mate
45 Youngest player
elected to the Pro
Football Hall of
Fame at age 34
47 Cornerback Clark
49 NFL contests
50 Signal caller Jeff in
Cincinnati
51 Heavens
52 Lake in Africa
53 Tim at short for 15
seasons
54 Wideouts
55 Bear guard Jackson
1975-82
56 Mexican coin
57 No good
59 Zero

Pro Basketball

ACROSS

1 Judo gi obi
5 Eject
10 Center Kauahi
14 Willie was the NHL's first black player
15 Backstop Buddy fielded a record 1.000 in 1946
16 Turkish chief
17 NBA ref Bill caught in the minors
18 Lake in Russia
19 CBA Bighorns
20 He coached the Magic to the '97 playoffs
22 NBA Rookie Of The Year in 1997
24 Big man's pos.
25 Cedric Ceballos
26 CART driver Luyendyk
28 NBA's "Spider"
33 Dean or Hakeem
37 Spur Johnny was the NBA assists leader in 1982
38 Earth crust
39 Coll. of So. Idaho
40 Victories
41 Where Danny Ferry & Brian Shaw played
43 Sampson's sub was '87 NBA All-Star MVP
46 League-leading rebounder for Pistons, Spurs and Bulls
48 Don in the pen
49 Jim was NBA trey leader for the '91 Kings
51 Old Dominion Univ.
52 Timberwolf drafted out of high school
56 Hoopster Hunter
61 Before USOC
62 Alex won the Preakness on Snow Chief
64 Abdelnaby in the NBA
65 Bird's home
66 Kevin Grevey
67 Goalie's wear
68 Podium
69 Runners aboard
70 Chooses

DOWN

1 Cubs' first 30/30 man (1993)
2 McCutchan won 504 while coaching at Evansville
3 Junior at Jack Murphy
4 Coach Brown
5 Harlem hoopster
6 Tribute
7 Illegal —— of the hands
8 Earvin Johnson
9 Buffalo NBA squad
10 Bull whose hoop clinched the NBA title for the '97 Bulls
11 Iowa State's home-town
12 Boxer Benvenuti
13 Hoop rim
21 Sour substance
23 Dutch cheese
26 Receiver Rashad
27 Kingdom
29 NBA little man Moore in the '80s
30 River in France
31 Sea eagles
32 Marv Albert's byword
33 John Francona
34 East Coast Conf.
35 Bat wood
36 Farrow in flicks.
38 "—— Charles" Barkley
42 Chris Dudley's alma mater
44 —— Square Garden
45 Bobby in the NHL 1956-71
47 Willis Reed's job in Jersey
50 Shop or market
51 Chi Chi for the orig-inal Atlanta Braves
52 Cleveland arena
53 Sailing
54 Jr. middleweight champ Gianfranco
55 Syracuse Nationals
57 Damaso Garcia
58 Duel challenge
59 NBA All-Star Game team
60 Asian oxen
63 "Truck" Robinson

Hockey

ACROSS

1 NBA GM John
5 Faceoff
9 Trade
13 Fencing sword
14 Goodfellow in the Hockey Hall Of Fame
16 Plant in Polynesia
17 Taffy was the NHL's first American-born skater
18 Pitching Cuban cigar smoker
19 Winger Kerr
20 Steve played in 884 consecutive games for the Blackhawks
22 NHL career scoring leader
24 Love archer
26 East. Ill. Univ.
27 Skater with a C on his sweater
30 TV repeat
33 Tie word
34 Dallas hockey team logo
36 Goalie for the original Caps & Nordiques
39 Pair to stay on
41 Netter Casale
43 Tremendous
44 Six brothers in the NHL
47 Throws
50 Injury exam
51 Stars' state
53 Slap shot
55 Rink
56 Hindu garment
57 Hockey shirt
61 Kamensky in Colorado
65 Glenn was "Mr. Goalie"
66 Mike traded for Lindros
69 Blue Moon
70 Willie was the NHL's first black skater
71 Digit retired for Phil Esposito
72 City in New Mexico
73 Tea Men
74 Team
75 Hobey Baker winner David

DOWN

1 Hobey Baker winner Broten
2 Amer. Power Boat Assn.
3 Prophet
4 Hockey headgear
5 Team that set NHL record with 62 wins in 1995-96
6 Run batted in
7 Old hoop loop
8 Line skater
9 Number on the stat sheet
10 Wes on ice
11 City in Iran
12 Youth baseball league
15 Mountaineer's rope ladder
21 Periods
23 European prefix
25 Wrist action on a shot
27 Felines
28 Felipe or Matty
29 Willi was NHL Rookie of the Year in 1977
31 Hockey East Wildcats
32 Senior circuit arbiter
35 Shaq's music
37 Monster
38 Stan skated for the original Edmonton Oilers
40 Sault —— Marie, Michigan
42 Mark Messier's nickname
45 Way out
46 Indianapolis team in the WHA
48 Cy Young Award winner drafted by the Los Angeles Kings in 1984
49 Netter Gomer
52 Four out of seven
54 Hall Of Fame Puckster Pierre
57 Shooter's attempt
58 Quarterback who won the Heisman at Houston
59 Greek colony
60 Pub pints
62 Dutch cheese
63 Den or study
64 Int'l. Motor Sports Assn.
67 Roman 106
68 Cedric Ceballos

College Football

ACROSS

1 Walked over
5 QB'd Canes to #1 in '83
10 Route
14 Sox
15 Head coach Harland
16 Ms. Fitzgerald
17 Int'l. Motor Contest Assn.
18 Actor Savalas
19 Puckster Per- —— Brasar
20 Stephen on the screen
21 Point after
22 Kicker's digit
24 Tropical bird
25 Set NCAA career rushing record at Pitt
27 College bowl
29 All-American Edgar Allan
30 Bowdoin's —— Bears
32 QB who won the Heisman at UCLA in '67
35 Social flop
36 Burl played football at Eastern Illinois
40 Bama's Bryant
41 Norfolk team
42 28 Down, for short
43 Pine place
44 Old matter
45 Spoiled
46 Writer W.H.
48 Family
49 Red was three-time Illini All-American
52 Oscar winner who was UNC football player
56 Tennis' Tiriac
57 All-terrain vehicle
59 Before
60 Tax-free acct.
61 Tourney passes
63 UTEP player
65 Show jumping obstacle
66 Lessen
67 Madonna role
68 Christmas song
69 Line gap
70 Prices
71 Bean on 18

DOWN

1 Passing down
2 After Alfa
3 Sportswriter Madison
4 Narc's agy.
5 First Division I team to lose 500 football games
6 Steve set the world mile mark twice
7 Bando brother
8 Guitarist Guthrie
9 Burt played football at FSU
10 —— Speedwagon
11 TAC's Cassell
12 —— for the ride
13 Succeeded Holtz at Notre Dame
21 Laborer
23 Pitching stat
26 Michigan State stadium
28 The only Pac-10 team that's never won a Rose Bowl
30 Ohio University stadium
31 Utah town
32 Fast fastballs
33 Wide shoe width
34 Boston ath. assn.
35 Iowa Heisman winner Kinnick
37 Tenn. player
38 Receiver
39 "—— hey!", Willie Mays
41 Quarterback who set 59 NCAA records at BYU
45 Distance in the decathlon
47 Georgia's bulldog
48 Alex won the Outland Trophy at Iowa
49 Gary succeeded Switzer as coach of the Sooners
50 The winningest football coach for the Longhorns (167-47-5)
51 Peak in Spain
52 Calvin or Rodney
53 United States president who played freshman football at Whittier
54 Apollo in *Rocky*
55 Quinn or Wynn
58 Elvis in —— *Las Vegas*
62 Football formation
64 New York City tourney
65 Stopped —— dime

College Basketball

ACROSS

1 Davidson arena
5 Defunct sports news ntwk.
8 Point guard on 1995 UCLA title team
13 Great Lake
14 Bill Shoemaker
15 Coach Carnesecca
16 Upset Hoyas in 1985 NCAA tourney finals
18 Richard Blackmore classic (with 9 Down)
19 After Sept.
20 Kareem in college
22 Virginia team
23 Employ
24 Rosie Perez role in White Men Can't Jump
27 Mexican coin
29 Japanese volcano
32 French artist
33 First to play on and later coach an NCAA title team in hoops
35 Claim
36 SEC state
37 Reserved one
38 1997 NCAA College Player of The Year
41 Infielder Denis 962-74
42 Print measures
43 Billy no-hit the Yanks for 8 $^2/_3$ innings in his debut
44 Dick coached Penn to 28-1 in 1971
45 Sun Devils
46 Jason was AL best 12-2 in '94
47 NCAA career scoring leader (4,045 points)
52 Actor Stephen
55 Bronco Super Bowl booter
56 Led Indiana State to 33 straight
58 Visiting 56 Across' school
59 City in China
60 Wooden team
61 —— Foot oil
62 Mr. Majerle
63 Appear

DOWN

1 Francis scored NCAA record 113 points against Hillsdale College in '54
2 Friar Murdock set NCAA steals record (376)
3 Happy tune
4 Golfer Nagle
5 Comes in third
6 16 Across for short
7 Curly with the Globetrotters
8 Freshman who was the NCAA tourney Most Outstanding Player for Louisville
9 See 18 Across
10 Quebec skater
11 Oksanen won the Boston Marathon three times
12 Season for an athlete
14 Tom won the Indy 500 in 1983
17 Grand Prix driver Prost
21 Atlantic fish
22 Attendance
24 Gridwork
25 Irv traded the Boston Celtics for the Buffalo Braves
26 Bronco Riley
27 Bowdoin College's Bears
28 Israel's Abba
29 Player's lawyer
30 —— & bake
31 Aquatic mammal
33 John coached basketball at Fordham and Penn State 1950-78
34 River in France
39 College in Pennsylvania
40 Entre ——
41 Journeyman Conlon in the NBA
44 Coach Iba
45 Command at sea
46 Adolph Rupp
47 Comparison word
48 Kyle or Kyle, Jr.
49 Fat lady's song
50 Happy
51 Hindu deity
52 Owls
53 Perry Mason creator —— Stanley Gardner
54 Guy in the Garden
57 Team transport

Baseball

ACROSS

1 AL president in the '90s
6 Sunday night baseball ntwk.
10 Florida football squad
14 Visiting the Monarchs
15 Last place
16 Chucker Chad
17 Forbidden
18 Shutout score in the Mexican League
19 Untouchable Eliot
20 Short
21 Baseball uniforms
23 Extra inning
24 Wanna make ——?
25 0-2 pitch
26 Tony La ——
29 Third baseman Gene sounds like a plant
31 Parched
32 NHL skater Stephane
33 Grapefruit League st.
36 Judge Landis
40 Fingers but not Rollie
41 Highway to Fairbanks
42 Jorge had a 15 year career at second, OF and DH
43 Hot streak
44 Slugger at the corners in Cleveland
46 Hose in New England
49 Four-for-four
51 When a player gets named
52 Argenis Salazar
53 Preacher
56 Leeward
57 Old
58 Hill for Ken Hill
60 Mindy's man
61 ChiSox hurler who led the AL at 12-2 (.857) in '94
62 Baltimore —— Giants of the Negro Leagues
63 Major leaguers
64 New England Sports Ntwk.
65 Al Lopez

DOWN

1 Hits
2 Jazz
3 Larry broke the color line in the AL in 1947
4 What Berry told Justice
5 Matt Jr. & Sr. in the NBA
6 ERA
7 First major league team to host a regular season game in March (3-31-96)
8 Catcher's wear
9 Shooter's org.
10 Chipper
11 Player's lawyer
12 Beau ——
13 Waist band
22 Stern league
23 Let go
25 Bowler Billy
26 Hurler Ron or Rick
27 Vases
28 View
30 North Carolina college
31 Head downhill
32 Rec. center
33 Minor league team

34 Lo cal beer
35 Santa ——, CA
37 Ted coached New York and Buffalo
38 Rodriguez was the AL Rookie of the Year
39 Also
44 Dizzy Dean broke his in the All-Star Game
45 Darren had the first save for the original Rockies
46 Moore on the mound 1970-80
47 OF Ricky in Philly
48 Looks for
50 Nash or Utah
51 Reliever who led the AL at 11-0 for the '85 Blue Jays
52 AL Rookie of the Year whose son played in the NFL
53 Destroy
54 On top of
55 Featherweight champ Jofre
57 Flyers' abbr.
59 John Olerud

Pro Football

ACROSS

1 Joe was the first lightweight champ elected to the Boxing Hall of Fame
5 Army movie with a football game
9 Team transport
12 Montreal manager
13 Nomo with a no-no
14 Remedy
15 Fashion mag
16 Clicking —— cylinders
17 Cub Kevin
18 Lack of emotion after a big game
20 Biochemist who won a Nobel Prize
22 Thread the ——
23 All-Pro Ram Robertson
24 Darrell at guard for 12 seasons
26 Natl. Scouting Serv.
27 QB with record six TD passes in a Super Bowl
32 Morrall or Farrell

36 Caps' arena
37 Sammy Baugh's alma mater
38 Lio in the Football Hall of Fame
39 NHL center Shawn
40 Set NFL mark with 404 pass completions in 1991
42 Johnny or Walker but not Johnny Walker
44 Jacob's brother
45 First Blue Jay to hurl a no-hitter (1990)
47 Mr. Maserati
51 Brown Byner
53 Bring out the chains
55 Packers 33-Raiders 14 Jan. 14, 1968
56 Turkic tongue
58 Hennings won the Outland at Air Force
59 Appeal
60 Grooms in the NFL
61 —— ran
62 Hurler Garver
63 Bill Andre
64 Globetrotters' gag

DOWN

1 Iona athlete
2 Marcus or Lucius
3 Nick in North Dallas Forty
4 Blue shoes for Elvis
5 First NFL team to lose four Super Bowls
6 Home of Ohio Northern Univ.
7 Hurler Aaron
8 Ten-yard penalty in the pros
9 Rangoon's country
10 Danny Heep
11 Noticed
13 Cowboy who was the first defensive Super Bowl MVP
14 Memorial for the Los Angeles Raiders
19 Stranger
21 Turn on the auto track
25 Legal capital of Bolivia
27 Second stringer
28 Texas So. Univ.

29 Tyson bit Holyfield's
30 Herman Moore's alma mater
31 Children's caretaker
33 Time past
34 Linebacker Jack Del ——
35 Chief Dawson
38 Catuna won the 1996 New York City Marathon
40 Slaughter in the NFL
41 Vikings' Purple People ——
43 Shoe width
45 Coat fur
46 Attempted
48 Vike running back Reed
49 Hurler Vern 1974-86
50 Wipe out
51 Sunday night NFL network
52 Tall story
54 Ancient land
57 Groza's digit

Pro Basketball

1	2	3	4		5	6	7	8		9	10	11
12					13					14		
15					16					17		
18				19		20		21				
		22				23						
	24	25				26				27	28	
29				30	31	32		33				34
35				36						37		
38			39	40	41		42	43	44			
	45			46			47	48				
		49				50						
51	52	53				54			55	56	57	
58				59	60		61					
62				63			64					
65				66			67					

ACROSS

1 Elitist
5 Teo on the auto track
9 Shooting stat.
12 Unit of time
13 Big man's basket
14 Anchor a boat
15 Dream Mile city
16 Free
17 Uncle's wife
18 "—— Dan" Majerle
20 Center on the Bulls' title teams
22 Illegal defense
23 Young horse
24 Heads up
26 George coached the Pacers in the '80s
29 Old hoop loop
30 Glenn caught for 16 seasons
33 Hoopster's seasons
35 Batting guru Charley
36 First name of 20 Across
37 "—— the greatest!"
38 Slope rocks
41 Turkish leaders
44 Shaq's school
45 Nineteen-time NBA All-Star
47 Two-team bet
49 Pilot's prefix
50 Utah ABA logo
51 First place team at playoff time
54 Kings made him the first pick in the '89 NBA draft
58 Sting like ——
59 Ron set a pro record by playing in 1,041 consecutive games
61 Isiah Thomas
62 Arena sound
63 Marcus Camby's college
64 Play —— it lies
65 Golfer Nagle
66 Dried up
67 No votes

DOWN

1 Field goal attempt
2 Deli snack
3 City in Finland
4 Olympic medal
5 Ted was first coach to take St. Peter's to the NCAA tourney (1991)
6 Credit card loan rate (abbr.)
7 First coach to take teams in in all four NBA divisions to the playoffs
8 Duke's Cameron —— Stadium
9 Personal
10 Fouled out
11 Avant-garde
13 Time out in the NBA
14 Barber in New York?
19 College jock's quarters
21 David Robinson's alma mater
24 Place to be taken?
25 Golfer Davies
27 Lenny Dykstra
28 Block a shot
29 Gehrig's disease
31 Spurs' arena
32 Frank McGraw
34 Jon Koncak's college
39 Shot blocker
40 Wide shoe size
42 Player, coach, general manager and vice president for the Warriors
43 Block
46 Volcanic peak in Antarctica
48 First player to lead both the NCAA and the NBA in scoring
50 Horse or sixth
51 Jerry Tarkanian
52 Woodwind
53 Ring the bell
55 Bristle
56 Not hurt
57 Famous loch in Scotland
60 Rowing pole

Hockey

ACROSS

1 NHL division of old
6 Sox
10 Flightless birds
14 President of Egypt who won a Nobel prize
15 Red army
16 Allergic reaction
17 Trophy awarded since 1894
19 Gretzky tied Howe's record with goal #801 against this netminder in '94
20 SE Asian front
21 Willie was the NHL's first black skater
22 Doctor's status
24 Towboats
25 Hockey league in the '40s
26 Boxer Buster
29 Jack-of-all-trades position
32 Hurts
33 Surplus
34 Require
36 Math. course
37 Computer instruction
38 Test car
39 Forecaster
40 Sign
41 Carrying a weapon
42 Hockey hanger
44 Short time
45 Major river in Asia
46 Tennessee team
47 Put on the sweater
50 Town in Kansas
51 Owns
54 Therefore
55 Ten-minute penalty
58 Conflict
59 Visiting the Kings
60 Laroupe won back-to-back New York City Marathons in 1994 & 1995
61 Scant
62 Christmas carol
63 Flyer Rod Brind'——

DOWN

1 WHA word (abbr.)
2 Statistics
3 Oates on ice
4 Defensive responsibility
5 Expansion team that made the Stanley Cup finals in its first season (1967-68)
6 Woody or Wendell
7 Number of times a player can win the Calder Trophy
8 Nahan was the original voice for NHL hockey on CBS in '67
9 He was the first NHL skater to score 100 points in a season (1968-69)
10 The NHL's top draft pick, he was traded for six players, two draft picks & $15 million
11 Giant family
12 Basketball league
13 Poet Silverstein
18 Units of energy
23 League formed in 1917
24 Wayne Gretzky
25 Direction reversal
26 Swede Sundin
27 Mark of the original Magic
28 Pennsylvania college
29 Coach's malady
30 Skater Selanne
31 Arabian land
33 Tough player
35 Georgia Tech's ——/Grant Stadium
37 Reliever in a blowout
41 Flames for 636 regular season games
43 Hurons' univ.
44 Unassisted
46 Like loud fans
47 Zone weakness
48 Encourage
49 Winger Liba
50 New York skater
51 Mascot for the Charlotte Hornets
52 Union for liberty
53 Dallas NHL logo
56 Midori on ice
57 Rep's rival

Chapter 16 answers begin on page 317.

Five's a Crowd

Five prominent former and current baseball personalities are lost in this crowd. Can you spot them? Identities and locations are revealed on page 319.

Mystery Guests

Page 10:
Jerry Rice.

Page 28:
Steve Spurrier.

Page 52:
Larry Bird.

Page 70:
George Mikan.

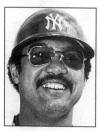

Page 88:
Reggie Jackson.

Page 106:
Doug Flutie.

Page 126:
Bobby Knight.

Page 144:
Mark Messier.

Page 160:
Kirby Puckett.

Page 178:
Jim Brown.

Page 184:
Reggie White.

Page 202:
Bobby Orr.

Page 218:
Patrick Roy.

Page 248:
Pete Maravich.

Page 260:
Karl Malone.

Page 272:
Roger Maris.

Where's Yogi?

Chapter 1: Baseball

Firsts (Warming up): 1. Ron Blomberg. 2. Hoyt Wilhelm. 3. Roberto Clemente. 4. Larry Doby. 5. The Baltimore Orioles. 6. Colt .45s. 7. Chicago's Comiskey Park and Babe Ruth. 8. Outfielder Elmer Smith and pitcher Jim Bagby. 9. The Boston Braves. 10. The Boston Red Sox.

Firsts (Getting serious): 1. The day Jackie Robinson broke baseball's color barrier as a member of the Brooklyn Dodgers. 2. The first night game, at Cincinnati's Crosley Field. 3. The first All-Star Game, at Chicago's Comiskey Park. 4. The first World Series game, Boston vs. Pittsburgh. 5. The first indoor game, at Houston's Astrodome. 6. The first West Coast game, at San Francisco. 7. Frank Robinson's Cleveland debut as the first black manager. 8. The first televised game, at Brooklyn's Ebbets Field. 9. The first night game at Chicago's Wrigley Field. 10. The first game by a transplanted team, at Milwaukee's County Stadium. 11. The first World Series perfect game, by Yankees pitcher Don Larsen. 12. The day Cleveland shortstop Ray Chapman was beaned by Yankees pitcher Carl Mays. Chapman later died, the first major league baseball player to die from injuries suffered on the field. 13. The first game on foreign soil, at Montreal. 14. The first game by an expansion team, Washington vs. Chicago. 15. The first League Championship Series games.

Lasts (Warming up): 1. The Chicago Cubs. 2. The Boston Red Sox and Boston Braves. 3. Jeff Bagwell. 4. Bob Welch and Dave Stewart. 5. Tom Browning. 6. Carl Yastrzemski. 7. Mark Whiten. 8. Tony Oliva. 9. The Boston Red Sox. 10. Carlton Fisk.

Lasts (Getting serious): 1. The last game at Ebbets Field. 2. The 30th victory for Denny McLain, the last 30-game winner. 3. Ted Williams completing baseball's last

.400 season. 4. The victory that clinched Boston's last World Series championship. 5. Ted Williams' last at-bat and game. 6. The Red Sox become the last team to break the color barrier. 7. Roberto Clemente's last game. 8. Hank Aaron hit his last home run. 9. Carl Yastrzemski completed baseball's last Triple Crown season. 10. He was the last out in Catfish Hunter's perfect game.

Famous Home Runs (Warming up): 1. Mickey Mantle. 2. Reggie Jackson. 3. Bucky Dent. 4. Gene Tenace. 5. Tom Niedenfuer. 6. Dave Henderson. 7. Goose Gossage. 8. Nate Colbert. 9. Babe Ruth. 10. Willie Mays.

Famous Home Runs (Getting serious): 1. Berra was the Yankees left fielder when Pittsburgh's Bill Mazeroski hit his World Series-winning home run in 1960 and he was watching from the dugout when Roger Maris hit his 60th and 61st home runs in 1961. 2. Hartung was the Giants runner at third base when Bobby Thomson hit his pennant-winning home run in 1951. 3. House was the Atlanta relief pitcher who stood in the bullpen and caught Hank Aaron's record 715th home run. 4. Molitor was Toronto's runner at first base when Joe Carter hit his World Series-winning home run in 1993. 5. Durante was the Yankees fan who caught Maris' 61st home run in 1961. 6. Davis was the Dodgers runner at second base when Kirk Gibson hit his Game 1-winning home run against Oakland in the 1988 World Series. 7. Bench was the Reds catcher when Boston's Carlton Fisk hit his dramatic Game 6 homer in the 1975 World Series. He also was catching when Aaron tied Babe Ruth's all-time home run record in 1974 with No. 714. 8. Yankees manager Huggins was in the dugout when Babe Ruth hit his 60th home run in 1927. 9. Root was the Cubs pitcher who surrendered Babe Ruth's called-shot home run in the 1932 World Series. 10. Trillo, Carew and Yount were the baserunners when Fred Lynn hit the first grand slam in All-Star Game history in 1983.

One Brief, Shining Moment: 1. Bob Nieman. 2. Larry Jaster. 3. Bobo Holloman. 4. Tom Cheney. 5. Babe Dahlgren. 6. Pat Seerey. 7. Rennie Stennett. 8. Floyd Giebell. 9. Al Gionfriddo. 10. Bill Wambsganss. 11. Gene Stephens. 12. Eddie Gaedel. 13. Dickie Kerr. 14. Wally Pipp. 15. Sandy Amoros.

Seasonal Offerings: 1. 1965. 2. 1979. 3. 1982. 4. 1957. 5. 1960.

Honors (Warming up): 1. The Cincinnati Reds. 2. Al Kaline. 3. Willie Stargell and Keith Hernandez. 4. Steve Carlton and Greg Maddux. 5. Frank Robinson. 6. Barry Bonds. 7. Tony La Russa. 8. Third baseman Brooks Robinson and pitcher Jim Kaat. 9. The Los Angeles Dodgers. 10. Denny McLain.

Honors (Getting serious): 1. The only relief pitchers who have won MVPs. 2. The charter class of the Hall of Fame. 3. World Series MVPs in the 1990s. 4. The first winners of the BBWAA's major awards. 5. Players who have won MVPs and Cy Youngs in the same season. 6. Washington/Minnesota Rookie of the Year winners. 7. The only multiple winners of the World Series MVP. 8. The only Rookie of the Year winners to also win a major award—Valenzuela Cy Young, Lynn MVP. 9. The only multiple winners of the All-Star Game MVP. 10. Players who have won consecutive MVPs. 11. Cleveland players who have had their numbers retired. 12. The only Montreal Expos to win major awards. 13. Players who won five or more batting championships. 14. The only multiple winners of the League Championship Series MVP. 15. Multiple Cy Young Award winners.

Milestones (Warming up): 1. Tom Seaver and Rod Carew. 2. George Brett. 3. Rickey Henderson. 4. Steve Garvey. 5. Lou Brock. 6. Ted Williams. 7. Bob Horner. 8. Cy Young. 9. Jimmie Foxx. 10. Lee Smith.

Milestones (Getting serious): 1. Players who have 3,000 career hits. 2. The only members of the 40-40 club. 3. Players who have hit four home runs in a game. 4. Pitchers who have 300 career victories. 5. Players with 4,000 hits. 6. Players who have won Triple Crowns. 7. Players with 600 home runs. 8. Players who have compiled hitting streaks of 40 or more games. 9. Players with 400 career victories. 10. Players with 500 home runs. 11. Pitchers with more than 3,000 career strikeouts. 12. Players who have stolen 100 bases in a season.

Peripheral Visions: 1. Ed Armbrister. 2. Hugh Casey. 3. Ken Keltner. 4. Bernie Carbo. 5. Burt Hooton, Elias Sosa and Charlie Hough. 6. Gene Garber. 7. Johnny Pesky. 8. Joe Adcock. 9. Sal Maglie. 10. Ron Swoboda.

Memorable Numbers (Warming up): 1. The Cleveland Indians. 2. Ron Guidry. 3. Rickey Henderson and Vince Coleman. 4. The 1975 Boston Red Sox. 5. The 1973 New York Mets. 6. Chicago White Sox vs. Los Angeles Dodgers in 1959. 7. They were the only two American League victories in a 23-year span. 8. The Kansas City Royals and Philadelphia Phillies. 9. Fred Lynn won in 1979. 10. The Chicago Cubs (1908), Chicago White Sox (1917), Boston Red Sox (1918), Cleveland Indians (1948) and New York/San Francisco Giants (1954).

Memorable Numbers (Getting serious): 1. Years the Dodgers have won World Series. 2. Expansion seasons. 3. The eight totals for players who have stolen 100 bases in a season. 4. The five highest single-season RBI totals. 5. Years the playoff formula was expanded. 6. The seven top career strikeout totals. 7. Years in which pennant and division playoffs were needed. 8. Babe Ruth's home run totals in the 1920s. 9. Seasons in which players posted four-home run games. 10. Years the Red Sox have won World Series. 11. The average, home run and RBI totals for Ted Williams' Triple Crown seasons. 12. Years Ty Cobb won American League batting titles. 13. Years in which the Yankees and Dodgers met in the World Series. 14. New York Yankees retired numbers. 15. Seasons in which players won Triple Crowns.

Chapter 2: Who Are These Guys?

Silhouettes in the Shade:

1. Babe Ruth.
2. Johnny Bench.
3. Steve Carlton.
4. Ty Cobb.
5. Yogi Berra.
6. Wade Boggs.
7. Cy Young.
8. Carl Yastrzemski.
9. Dan Quisenberry.
10. Yogi Berra and Don Larsen hugging after Larsen's World Series perfect game.
11. Dennis Eckersley.
12. Dave Parker.
13. Eddie Gaedel.
14. Don Mattingly.
15. Fernando Valenzuela.
16. Eric Davis.
17. Dave Winfield.
18. Cecil Fielder.
19. Joe DiMaggio.
20. Reggie Jackson.
21. Fred McGriff.
22. Bob Gibson.
23. Julio Franco.
24. Rickey Henderson.
25. Willie McCovey.
26. Mickey Mantle.
27. Willie Mays making his spectacular catch in Game 1 of the 1954 World Series.
28. Sandy Koufax.
29. Juan Marichal.
30. Randy Johnson.
31. Connie Mack.
32. Roberto Clemente.
33. Kirby Puckett.
34. Stan Musial.
35. Phil Niekro.
36. Pete Gray.
37. Jim Palmer.
38. Tony Pena.
39. Marge Schott and Schottzie.
40. Brooks Robinson.
41. Ted Williams.
42. Frank Robinson.
43. Tom Seaver.
44. Darryl Strawberry.

45. U.L. Washington.
46. Pete Rose.
47. Brett Favre.
48. Lawrence Taylor.
49. Don Shula.
50. Bear Bryant.
51. The Four Horsemen of Notre Dame.
52. Joe Paterno.
53. Joe Montana.
54. O.J. Simpson.
55. William "Refrigerator" Perry.
56. Marty Schottenheimer.
57. Barry Sanders.
58. George Seifert.
59. Tom Dempsey.
60. Wilt Chamberlain.
61. George Mikan.
62. Artis Gilmore.
63. Larry Bird.
64. Bill Russell.
65. Manute Bol (right) and Muggsy Bogues.
66. Julius Erving.
67. Red Auerbach.
68. Kareem Abdul-Jabbar.
69. Chris Mullin.
70. Pete Maravich.
71. Michael Jordan.
72. Kevin McHale.
73. Oscar Robertson.
74. Magic Johnson.
75. Bob Knight.
76. Gordie Howe.
77. Brett Hull.
78. Toe Blake.
79. Jaromir Jagr.
80. Ken Dryden.

Chapter 3: Pro Football

Firsts (Warming up): 1. The Tampa Bay Buccaneers. 2. Eric Dickerson. 3. Paul Brown. 4. Bob Lilly. 5. The Baltimore Colts used the first overall pick on Elway in 1983. 6. The Tampa Bay Buccaneers. 7. The Houston Oilers. 8. Honolulu, Hawaii. 9. Tony Dorsett. 10. Dick Butkus, Gale Sayers.

Firsts (Getting serious): 1. Chicago's Feathers became the NFL's first 1,000-yard rusher. 2. Berwanger was the NFL's first-ever draft pick. 3. The participants in the first Monday Night Football telecast. 4. Boston's Battles became the NFL's first player to rush for 200 yards in one game. 5. The final score in the first Super Bowl. 6. The players who returned the first kickoffs in franchise history for touchdowns—Auer for Miami and Gilliam for New Orleans. 7. Buffalo's Gogolak was pro football's first soccer-style kicker. 8. Denver's Taylor was the first AFL or NFL player to catch 100 passes in a season. 9. The first black player to gain election to the Pro Football Hall of Fame. 10. The first United States Football League champions. 11. The first regular-season overtime game in NFL history ended in a tie. 12. Green Bay's Hutson was the first player to gain 1,000 yards in receptions in a season.

Out Patterns (Warming up): 1. David Woodley. 2. Pittsburgh selected Johnny Unitas; Green Bay picked Bart Starr. 3. The St. Louis Cardinals. 4. The Baltimore Colts and Earl Morrall. 5. Vince Ferragamo. 6. Y.A. Tittle. 7. Otto Graham. 8. Sammy Baugh. 9. Bobby Douglass. 10. Jim Plunkett, Archie Manning, Dan Pastorini.

Out Patterns (Getting serious): 1. The six quarterbacks selected in the first round of the 1983 draft. 2. Quarterbacks who have thrown for 40,000 or more yards in their careers. 3. Quarterbacks who have thrown seven touchdown passes in a game. 4. Quarterbacks who have thrown for 500 yards in a game. 5. Former Kansas City Chiefs quarterbacks. 6. Quarterbacks who were Super Bowl MVPs. 7. Lefthanded quarterbacks. 8. Former Dallas Cowboys quarterbacks. 9. Quarterbacks who have lost three or more times in the Super Bowl. 10. Cardinals quarterbacks selected on the first round.

Famous Plays (Warming up): 1. Jim Marshall. 2. Jack Tatum. 3. Gale Sayers. 4. Earnest Byner. 5. Ron Meyer. 6. Joe Pisarcik. 7. Matt Bahr. 8. Billy Cannon. 9. Sammy Baugh. 10. Chris Boniol.

Famous Plays (Getting serious): 1. Starr made the game-winning touchdown plunge behind Kramer's block in the 1967 Ice Bowl championship game in which Green Bay defeated Dallas. 2. The 1972 Immaculate Reception. Pittsburgh QB Bradshaw threw the pass, Raiders defender Tatum tipped it and Steelers running back Harris caught it and ran for the winning touchdown in an AFC playoff game. 3. The Catch. San Francisco QB Montana threw the end zone pass and Clark made the leaping catch to give the 49ers a 28-27 victory over Dallas in the 1981 NFC title game. 4. The Hail Mary Pass. Dallas QB Staubach made a desperation heave and Pearson outfought Minnesota defenders Wright and Brown for the game-winning TD in a 1975 NFC playoff game. 5. Morrall was the holder when Baltimore's O'Brien kicked his Super Bowl V-deciding 32-yard field goal against Dallas. 6. The three Raiders who fumbled, batted and kicked the ball into the end zone where Oakland recovered for a final-play touchdown and a 21-20 victory over San Diego in a 1978 contest. 7. Baltimore QB Unitas handed off to running back Ameche for the NFL championship-deciding touchdown in a sudden-death 1958 overtime victory over the Giants. 8. Miami kicker Yepremian, whose field-goal attempt was blocked by Washington's Brundige, picked up the ball and threw a desperation pass that was intercepted and returned for a Super Bowl VII touchdown by Bass. 9. Scarpati was the holder when New Orleans' Dempsey booted his record 63-yard field goal to defeat Detroit in a 1970 game. 10. 49ers QB Montana connected with Taylor on a Super Bowl XXIII-deciding 10-yard TD pass that defeated Cincinnati with 34 seconds remaining.

Milestones (Warming up): 1. Jim Brown. 2. Steve Largent. 3. Joe Namath. 4. Marino threw for more than 5,000 yards; Dickerson rushed for more than 2,000 yards. 5. John Riggins. 6. The New York Giants. 7. Walter Payton, Eric Dickerson and Tony Dorsett. 8. Johnny Unitas. 9. Jim Marshall. 10. Jan Stenerud, Nick Lowery.

Milestones (Getting serious): 1. Jerry Rice, Marcus Allen, Jim Brown, Walter Payton, John Riggins, Emmitt Smith, Lenny Moore, Don Hutson, Steve Largent, Franco Harris. 2. George Blanda, Nick Lowery, Jan Stenerud, Gary Anderson, Morten Andersen. 3. Walter Payton, Eric Dickerson, Tony Dorsett, Jim Brown, Franco Harris, Marcus Allen, Barry Sanders, John Riggins, O.J. Simpson, Thurman Thomas, Ottis Anderson, Emmitt Smith. 4. Dan Marino, Fran Tarkenton, Dan Fouts, Warren Moon, John Elway, Joe Montana, Johnny Unitas. 5. Dan Marino, Fran Tarkenton, Johnny Unitas, Joe Montana, Dave Krieg, Sonny Jurgensen, Dan Fouts, Warren Moon, John Elway. 6. Jerry Rice, Art Monk, Steve Largent, Henry Ellard, Andre Reed, James Lofton, Charlie Joiner. 7. Reggie White, Lawrence Taylor, Rickey Jackson, Richard Dent, Bruce Smith, Kevin Greene. 8. Jerry Rice, Emmitt Smith, Franco Harris, Roger Craig, Thurman Thomas. 9. George Blanda, Earl Morrall, Jim Marshall, Jackie Slater. 10. Jim Brown, Steve Van Buren, O.J. Simpson, Eric Dickerson, Emmitt Smith.

Super Intense (Warming up): 1. Don Shula, Bud Grant, Marv Levy. 2. The 1980 Raiders won Super Bowl XV. 3. The Dallas Cowboys. 4. Joe Montana. 5. The Raiders won Super Bowl XVIII. 6. Scott Norwood. 7. Doug Williams. 8. Chuck Howley. 9. Harvey Martin, Randy White. 10. Tom Flores, Mike Ditka.

Super Intense (Getting serious): 1. Marcus Allen. 2. Timmy Smith. 3. Jake Scott. 4. Max McGee. 5. Duane Thomas. 6. John Stallworth. 7. Jim Plunkett. 8. Roger Craig. 9. Larry Csonka. 10. Mark Rypien. 11. Matt Snell. 12. Larry Brown.

Memorable Numbers (Warming up): 1. Tom Flores guided the Raiders to the AFC's only two titles in the 1980s. 2. 324. 3. 27 points for the winners; 10 for the losers. 4. Starr wore 15, Unitas 19. 5. 17—11 players, 6 founding fathers. 6. 31. 7. Seven. 8. Three—Tom Landry, Jimmy Johnson, Barry Switzer. 9. 48. 10. The Super Bowls played in 1972, 1973, 1974.

Memorable Numbers (Getting serious): 1. O.J. Simpson's record rushing total in 1973. 2. The width, in yards, of a football field. 3. The final score in Chicago's 1940 NFL championship game victory over Washington. The most lopsided shutout in NFL history was engineered by Halas and Luckman, who are pictured on the page. 4. The total minutes and seconds of the Miami-Kansas City Christmas Day playoff game in 1971—the longest game in NFL history. 5. The Dolphins' final record in their unprecedented perfect 1972 season. 6. The length, in yards, of Tom Dempsey's record 1970 field goal. 7. The record number of yards compiled by Chicago's Walter Payton in a 1977 game against Minnesota. 8. Don Shula's record total of NFL coaching victories. 9. The record number of yards Miami's Dan Marino passed for in 1984. 10. The Super Bowl records of the Vikings, Broncos and Bills.

Seasonal Offerings: 1. 1981. 2. 1987. 3. 1971. 4. 1968. 5. 1950.

Double and Triple Vision (Warming up): 1. Tampa Bay, 1984. 2. Arizona, 1989. 3. Atlanta, 1989. 4. Green Bay, 1978. 5. Buffalo, 1982. 6. Baltimore Colts, 1983. 7. New Orleans, 1976. 8. New York Jets, 1980. 9. Cincinnati, 1993. 10. New England, 1973.

Double and Triple Vision (Getting serious): 1. Charlie Brown, John Riggins. 2. Cliff Branch, Mark van Eeghen. 3. Drew Pearson, Tony Dorsett. 4. Otis Taylor, Mike Garrett. 5. Jerry Rice, Roger Craig. 6. Mark Bavaro, Joe Morris. 7. Todd Christensen, Marcus Allen. 8. Michael Irvin, Emmitt Smith. 9. Don Maynard, Matt Snell. 10. Carroll Dale, Jim Taylor. 11. Gary Clark, George Rogers. 12. Dwight Clark, Wendell Tyler.

Running in Place (Warming up): 1. Jim Brown. 2. Walter Payton. 3. Earl Campbell. 4. O.J. Simpson. 5. Eric Dickerson. 6. Gale Sayers. 7. Thurman Thomas. 8. Steve Van Buren. 9. Emmitt Smith. 10. John Brockington. 11. Barry Sanders. 12. Floyd Little.

Running in Place (Getting serious): 1. G. 2. J. 3. E. 4. F. 5. I. 6. A. 7. D. 8. B. 9. C. 10. H.

Chapter 4: Venues

The Eyes Have It: 1. Actor Jack Nicholson is a familiar figure at The Great Western Forum when the NBA's Los Angeles Lakers play their games. 2. A gondola that formerly was located at the apex of Houston's Astrodome, 208 feet above second base. New York broadcaster Lindsey Nelson and producer Joel Nixon once called a Mets-Astros game from that lofty perch. 3. The Sym-Phony Band stayed out of tune for two decades as part of the entertainment fare at Brooklyn's Ebbets Field in the 1940s and '50s. 4. The "Green Monster" left-field wall at Boston's Fenway Park stands as a monument to baseball past and present. 5. Uga, the University of Georgia's bulldog mascot, is a familiar sight during football games at Sanford Stadium. 6. The decorative facade that spans the upper rim of Yankee Stadium. 7. The Forum, now known as the Great Western Forum, has served as home of the NBA's Los Angeles Lakers and the NHL's Los Angeles Kings since 1967. 8. "The Bull Ring" was a former section of the upper left-field deck at Philadelphia's Veterans Stadium, which was usually populated by young fans who were guests of Phillies left fielder Greg "Bull" Luzinski. 9. The towering bat is a fixture in Yankee Stadium's parking area. 10. The smiling Indian delivered messages to customers who attended games at Cleveland's Municipal Stadium. 11. The decorative fountains in the right-center field area of Kansas City's Kauffman Stadium. 12. The "Dawg Pound" was the home of avid, barking fans who filled an end zone section at Municipal Stadium before the Cleveland Browns franchise was shifted to Baltimore. 13. No game at Dodger Stadium is complete without Mike Brito and his radar gun behind home plate. 14. The 230-foot A-frame scoreboard was a feature of Anaheim Stadium before it was relocated to the parking lot. 15. A's owner Charles O. Finley and Charlie O. the Mule were regular companions at old Municipal Stadium in Kansas City. 16. Clemson football players rub Howard's Rock as a ritual before every pre-game run down the Hill into Memorial Stadium. 17. Bill the Goat, Navy's mascot since 1904, attends all games at Navy-Marine Corps Memorial Stadium. 18. The short pennant porch was a brief Charles O. Finley innovation at Kansas City's Municipal Stadium in 1964. 19. The football-shaped dome atop the Pro Football Hall of Fame at Canton, Ohio. 20. A section of the outfield wall and bleachers at Chicago's Wrigley Field. 21. Ted Giannoulas entertained fans and harassed umpires at Jack Murphy Stadium as the San Diego Chicken before expanding his opportunities as The Chicken. 22. Super fan Hilda Chester and her ever-present cowbell were regular sights at Brooklyn's Ebbets Field. 23. Championship banners, both basketball and hockey, hung from the rafters, giving Boston Garden a nostalgic atmosphere. 24. The Clydesdales, pulling August A. Busch's beer wagon, made festive appearances at St. Louis' Busch Stadium. 25. The crown-shaped scoreboard at Kansas City's Kauffman Stadium. 26. The Schaefer Beer and Abe Stark signs sandwiched the scoreboard at Brooklyn's Ebbets Field. 27. The artificial carpet of the early Astrodome was cleaned between innings by several astronaut wannabes. 28. A bronze statue of Cardinals great Stan Musial stands guard outside the gates of St. Louis' Busch Stadium. 29. The columns at one end of the horseshoe-shaped Los Angeles Coliseum give the stadium a distinctive look. 30. County Stadium home runs by Milwaukee players are celebrated by Bernie Brewer, who slides from his chalet into a mug of beer. 31. Two of the three monuments that stood for years in center field at Yankee Stadium honored former New York greats Miller Huggins and Lou Gehrig. 32. The 31-foot center field fence at Washington's Griffith Stadium projected onto the field, forming a peculiar angle for ball-chasing outfielders. 33. The Big Apple at New York's Shea Stadium rises in celebration whenever a Mets player hits a home run. 34. The left field scoreboard at Cleveland's Jacobs Field. 35. The rearing Bronco oversees football activity from atop the scoreboard at Denver's Mile High Stadium during NFL games. 36. How bad were the 1980 New Orleans Saints? Bad enough that fans at the New Orleans Superdome, billing themselves as the Aints, attended games wearing bags over their heads. 37. The Lakers Girls are a mainstay at the Great Western Forum during basketball games. 38. Ralphie the buffalo runs rampant before and during breaks in college football games at Colorado's Folsom Field. 39. The office tower was the distinguishing feature at Wrigley Field in Los Angeles—the first home of the Los Angeles Angels. 40. This overhead shot shows the close proximity of Yankee Stadium (foreground) and the horseshoe-shaped Polo Grounds, located just across the river. 41. The helmets are a dead giveaway for football festivities at Michigan Stadium in Ann Arbor. 42. Chicago fans can watch Cubs games from the roofs of buildings across from Wrigley Field. 43. The left field scoreboard at Coors Field in Denver. 44. The white line on the concrete wall at Cincinnati's Crosley Field served as a home run marker in the late 1940s. The ground rule was spelled out on the wall. 45. The Boston Celtics' leprechaun was prominently displayed during games at Boston Garden. 46. Barrel Man is a regular during Denver Broncos' games at Mile High Stadium. 47. Touchdown Jesus presides over football destinies across from Notre Dame Stadium. 48. The scoreboard at Arlington Stadium, the facility used by the Texas Rangers before their move to The Ballpark in Arlington. 49. The center-court logo at Indiana's Assembly Hall. 50. Chief Noc-a-homa celebrated Braves home runs during his stay at Atlanta-Fulton County Stadium. 51. The victory cigar and championship ring belong to long-time Boston Celtics coach and front-office executive Red Auerbach, a fixture at Boston Garden. 52. The locker of former New York star Lou Gehrig was a clubhouse staple at Yankee Stadium before being moved to the Baseball Hall of Fame at Cooperstown, N.Y.

53. Harvey was the mechanical rabbit that rose out of the ground from his position behind home plate to deliver fresh balls to the home plate umpire at Kansas City's Municipal Stadium. Harvey was a Charles O. Finley innovation. 54. Chief Osceola traditionally rides his Appaloosa to the 50-yard line at Doak Campbell Stadium and plants a flaming spear into the ground, sending Florida State football fans into a pregame frenzy. 55. The Husky Helmet Car makes a parade lap on the track surrounding Husky Stadium after every University of Washington touchdown. 56. The CN Tower dominates the skyline around Toronto's SkyDome. 57. The "Chinese Screen" was a 40-foot detriment to home runs at the Los Angeles Coliseum, temporary home to the Dodgers from 1958-61. The screen was erected because the left field foul line measured only 251 feet from home plate. 58. The site of the Sun Bowl in El Paso, Texas, as one end zone section informs all football fans.

Stadium Composite No. 1: Base stadium: Boston's Fenway Park. 1. Outfielders at Cincinnati's Crosley Field had to deal with a slope leading up to the left field fence. 2. The ivy walls are still a feature at Chicago's Wrigley Field. 3. The left field wall at Boston's Fenway Park is known as the "Green Monster." 4. The Cathedral of Learning, located on the University of Pittsburgh campus, towered over the left field bleachers at Pittsburgh's Forbes Field. 5. The left field scoreboard at St. Louis' Sportsman's Park. 6. The center field clubhouse at New York's Polo Grounds, complete with its Chesterfield cigarette sign. 7. The monuments to Babe Ruth, Miller Huggins and Lou Gehrig were part of Yankee Stadium's center field for a number of years. 8. The right field scoreboard, complete with its Abe Stark sign, was a fixture at Brooklyn's Ebbets Field. 9. A seating section at Boston's Braves Field, known as the Jury Box, had a capacity of about 2,000. 10. Harvey, a mechanical rabbit that rose out of the ground to deliver fresh balls to the umpire, was a Charles O. Finley innovation at Kansas City's Municipal Stadium.

Stadium Composite No. 2: Base stadium: Baltimore's Oriole Park at Camden Yards. 1. The light standard and Indians sign that sits atop the left field scoreboard at Cleveland's Jacobs Field. 2. The decorative facade that outlines the upper rim of Yankee Stadium. 3. An outfield bleacher section from Detroit's Tiger Stadium. 4. The A-frame scoreboard was moved from the left center field area at Anaheim Stadium to its parking lot. 5. The Mets apple rises in celebration of New York home runs at Shea Stadium. 6. The decorative fountains from the right center field area at Kansas City's Kauffman Stadium. 7. The fireworks-spouting scoreboard that dominated the outfield area at old Comiskey Park in Chicago. 8. The right field bleacher section and scoreboard from Dodger Stadium. 9. The B&O Warehouse, located 432 feet from home plate at Camden Yards, provides office space for the Orioles and houses a souvenir shop, cafeteria and lounge for the general public. 10. The Gateway Arch dominates the skyline outside St. Louis' Busch Stadium.

Chapter 5: Pro Basketball

Firsts (Warming up): 1. Bob Pettit. 2. Pittsburgh (Pipers) and New Orleans (Buccaneers). 3. 30,000 points. 4. Bill Russell. 5. George Mikan. 6. Milwaukee Bucks. 7. It was the Lakers' first game on the West Coast after moving to Los Angeles. 8. Larry Bird. 9. Bill Walton. 10. Toronto.

Firsts (Getting serious): 1. The first NBA All-Star Game. 2. The first game in ABA history. 3. The first player to make a 3-point shot. 4. Moses Malone becomes the first player to jump from high school to the pros, signing with Utah of the ABA. 5. Lenny Wilkens earns his 1,000th NBA coaching victory. 6. Rochester beats Boston in the NBA's first game using the 24-second clock. 7. The Boston Celtics start their 11-of-13 championship streak with an NBA Finals Game 7 victory over St. Louis. 8. Leading scorer Fulks sparks the Warriors to a Game 5 victory over the Chicago Stags and the BAA/NBA's first championship. 9. The opening of the Naismith Memorial Basketball Hall of Fame in Springfield, Mass. 10. The first NBA draft.

Numero Uno (Warming up): 1. Elgin Baylor. 2. Vancouver Grizzlies. 3. Nate "Tiny" Archibald. 4. Sam Jones. 5. Karl Malone. 6. Patrick Ewing. 7. Oscar Robertson. 8. Scott Burrell. 9. Bernard King. 10. David Robinson.

Numero Uno (Getting serious): 1. The record number of points Philadelphia center Wilt Chamberlain scored in a March 2, 1962, victory over New York. 2. The lowest scoring game in NBA history, won by Fort Wayne over Minneapolis on November 22, 1950. 3. The only season the Boston Celtics failed to win a championship in the 1960s. 4. Philadelphia center Wilt Chamberlain's incredible scoring average in 1961-62. 5. The record number of championships won by the Boston Celtics. 6. The unprecedented record compiled by the 1995-96 Chicago Bulls. 7. The time span of Los Angeles' record 33-game winning streak. 8. The points scored by Kareem Abdul-Jabbar in his record-setting NBA career. 9. The record playoff won-lost total of the 1982-83 Philadelphia 76ers. 10. The height of Washington's Gheorghe Muresan, the tallest player in NBA history.

Uniformity (Warming up): 1. Kareem Abdul-Jabbar (33, Bucks and Lakers); Bob Lanier (16, Pistons and Bucks); Wilt Chamberlain (13, 76ers and Lakers); Nate Thurmond (42, Warriors and Cavaliers). 2. Julius Erving (32, Nets and 6, 76ers); Oscar Robertson (14, Cincinnati Royals/Sacramento Kings and 1, Bucks). 3. Celtics (Walter Brown) and Trail Blazers (Larry Weinberg). 4. 613 is the number of regular-season coaching victories Holzman compiled. 5. 77 honors the year (1977) Ramsay guided the Trail Blazers to their only championship. 6. Brad Davis. 7. The microphone honors longtime announcer Johnny Most and the nickname "Loscy" belonged to Jim Loscutoff. 8. The No. 6 honors Sacramento's fans. 9. George Mikan. 10. No. 5.

Uniformity (Getting serious): 1. Bill Russell (6), Bob Cousy (14), John Havlicek (17), Larry Bird (33). 2. Wilt Chamberlain (13), Elgin Baylor (22), Kareem Abdul-Jabbar (33), Jerry West (44). 3. Walt Frazier (10), Earl Monroe (15), Willis Reed (19), Bill Bradley (24). 4. Julius Erving (6), Wilt Chamberlain (13), Hal Greer (15). 5. Alex English (2), David Thompson (33), Dan Issel (44). 6. Oscar Robertson (1), Sidney Moncrief (4), Kareem Abdul-Jabbar (33). 7. Elvin Hayes (11), Wes Unseld (41). 8. Bob Lanier (16), Dave Bing (21). 9. Pete Maravich (7), Darrell Griffith (35). 10. Bob Pettit (9), Lou Hudson (23).

Offensive Patterns (Warming up): 1. Wilt Chamberlain and Wes Unseld. 2. Willis Reed. 3. Don Chaney. 4. Willis Reed (1970), Kareem Abdul-Jabbar (1971), Magic Johnson (1987) and Hakeem Olajuwon (1994). 5. Bill Russell (Celtics), Henry Bibby (Knicks), Magic Johnson (Lakers), Billy Thompson (Lakers). 6. Three times. 7. Bob McAdoo. 8. Rick Barry. 9. Swen Nater. 10. Don Buse.

Offensive Patterns (Getting serious): 1. Lefthanded centers. 2. Boston Celtics sixth men. 3. ABA scoring champions. 4. The men who compiled the top six single-game point totals in NBA history. 5. Milwaukee Bucks coaches. 6. The shortest and tallest players in NBA history. 7. Members of Dream Team I. 8. First-round draft picks of the Orlando Magic. 9. Nicknames of Chicago NBA teams. 10. Defensive stoppers.

That's Final (Warming up): 1. Elgin Baylor. 2. The Sacramento Kings. 3. The Los Angeles Lakers. 4. Alex Hannum (St. Louis, 1958, and Philadelphia, 1967). 5. Kareem Abdul-Jabbar. 6. The Washington Bullets and Seattle SuperSonics. 7. The Indiana Pacers. 8. Jerry West. 9. The 1977 Portland Trail Blazers. 10. The Philadelphia 76ers.

That's Final (Getting serious): 1. Dave DeBusschere. 2. Chet Walker. 3. Tom Heinsohn. 4. Gail Goodrich. 5. Bill Laimbeer. 6. Bob Dandridge. 7. Gus Williams. 8. Maurice Cheeks. 9. Kevin McHale. 10. Horace Grant. 11. Elvin Hayes. 12. James Worthy.

Seasonal Offerings: 1. 1975. 2. 1968. 3. 1988. 4. 1978. 5. 1960.

Sites and Sounds (Warming up): 1. Boston Garden. 2. The (Great Western) Forum in Los Angeles. 3. Chicago Stadium. 4. The Memorial Coliseum in Portland. 5. Madison Square Garden in New York. 6. The Philadelphia Spectrum. 7. The Los Angeles Sports Arena. 8. The Capital Centre/USAir Arena.

Sites and Sounds (Getting serious): 1. Atlanta Hawks. 2. Sacramento Kings. 3. Vancouver Grizzlies. 4. Phoenix Suns. 5. Houston Rockets. 6. Boston Celtics. 7. Dallas Mavericks. 8. Detroit Pistons. 9. Portland Trail Blazers. 10. Utah Jazz. 11. Seattle SuperSonics. 12. Cleveland Cavaliers. 13. Milwaukee Bucks. 14. Indiana Pacers. 15. Philadelphia 76ers.

Feeling a Draft (Warming up): 1. Lionel Simmons (La Salle), Travis Mays (Texas), Duane Causwell (Temple), Anthony Bonner (Saint Louis U.). 2. Patrick Ewing. 3. Phoenix Suns. 4. Ralph Sampson (1983), Hakeem Olajuwon (1984). 5. Chris Webber. 6. San Antonio picked David Robinson, who had played collegiately at Navy. 7. St. Louis Hawks. 8. Hayes. 9. Johnson. 10. Chamberlain was born and raised in Philadelphia.

Feeling a Draft (Getting serious): 1. 1985: Ewing, Tisdale, Benjamin, McDaniel, Koncak, Kleine, Mullin. 2. 1986: Daugherty, Bias, Washburn, Person, Walker, Bedford, Tarpley. 3. 1987: Robinson, Gilliam, Hopson, Williams, Pippen, Smith, Johnson. 4. 1988: Manning, Smits, Smith, Morris, Richmond, Hawkins, Perry. 5. 1989: Ellison, Ferry, Elliott, Rice, Reid, King, McCloud, White, Hammonds. 6. 1990: Coleman, Payton, Jackson, Scott, Gill, Spencer, Simmons, Kimble, Burton, Robinson, Hill. 7. 1991: Johnson, Anderson, Owens, Mutombo, S. Smith, D. Smith, Longley, Macon, Augmon, Williams, Brandon. 8. 1992: O'Neal, Mourning, Laettner, Jackson, Ellis, Gugliotta, Williams, Day, Weatherspoon, Keefe, Horry. 9. 1993: Webber, Bradley, Hardaway, Mashburn, Rider, Cheaney, Hurley, Baker, Rogers, Hunter, Houston. 10. 1994: Robinson, Kidd, Hill, Marshall, Howard, Wright, Murray, Grant, Montross, Jones, Rogers.

Odds and Ends (Warming up): 1. Jerry West. 2. Larry Brown. 3. 2,000 victories. 4. Julius Erving. 5. Bob Cousy and Oscar Robertson. 6. Charles Barkley. 7. Bill Russell and K.C. Jones. 8. It was David Robinson's first season. 9. John Stockton. 10. Toronto.

Odds and Ends (Getting serious): 1. Olajuwon, 7-0; Robinson, 7-1; Gilmore, 7-2; Sampson, 7-4; Bradley, 7-6. 2. Bogues, 5-3; Jennings, 5-7; Murphy, 5-9; Barros, 5-11; Archibald, 6-1. 3. Frazier, 6-4; Erving, 6-7; Cowens, 6-9; Malone, 6-11; Ewing, 7-0. 4. Cousy, 6-1; Dumars, 6-3; Rivers, 6-4; Robertson, 6-5; Miller, 6-7. 5. Buckner, Indiana; Lester, Iowa; Havlicek, Ohio State; Harper, Illinois; Grant, Michigan; Kelser, Michigan State. 6. Chapman, Kentucky; Pettit, Louisiana State; Morris, Auburn; Wilkins, Georgia; Schintzius, Florida; Houston, Tennessee. 7. Perkins, North Carolina; Thompson, North Carolina State; Parks, Duke; Scott, Georgia Tech; Lucas, Maryland; Stith, Virginia. 8. Hoiberg, Iowa State; Peeler, Missouri; White, Kansas; Blackman, Kansas State; Piatkowski, Nebraska; Tisdale, Oklahoma. 9. Magic Johnson. 10. Jerry West. 11. Julius Erving. 12. K.C. Jones.

Chapter 6: Sports Movies

Sports Movies: 1. Movie: *The Stratton Story*. Actor: Jimmy Stewart. 2. Movie: *Damn Yankees*. Actor: Tab Hunter. 3. Movie: *The Natural*. Actor: Robert Redford. 4. Movie: *Fear Strikes Out*. Actor: Anthony Perkins; Tab Hunter (TV version). 5. Movie: *The Pride of St. Louis*. Actor: Dan Dailey. 6. Movie: *Major League; Major League II*. Actors: Wesley Snipes, Omar Epps. 7. Movie: *A League of Their Own*. Actor: Tom Hanks. 8. Movie: *Field of Dreams*. Actor: Amy Madigan. 9. Movie: *The Natural*. Actor: Barbara Hershey. 10. Movie: *Major League; Major League II*. Actor: Tom Berenger.

11. Movie: *Hoosiers*. Actor: Gene Hackman. 12. Movie: *White Men Can't Jump*. Actor: Woody Harrelson. 13. Movie: *Brian's Song*. Actor: James Caan. 14. Movie: *The Mighty Ducks; D2, The Mighty Ducks; D3, The Mighty Ducks*. Actor: Emilio Estevez. 15. Movie: *The Natural*. Actor: Robert Duvall. 16. Movie: *Semi-Tough*. Actor: Burt Reynolds. 17. Movie: *Amazing Grace and Chuck*. Actor: Alex English. 18: Movie: *Bull Durham*. Actor: Susan Sarandon. 19. Movie: *Rookie of the Year*. Actor: Thomas Ian Nicholas. 20. Movie: *SpaceJam*. Actor: Danny DeVito. 21. Movie: *Jerry Maguire*. Actor: Tom Cruise. 22. Movie: *Field of Dreams*. Actors: Frank Whaley (Archie Graham) and Burt Lancaster (Dr. "Moonlight" Graham). 23. Movie: *Alibi Ike*. Actor: Joe E. Brown. 24. Movie: *White Men Can't Jump*. Actor: Rosie Perez. 25. Movie: *Slapshot*. Actor: Paul Newman. 26. Movie: *M*A*S*H*. Actor: Fred Williamson. 27. Movie: *Hoosiers*. Actor: Dennis Hopper. 28. Movie: *A League of Their Own*. Actor: Geena Davis. 29. Movie: *The Jackie Robinson Story*. Actor: Minor Watson. 30. Movie: *Cobb* or *Babe Ruth*. Actors: Tommy Lee Jones or Pete Rose. 31. Movie: *Forget Paris*. Actor: Billy Crystal. 32. Movie: *The Natural*. Actor: Joe Don Baker. 33. Movie: *The Bad News Bears; The Bad News Bears in Breaking Training; The Bad News Bears Go to Japan*. Actor: Chris Barnes. 34. Movie: *Knute Rockne: All American*. Actor: Pat O'Brien. 35. Movie: *The Big Leaguer*. Actor: Edward G. Robinson. 36. Movie: *Jerry Maguire*. Actor: Cuba Gooding, Jr. 37. Movie: *The Natural*. Actor: Kim Basinger. 38. Movie: *The Stratton Story*. Actor: June Allyson. 39. Movie: *It Happens Every Spring*. Actor: Ray Milland. 40. Movie: *Semi-Tough*. Actor: Jill Clayburgh. 41. Movie: *Blue Chips*. Actor: Shaquille O'Neal. 42. Movie: *Cobb*. Actor: Robert Wuhl. 43. Movie: *One in a Million*. Actor: LeVar Burton. 44. Movie: *The Longest Yard*. Actor: Burt Reynolds. 45. Movie: *It Happens Every Spring*. Actor: Paul Douglas. 46. Movie: *Damn Yankees*. Actor: Gwen Verdon. 47. Movie: *Knute Rockne: All American*. Actor: Ronald Reagan. 48. Movie: *The Fish That Saved Pittsburgh*. Actor: Julius Erving. 49. Movie: *The Bingo Long Traveling All-Stars and Motor Kings*. Actor: Billy Dee Williams. 50. Movie: *Major League; Major League II*. Actor: Corbin Bernsen. 51. Movie: *The Bad News Bears; The Bad News Bears in Breaking Training; The Bad News Bears Go to Japan*. Actors: Gary Lee Cavagnaro; Jeffrey Louis Starr. 52. Movie: *Everybody's All-American*. Actor: Dennis Quaid. 53. Movie: *White Men Can't Jump*. Actor: Wesley Snipes. 54. Movie: *A League of Their Own*. Actor: Rosie O'Donnell. 55. Movie: *Field of Dreams*. Actor: Kevin Costner. 56. Movie: *Brian's Song*. Actor: Billy Dee Williams. 57. Movie: *Brewster's Millions*. Actors: Richard Pryor, Dennis O'Keefe. 58. Movie: *Bull Durham*. Actor: Kevin Costner. 59. Movie: *One On One*. Actor: Robby Benson. 60. Movie: *Horse Feathers*. Actor: Groucho Marx. 61. Movie: *The Bad News Bears*. Actor: Walter Matthau. 62. Movie: *The Pride of St. Louis*. Actor: Richard Crenna. 63. Movie: *Angels in the Outfield*. Actor: Paul Douglas. 64. Movie: *Rudy*. Actor: Sean Astin. 65. Movie: *Kill the Umpire*. Actor: William Bendix. 66. Movie: *The Babe Ruth Story* or *Babe Ruth* or *The Babe*. Actors: Charles Bickford, William Lucking, James Cromwell. 67. Movie: *Field of Dreams*. Actor: James Earl Jones. 68. Movie: *A League of Their Own*. Actor: Madonna. 69. Movie: *The Longest Yard*. Actor: Eddie Albert. 70. Movie: *The Babe Ruth Story* or *Babe Ruth* or *The Babe*. Actors: William Bendix; Stephen Lang; John Goodman. 71. Movie: *Hoosiers*. Actor: Barbara Hershey. 72. Movie: *The Natural*. Actor: Glenn Close. 73. Movie: *The Kid From Left Field*. Actors: Dan Dailey (1953); Robert Guillaume (1979). 74. Movie: *Eddie*. Actor: Whoopi Goldberg. 75. Movie: *Brian's Song*. Actor: Jack Warden. 76. Movie: *Rookie of the Year*. Actor: Daniel Stern. 77. Movie: *Mr. Baseball*. Actor: Tom Selleck. 78. Movie: *The Best of Times*. Actor: Kurt Russell. 79. Movie: *Major League; Major League II*. Actor: Charlie Sheen. 80. Movie: *Damn Yankees*. Actor: Ray Walston. 81. Movie: *Bang the Drum Slowly*. Actors: Albert Salmi (1956); Robert De Niro (1973). 82. Movie: *Field of Dreams* or *Eight Men Out*. Actors: Ray Liotta; D.B. Sweeney. 83. Movie: *Blue Chips*. Actor: Nick Nolte. 84. Movie: *Semi-Tough*. Actor: Kris Kristofferson. 85. Movie: *Necessary Roughness*. Actor: Scott Bakula. 86. Movie: *Field of Dreams*. Actor: Gaby Hoffmann. 87. Movie: *The Bad News*

Bears. Actor: Tatum O'Neal. 88. Movie: *The Fish That Saved Pittsburgh.* Actor: Jonathan Winters. 89. Movie: *Brian's Song.* Actor: Shelley Fabares. 90. Movie: *Black Sunday.* Actor: Robert Shaw. 91. Movie: *The Natural.* Actor: Wilford Brimley. 92. Movie: *Eight Men Out.* Actor: John Cusack. 93. Movie: *Bull Durham.* Actor: Tim Robbins. 94. Movie: *Rudy.* Actor: Chelcie Ross. 95. Movie: *Don't Look Back.* Actor: Louis Gossett, Jr. 96. Movie: *Semi-Tough.* Actor: Brian Dennehy. 97. Movie: *The Bad News Bears; The Bad News Bears in Breaking Training; The Bad News Bears Go to Japan.* Actor: Jackie Earle Haley. 98. Movie: *The Program.* Actor: James Caan. 99. Movie: *The Longest Yard.* Actor: Richard Kiel. 100. Movie: *Brewster's Millions.* Actor: John Candy. 101. Movie: *Sudden Death.* Actor: Jean-Claude Van Damme. 102. Movie: *The Best of Times.* Actor: Robin Williams. 103. Movie: *Slapshot.* Actor: Jeff Carlson. 104. Movie: *Slapshot.* Actor: Steve Carlson. 105. Movie: *Slapshot.* Actor: David Hanson. 106. Movie: *That's My Boy.* Actor: Jerry Lewis. 107. Movie: *Youngblood.* Actor: Rob Lowe. 108. Movie: *Bang the Drum Slowly.* Actor: Paul Newman (1956) or Michael Moriarty (1973). 109. Movie: *Major League; Major League II.* Actor: Bob Uecker. 110. Movie: *Blue Chips.* Actor: Anfernee "Penny" Hardaway. 111. Movie: *Pistol Pete—Birth of a Legend.* Actor: Adam Guier. 112. Movie: *The Fan.* Actor: Wesley Snipes.

Sports Movies (Photos): Page 107: Baseball action in *The Natural* was filmed at War Memorial Stadium in Buffalo, N.Y. Page 108: The man autographing a ball for Semon is Hall of Fame pitcher Grover Cleveland Alexander. Page 109: De Niro was a catcher, Moriarty a pitcher. Page 110: Pirates second baseman Mazeroski bounced into a triple play in a scene for the movie. Page 111: Minor Watson played the role of Brooklyn executive Branch Rickey. Page 112: Dizzy and Paul Dean were the focus in *The Pride of St. Louis.* Page 113: Tab Hunter's Joe Hardy character sold his soul to the Devil. Page 114: Former New York Yankees first baseman Lou Gehrig. Page 115: William Frawley, better known for his portrayal of Fred Mertz on the hit television series *I Love Lucy.* Page 116: Gehrig's former teammate Babe Ruth offered insight for the director. Page 117: Cooper was preparing for his role as Lou Gehrig. Page 118: William Bendix portrayed Ruth in the movie. Page 119: Trevor portrayed Mrs. Babe Ruth. Page 120: Robinson portrayed a tryout camp supervisor for the New York Giants. Page 121: Vera-Ellen. Page 122: Real-life Pittsburgh slugger Ralph Kiner. Page 123: Lancaster's Moonlight Graham character was a doctor. Page 124: The real Monty Stratton. Page 125: New York Yankees catcher Bill Dickey.

Chapter 7: Hockey

The Great Ones (Warming up): 1. The Indianapolis Racers. 2. Pittsburgh's Mario Lemieux. 3. 51 games. 4. 92. 5. 215. 6. 61. 7. Four times. 8. Janet Jones. 9. Four—1984, 1985, 1987, 1988 with Edmonton. 10. Boston's Bobby Orr, 1970-71; Pittsburgh's Mario Lemieux, 1988-89.

The Great Ones (Getting serious): 1. Chicago Blackhawks. 2. New York Rangers. 3. Hartford Whalers. 4. Quebec Nordiques. 5. Detroit Red Wings. 6. Chicago Blackhawks. 7. Boston Bruins. 8. Edmonton Oilers. 9. New York Rangers. 10. Hartford Whalers. 11. New York Rangers. 12. Detroit Red Wings.

Net Worth (Warming up): 1. Ron Hextall. 2. Edmonton's Grant Fuhr. 3. Jeff Reese. 4. Buffalo's Dominik Hasek, 1.95, in 1993-94; New Jersey's Martin Brodeur, 1.88, 1996-97. 5. Bernie Parent. 6. Bill Durnan. 7. Chicago's Tony Esposito. 8. Terry Sawchuk. 9. Chuck Gardiner. 10. Toronto and Johnny Bower defeated Detroit and Terry Sawchuk in the 1964 Cup finals. A year later, they were teammates in Toronto.

Net Worth (Getting serious): 1. Philadelphia's Bernie Parent. 2. Montreal's Ken Dryden. 3. Edmonton's Bill Ranford. 4. Chicago's Glenn Hall. 5. Calgary's Mike

Vernon. 6. Montreal's Rogie Vachon. 7. Edmonton's Grant Fuhr. 8. Detroit's Terry Sawchuk. 9. New York Rangers' Dave Kerr. 10. Pittsburgh's Tom Barrasso. 11. Boston's Gerry Cheevers. 12. Montreal's Patrick Roy.

Expanding Horizons (Warming up): 1. The California Seals and Minnesota North Stars. 2. Terry Sawchuk (pictured on page). 3. The Chicago Blackhawks. 4. The Washington Capitals. 5. The Philadelphia Flyers. 6. Philadelphia defeated Buffalo. 7. Gordie Howe and Bobby Hull. 8. The Winnipeg Jets. 9. Philadelphia goalie Bernie Parent. 10. Edmonton's Glen Sather.

Expanding Horizons (Getting serious): 1. Bulls. 2. Cowboys. 3. Cougars. 4. Stingers. 5. Crusaders. 6. Aeros. 7. Racers. 8. Sharks. 9. Blazers. 10. Mariners.

The 50-500 Club (Warming up): 1. Bobby and Brett Hull. 2. Bernie "Boom Boom" Geoffrion. 3. Scoring 50 or more goals in the first 50 games of a season. 4. Mario Lemieux and Kevin Stevens. 5. Brendan Shanahan and Mike Modano. 6. Wayne Gretzky, Jari Kurri and Glenn Anderson. 7. Craig Simpson scored 13 goals for Pittsburgh and 43 for Edmonton. 8. Dave Andreychuk scored 29 goals for Buffalo, 25 for Toronto. 9. Blaine Stoughton. 10. Joe Mullen.

The 50-500 Club (Getting serious): 1. Gordie Howe. 2. Guy Lafleur. 3. Bobby Hull. 4. Bryan Trottier. 5. Jari Kurri. 6. Marcel Dionne. 7. Phil Esposito. 8. Wayne Gretzky. 9. Frank Mahovlich. 10. Dale Hawerchuk.

He Shoots, He Scores (Warming up): 1. Boston's Phil Esposito. 2. Denis Potvin of the New York Islanders. 3. Darryl Sittler. 4. Bobby Orr, Phil Esposito, John Bucyk, Ken Hodge and Wayne Cashman finished 1 through 5 in the final assist standings for Boston in 1970-71. Orr, Esposito, Bucyk and Hodge all topped 100 points. 5. Brian Bradley. 6. It took them 5 seconds. 7. Bill Mosienko. 8. Four times. 9. Ian Turnbull. 10. Joe Malone. 11. Marc Tardif. 12. All have managed 50-goal seasons for two different teams. 13. They are the only goalies to score goals in NHL action. 14. Kevin Stevens. 15. Bobby Carpenter.

He Shoots, He Scores (Getting serious): 1. Gordie Howe (1960). 2. Henri Richard (1973). 3. Rod Gilbert (1977). 4. Bobby Clarke (1981). 5. Wayne Gretzky (1984). 6. Mike Bossy (1986). 7. Bernie Federko (1988). 8. Peter Stastny (1989). 9. Paul Coffey (1990). 10. Mario Lemieux (1992). 11. Steve Yzerman (1993). 12. Steve Larmer (1995).

What's My Line? (Warming up): 1. Winnipeg Jets. 2. Quebec Nordiques. 3. Minnesota North Stars. 4. Colorado Rockies. 5. Kansas City Scouts. 6. Atlanta Flames. 7. The Ottawa Senators. 8. California Golden Seals.

What's My Line? (Getting serious): 1.Buffalo's French Connection Line. 2. Detroit's Production Line. 3. The New York Rangers' GAG (Goal-A-Game) Line. 4. Chicago's MPH Line. 5. Los Angeles' Triple Crown Line. 6. Chicago's Million Dollar Line. 7. Philadelphia's LCB Line. 8. The New York Islanders' Long Island Lighting Co. Line. 9. Toronto's Kid Line. 10. Philadelphia's Legion of Doom Line.

A Trophy Case (Warming up): 1. Pittsburgh's Mario Lemieux in 1993. 2. Stan Mikita (1967 and 1968). 3. Philadelphia's Bobby Clarke. 4. Philadelphia's Eric Lindros. 5. The Minnesota North Stars. 6. Pelle Lindbergh (pictured in accompanying photo). 7. Tom Barrasso. 8. Ken Dryden in 1970-71 and 1971-72. 9. Al Rollins. 10. Ken Dryden and Michel "Bunny" Larocque.

A Trophy Case (Getting serious): 1. Wayne Gretzky (10), Gordie Howe (6), Mario Lemieux (6), Phil Esposito (5), Stan Mikita (4). 2. Bobby Orr (1970 and 1972), Guy Lafleur (1977), Wayne Gretzky (1985). 3. Roger Crozier (1966), Glenn Hall (1968), Reggie Leach (1976), Ron Hextall (1987). 4. Bryan Trottier and Glenn "Chico" Resch in 1976 for the Islanders. 5. Jacques Plante (7), Bill Durnan (6), Ken Dryden (5), Bunny

Larocque (4), Terry Sawchuk (4), Tiny Thompson (4). 6. Buddy O'Connor (1948), Bobby Hull (1965), Stan Mikita (1967, 1968), Wayne Gretzky (1980). 7. Bobby Orr (8), Doug Harvey (7), Ray Bourque (5). 8. Gilbert Perreault (Buffalo, 1970), Denis Potvin (N.Y. Islanders, 1973), Bobby Smith (Minnesota, 1978), Dale Hawerchuk (Winnipeg, 1981), Mario Lemieux (Pittsburgh, 1984), Bryan Berard (N.Y. Islanders, 1997). 9. Wayne Gretzky (9), Gordie Howe (6), Eddie Shore (4), Bobby Clarke (3), Mario Lemieux (3), Howie Morenz (3), Bobby Orr (3). 10. Bobby Orr (1970), Guy Lafleur (1977), Wayne Gretzky (1985), Mario Lemieux (1992).

Good Lord, Stanley (Warming up): 1. The New York Islanders in 1982 and 1983. 2. 1970. The Canadiens finished fifth and Toronto sixth in the East Division. 3. Ken Morrow. 4. It was halted because of a killer influenza epidemic in Canada. 5. Claude Lemieux. 6. Petr Klima. 7. Edmonton's Grant Fuhr. 8. Bill Barilko. 9. The Chicago Blackhawks. 10. Pat LaFontaine.

Good Lord, Stanley (Getting serious): 1. Montreal Canadiens. 2. Chicago Blackhawks. 3. St. Louis Blues. 4. Montreal Maroons. 5. New York Islanders. 6. Toronto Maple Leafs. 7. Montreal Canadiens. 8. Take your choice: Philadelphia, Chicago or Boston. 9. Edmonton Oilers. 10. Pittsburgh Penguins.

Behind the Bench (Warming up): 1. Scotty Bowman won four straight titles with Montreal from 1976-79 after watching his St. Louis Blues get swept in the 1968, 1969 and 1970 Cup finals. 2. Tommy Gorman. 3. Montreal's Toe Blake. 4. Bob Johnson guided the Pittsburgh Penguins to the 1991 championship. 5. Pete Muldoon. 6. Lester Patrick. 7. Hap Day. 8. Babe Siebert. 9. Bill Stewart. 10. Herb Brooks.

Behind the Bench (Getting serious): 1. St. Louis Blues. 2. New York Rangers. 3. Chicago Blackhawks. 4. Montreal Canadiens. 5. Detroit Red Wings. 6. Toronto Maple Leafs. 7. Philadelphia Flyers. 8. Buffalo Sabres. 9. Los Angeles Kings. 10. St. Louis Blues.

Chapter 8: Celebrities in Sports

Facing Facts: 1. Actor Tommy Lee Jones was an All-Ivy League offensive guard for Harvard in 1968. 2. Actor Bill Cosby was a running back for Temple in the early 1960s. 3. Lou Boudreau was a two-year varsity basketball player at Illinois before going on to a Hall of Fame baseball career from 1938-52. 4. John Beradino, long-time star of the daytime soap opera *General Hospital,* enjoyed a pre-acting major league career with the St. Louis Browns, Cleveland Indians and Pittsburgh Pirates. 5. Former U.S. Sen. Bill Bradley was an outstanding basketball player for Princeton and the New York Knicks before jumping into the political arena. 6. Danny Ainge played parts of three seasons for the Toronto Blue Jays, but his real success came during a 13-year NBA career with the Boston Celtics, Sacramento Kings, Portland Trail Blazers and Phoenix Suns. 7. Jim Brown, a basketball and football star at Syracuse University, rushed for a then NFL-record 12,312 yards before retiring at age 29 and becoming a successful actor. 8. John Elway played a season of minor league baseball for the Oneonta Yankees in 1982 before beginning his outstanding pro football career as quarterback of the Denver Broncos. 9. Rob Fitzgerald, known today for his "I love you, man" Bud Light television commercials, was a three-year letterman as a defensive back for the University of Missouri in the mid-1970s. 10. David Adkins, better know today as the comedian "Sinbad," played varsity basketball from 1974 through 1978 for the University of Denver. 11. Chuck Connors, best known as the star of the hit television series *The Rifleman,* was a two-sport professional. He played major league baseball for the Brooklyn Dodgers (1949) and Chicago Cubs (1951) and pro basketball with the NBL's Rochester Royals (1945-46) and the BAA/NBA's Boston Celtics (1946-48). 12. Dave Winfield played one year of varsity basketball at

Minnesota before starting his outstanding major league baseball career. 13. Fred Dryer was a Pro Bowl defensive end for the Los Angeles Rams in the 1970s before moving on to acting and the hit television show *Hunter.* 14. Gerald Ford, who was named the outstanding player of the 1934 Michigan team and played for the College All-Stars against the Chicago Bears in 1935, later served for 24 years in the U.S. House of Representatives before becoming vice president of the United States in 1973 and president in 1974. 15. Former New York Yankees ironman first baseman Lou Gehrig did a role reversal when he starred in the 1938 musical Western *Rawhide.* 16. George Bush, a first baseman for Yale in the late 1940s, later served as vice president of the United States under Ronald Reagan and was elected as the 41st president in 1988. 17. Hale Irwin, a three-time U.S. Open champion in golf, was an All-Big Eight Conference defensive back for Colorado in 1965 and 1966. 18. Dick Groat was a high-scoring college star for Duke from 1949-52 before an outstanding major league baseball career with Pittsburgh, St. Louis, Philadelphia and San Francisco. 19. Ted Kennedy, a long-time U.S. Senator from Massachusetts, played 14 games as an end for Harvard in 1954 and 1955, catching two touchdown passes. 20. George "Papa Bear" Halas played 12 major league games for the 1919 New York Yankees before his long and distinguished career as NFL founder, player, coach and owner. 21. James Dean was better known for his acting than his good-but-not-great performance as an Indiana prep basketball player. 22. Actor Kris Kristofferson competed as a 170-pound end for Pomona-Claremont in the late 1950s. 23. Kenny Lofton, an outstanding center fielder with the Atlanta Braves, set a single-season steals record while playing guard for the Arizona basketball team from 1985 through 1989. 24. California running back Jackie Jensen played in the 1949 Rose Bowl before going on to an outstanding 11-year major league career, most of which was spent with the Boston Red Sox. 25. Jack Kemp, who quarterbacked the Buffalo Bills to AFL championships in 1964 and 1965, gained even more national prominence in his long political career as a member of the U.S. House of Representatives out of New York. 26. Alex Karras was an outstanding defensive tackle at the University of Iowa and for 12 seasons with the NFL's Detroit Lions before beginning an equally outstanding career as an actor. 27. Actor Lee Majors was known during his early-1960s college football career at Eastern Kentucky as Harvey Lee Yeary. Television's *Six Million Dollar Man* was an offensive and defensive end. 28. Ed Marinaro, best known for his role as Joe Coffey in the hit television series *Hill Street Blues,* was the 1971 Heisman Trophy runnerup to Pat Sullivan as a running back out of Cornell. Marinaro also played professionally with Minnesota, the New York Jets and Seattle. 29. Bob Mathias, best known as a two-time Olympic gold medal-winning decathlete, lettered in 1951 and 1952 as a Stanford fullback and played against Illinois in the 1952 Rose Bowl. 30. Carl Weathers played two seasons of professional football for the Oakland Raiders (1970 and 1971) before rising to prominence as Apollo Creed in the *Rocky* movie series. 31. Richard Nixon was a reserve player for little Whittier College in California in the early 1930s before beginning a political career that would vault him all the way to the U.S. presidency. 32. Merlin Olsen gained acting fame in the television series *Father Murphy* and *Little House on the Prairie* after 15 outstanding NFL seasons as a defensive tackle for the Los Angeles Rams. 33. Buddy Reynolds, who changed his name to Burt when he began his long and successful acting career, earned varsity letters as a part-time running back for the 1955 and 1957 Florida State football teams. 34. After graduating from Eureka College in Illinois in 1932, former football player Ronald Reagan became a broadcaster, a motion-picture actor, a television-show host, the governor of California and the 40th president of the United States. 35. Jackie Robinson was an outstanding running back at UCLA in the early 1940s before vaulting into prominence as the man who would break baseball's color barrier. 36. Ted Cassidy averaged 17.7 points and 10.7 rebounds for Stetson in 1954-55 before going on to prominence as the character Lurch in television's *The Addams Family* series. 37. Stone Phillips, known today as the co-anchor of television's *Dateline NBC,* was known as a quarterback in 1975 and 1976 when he attended Yale. 38. Paul Robeson was a former Rutgers (1917 and 1918) and early NFL star who went on to prominence as a singer, actor and black activist. 39. Lee Smith, baseball's all-time saves leader, averaged 3.4 points in his only college basketball season for Northwestern (La.) State. 40. Although Ron Luciano was a solid football lineman for Syracuse from 1956-58, he was better known for his performance as an animated American League umpire from 1968-79. 41. Michael Warren, who achieved acting fame in his role as Bobby Hill in the television series *Hill Street Blues,* was a starting guard on UCLA's 1967 and 1968 NCAA Tournament championship teams. 42. Mark Harmon quarterbacked the UCLA football team in 1972 and 1973 before embarking on his successful acting career. 43. Tom Selleck, known to millions of television viewers as Thomas Magnum for his role in *Magnum, P.I.,* played a total of 10 games for Southern California in the 1965-66 and 1966-67 seasons, scoring four points. 44. Perennial National League batting champion Tony Gwynn averaged 8.6 points and 5.5 assists over four seasons as a guard for San Diego State University from 1977-81. 45. Known during his football-playing days at USC (1925 and 1926) as Marion Morrison, he went on to greater fame as actor John Wayne.

Chapter 9: College Football

One Fine Day (Warming up): 1. Sands, playing for the University of Kansas in 1991. 2. Houston quarterback Klingler in 1990. 3. UNLV wide receiver Gatewood in 1994. 4. Illinois running back Griffith in 1990. 5. Wake Forest quarterback LaRue in 1995. 6. Illinois' Grange in 1924. 7. Syracuse's Brown in 1956. 8. Southern Cal's Davis in 1972. 9. Texas A&M's Franklin in 1976. 10. Kansas' Cromwell in 1975.

One Fine Day (Getting serious): 1. Tony Sands, Kansas. 2. Marshall Faulk, San Diego State. 3. Troy Davis, Iowa State. 4. Anthony Thompson, Indiana. 5. Mike Pringle, Cal State Fullerton. 6. Rueben Mayes, Washington State. 7. Brian Pruitt, Central Michigan. 8. Eddie Lee Ivery, Georgia Tech. 9. Scott Harley, East Carolina. 10. Eric Allen, Michigan State.

Scenarios: 1. Georgia Tech defeated Cumberland College. 2. Notre Dame defeated Army. 3. Michigan defeated arch-rival Ohio State. 4. Notre Dame upset Oklahoma. 5. Cannon and LSU defeated Mississippi. 6. Southern Cal upset Notre Dame. 7. No. 1 Notre Dame tied with No. 2 Michigan State. 8. Southern Cal and O.J. Simpson defeated No. 1 UCLA. 9. Harvard rallied for 16 points in the final minute to tie Yale. 10. Houston pounded Tulsa. 11. Texas rallied to defeat Arkansas. 12. Nebraska defeated Oklahoma. 13. Southern Cal blitzed Notre Dame. 14. California defeated Stanford. 15. Boston College and Doug Flutie defeated Miami and Bernie Kosar.

Statue of Liberty (Warming up): 1. Ed Smith served as the model for the Heisman Trophy. 2. Stanford's Jim Plunkett. 3. Jake Gibbs. 4. Oregon State quarterback Terry Baker. 5. Pat Sullivan. 6. Larry Kelley and Clint Frank, both of Yale, won in 1936 and '37. 7. Auburn running back Bo Jackson (1985) and Florida State quarterback Charlie Ward (1993). 8. Nebraska flanker Johnny Rodgers (1972) and Boston College quarterback Doug Flutie (1984). 9. Desmond Howard. 10. Michigan's Desmond Howard in 1991.

Statue of Liberty (Getting serious): 1. Berwanger, a University of Chicago halfback, won the first Heisman Trophy in 1935. 2. Ohio State running back Griffin is the only two-time Heisman winner, capturing the award in 1974 and '75. 3. Syracuse halfback Davis became the first black Heisman winner in 1961. 4. Notre Dame quarterback Hornung became the first Heisman winner from a losing team in 1956.

5. Yale's Kelley (1936) and Notre Dame's Hart (1949) are the only two Heisman winners who did not play quarterback, running back or wide receiver. 6. The only Heisman winners from service academies. Blanchard, Davis and Dawkins played at Army; Bellino and Staubach played at Navy. 7. Texas Christian quarterback O'Brien (1938) was the shortest Heisman winner at 5-foot-7. 8. Army fullback Blanchard (1945) was the first underclassman (junior) to win the Heisman. 9. Pittsburgh defensive end Green finished as Heisman runner-up in 1980—the only time a defensive player has finished in the second position. 10. Heisman winners who never played in the National Football League.

School Spirit (Warming up): 1. Dick Butkus, Illinois; Len Dawson, Purdue; Otto Graham, Northwestern; Bob Griese, Purdue; Paul Warfield, Ohio State. 2. George Blanda, Kentucky; Joe Namath, Alabama; Fran Tarkenton, Georgia; Jim Taylor, LSU; Bart Starr, Alabama; Doug Atkins, Tennessee. 3. Dan Fouts, Oregon; Frank Gifford, USC; Ernie Nevers, Stanford; Norm Van Brocklin, Oregon; O.J. Simpson, USC. 4. Lance Alworth, Arkansas; Bob Lilly, TCU; Doak Walker, SMU; Sammy Baugh, TCU; Earl Campbell, Texas. 5. John Riggins, Kansas; Kellen Winslow, Missouri; Gale Sayers, Kansas. 6. Sonny Jurgensen, Duke; Randy White, Maryland; Henry Jordan, Virginia. 7. Franco Harris, Penn State; Johnny Unitas, Louisville; Paul Hornung, Notre Dame; Fred Biletnikoff, Florida State; Mike Ditka, Pittsburgh; Jim Otto, Miami.

School Spirit (Getting serious): 1. Terry Bradshaw. 2. Willie Lanier. 3. Roger Staubach. 4. Walter Payton. 5. Art Shell. 6. Deacon Jones. 7. Joe Greene. 8. Larry Little. 9. Ken Houston. 10. Mel Blount.

Whistle Blowers (Warming up): 1. Bo Schembechler. 2. Lou Holtz. 3. Bear Bryant. 4. Woody Hayes. 5. Bobby Bowden. 6. Amos Alonzo Stagg. 7. Hayden Fry. 8. Jim Sweeney. 9. Pop Warner. 10. Darrell Royal.

Whistle Blowers (Getting serious): 1. Bear Bryant at Alabama. 2. John McKay at USC. 3. Darrell Royal at Texas. 4. Bud Wilkinson at Oklahoma. 5. Bo Schembechler at Michigan. 6. Red Blaik at Army. 7. Woody Hayes at Ohio State. 8. Johnny Majors at Tennessee. 9. Knute Rockne at Notre Dame. 10. Vince Dooley at Georgia. 11. Frank Howard at Clemson. 12. Terry Donahue at UCLA.

The Match Game (Warming up): 1. California and Stanford. 2. Indiana and Purdue. 3. Yale and Harvard. 4. Lafayette and Lehigh. 5. The Little Brown Jug. 6. Army (Doc Blanchard and Glenn Davis) vs. Notre Dame (Johnny Lujack and Leon Hart). 7. Michigan and Michigan State have met 89 times. UCLA has played USC 66 times and Alabama and Auburn have faced off 61 times. 8. Illinois defeated UCLA in the first Rose Bowl game that pitted the Big Ten Conference against the Pacific-10 under a long-term contract that would run for more than half a century. 9. Tulane beat Temple in the first Sugar Bowl game and Bucknell beat Miami in the first Orange Bowl. 10. Princeton and Yale.

The Match Game (Getting serious): 1. Southern Cal (20 Rose Bowl wins) vs. Oklahoma (11 Orange Bowl wins). 2. Nebraska (103 wins) vs. BYU (102). 3. Minnesota vs. Wisconsin (106 games). 4. Michigan (764) vs, Notre Dame (746). 5. Texas (9 Cotton Bowl wins) vs. Alabama (8 Sugar Bowl wins). 6. Kansas vs. Missouri (105 games). 7. Alabama (103 wins) vs. Oklahoma (102). 8. Notre Dame (8) vs. Oklahoma or Alabama (6). 9. Oklahoma (47) vs. Washington (39). 10. Florida State (75 wins) vs. Nebraska (74).

Let's Go Bowling (Warming up): 1. The Rose Bowl dates back to 1902. The Orange Bowl and Sugar Bowl played their first games in 1935, the Cotton Bowl in 1937. 2. Alabama. 3. The 1942 Rose Bowl was moved to Durham because military conditions during World War II forbade the gathering of large crowds on the West Coast. It was the only Rose Bowl not played at Pasadena. 4. Alabama. Michigan won the first Rose Bowl, Bucknell the first Orange Bowl, Tulane the first Sugar Bowl and TCU the first Cotton Bowl. 5. The California Golden Bears. 6. Arizona. 7. Missouri lost to Penn State in 1970. 8. BYU as champion of the Western Athletic Conference. 9. The Florida Gators. 10. Mississippi State and Vanderbilt.

Let's Go Bowling (Getting serious): 1. Ohio State coach Hayes punched Clemson defender Charlie Bauman, who had just made a game-saving interception in the Gator Bowl. 2. California defender Riegels picked up a Georgia Tech fumble and advanced the ball 65 yards—the wrong way—in the Rose Bowl. 3. Kansas, using a 12-man defense on Penn State's potential game-winning two-point conversion attempt in the Orange Bowl, was whistled for a penalty after stopping the Nittany Lions. Penn State scored on the replay and won the game, 15-14. 4. The Pittsburgh passing combination that clicked for 33 yards and the winning touchdown with 35 seconds remaining in the Sugar Bowl against Georgia. 5. Florida State defeated Nebraska, 18-16, in a national championship-deciding Orange Bowl game. 6. Rice's Moegle was on his way to a 95-yard touchdown run when Alabama's Lewis stepped off the bench and tackled him in a Cotton Bowl game. Moegle was awarded a TD. 7. Penn State defeated Miami on the late interception in the national championship-deciding Fiesta Bowl. 8. The Schooner, a horse-drawn covered wagon belonging to Oklahoma's spirit group, was penalized 15 yards for charging onto the field during an Orange Bowl game against Washington. The penalty cost the Sooners a field goal. 9. Speyrer's diving fourth-down catch of a James Street pass kept alive the desperation drive that helped Texas defeat Notre Dame 21-17 in the Cottom Bowl and win a national championship. 10. Bosco's TD pass to Smith secured BYU's 24-17 Holiday Bowl victory over Michigan and the school's first national championship. 11. The end zone play on a Nebraska conversion attempt secured Miami's 31-30 victory in the Orange Bowl and the Hurricanes' first national championship. 12. UCLA defender Stiles stopped Michigan State's Apisa short on a two-point conversion attempt that would have given the No. 1-ranked Spartans a Rose Bowl tie. Stiles was knocked out on the game-saving play.

Sites and Sounds (Warming up): 1. Washington. 2. Tennessee. 3. Iowa. 4. Colorado. 5. Florida State. 6. Auburn. 7. Texas A&M. 8. East Carolina. 9. Penn State. 10. Missouri. 11. Northwestern. 12. Kentucky.

Sites and Sounds (Getting serious): 1. Neyland Stadium, 102,485. 2. Dowdy-Ficklen Stadium, 35,000. 3. Kinnick Stadium. 4. Faurot Field. 5. Husky Stadium, built in 1920. 6. Commonwealth Stadium, built in 1973. 7. Jordan-Hare Stadium, after long-time coach Shug Jordan. 8. Folsom Field. 9. Florida State's Doak-Campbell Stadium. 10. Kyle Field. 11. Beaver Stadium. 12. Dyche Stadium.

Conference Calls (Warming up): 1. The Big Ten. 2. The Pacific-10 Conference. 3. University of Chicago. 4. The Big West Conference. 5. The Big 12, Pacific-10 and Western Athletic. 6. Southern California. 7. The Ivy League. 8. Arkansas won 13 SWC titles before moving to the Southeastern Conference. 9. Purdue. 10. Colorado.

Conference Calls (Getting serious): 1. Oklahoma was a Southwest Intercollegiate Athletic Conference (the Southwest Conference) charter member and now plays in the Big 12. 2. Georgia Tech from the Southeastern to the Atlantic Coast. 3. South Carolina from the Atlantic Coast to the Southeastern. 4. Arkansas from the Southwest to the Southeastern. 5. Oklahoma State from the Southwest Intercollegiate Athletic Conference (the Southwest Conference) to the Missouri Valley Intercollegiate Athletic Association (the current Big 12). 6. Arizona State from the Western Athletic to the Pacific-10. 7. Texas from the Southwest to the Big 12. 8. Fresno State from the Big West to the Western Athletic. 9. Iowa from the Missouri Valley Intercollegiate Athletic Association (the current Big 12) to the Big Ten. 10. Rice from the Southwest to the Western Athletic.

Chapter 10: Photo Morphing

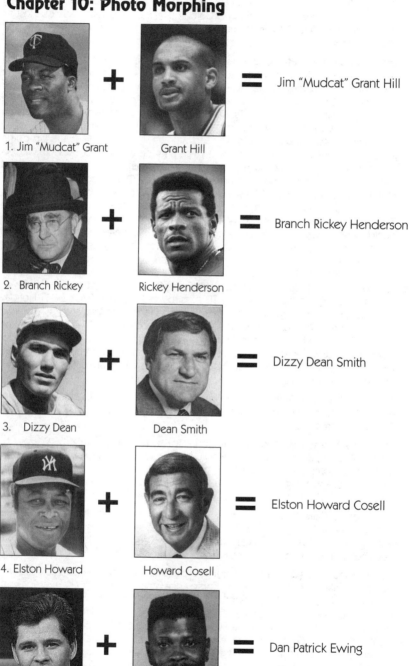

1. Jim "Mudcat" Grant + Grant Hill = Jim "Mudcat" Grant Hill

2. Branch Rickey + Rickey Henderson = Branch Rickey Henderson

3. Dizzy Dean + Dean Smith = Dizzy Dean Smith

4. Elston Howard + Howard Cosell = Elston Howard Cosell

5. Dan Patrick + Patrick Ewing = Dan Patrick Ewing

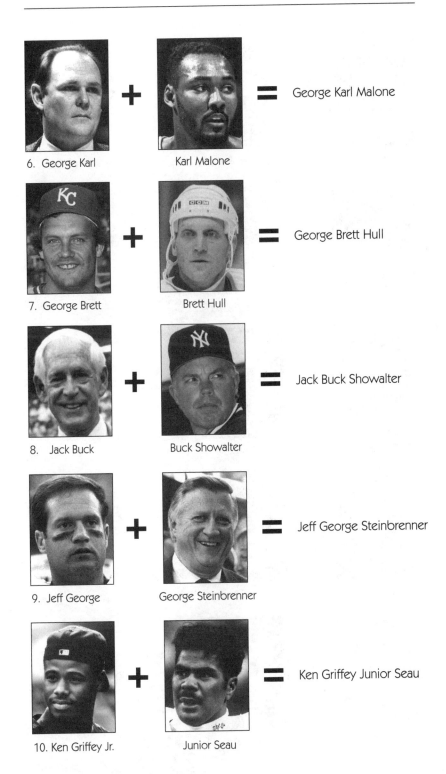

6. George Karl   Karl Malone   =   George Karl Malone

7. George Brett   Brett Hull   =   George Brett Hull

8. Jack Buck   Buck Showalter   =   Jack Buck Showalter

9. Jeff George   George Steinbrenner   =   Jeff George Steinbrenner

10. Ken Griffey Jr.   Junior Seau   =   Ken Griffey Junior Seau

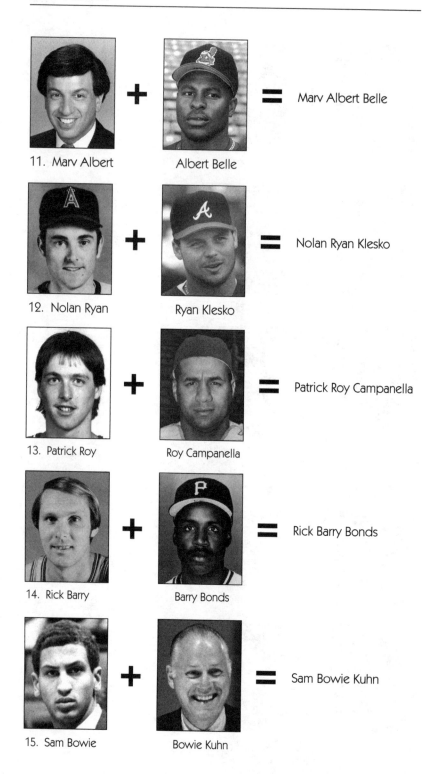

11. Marv Albert   Albert Belle   =   Marv Albert Belle

12. Nolan Ryan   Ryan Klesko   =   Nolan Ryan Klesko

13. Patrick Roy   Roy Campanella   =   Patrick Roy Campanella

14. Rick Barry   Barry Bonds   =   Rick Barry Bonds

15. Sam Bowie   Bowie Kuhn   =   Sam Bowie Kuhn

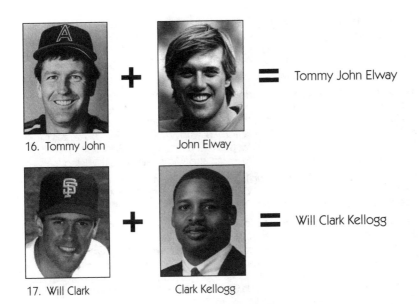

16. Tommy John   John Elway   = Tommy John Elway

17. Will Clark   Clark Kellogg   = Will Clark Kellogg

Chapter 11: College Basketball

First and Foremost (Warming up): 1. Temple defeated Colorado. 2. Arkansas' Nolan Richardson. 3. North Carolina's Dean Smith played for Kansas' national championship team in 1952 and Indiana's Bobby Knight played for national champion Ohio State in 1960. 4. Stanford. 5. City College of New York (CCNY) in 1950. 6. Kentucky had 1,685 victories, 10 more than second-place North Carolina. 7. North Carolina State. 8. UCLA. 9. North Carolina. 10. Kansas.

First and Foremost (Getting serious): 1. Freeman Williams. 2. Pete Maravich. 3. Sherman Douglas. 4. Shawn Bradley. 5. Steve Nash. 6. Mookie Blaylock. 7. Bill Chambers. 8. Calvin Murphy. 9. Askia Jones. 10. Clifford Rozier.

Magic Numbers (Warming up): 1. UCLA. 2. No. 33. Teammate Greg Kelser wore No. 32. 3. Chris Jackson. 4. Bob Kurland (see accompanying photo). 5. Dean Smith. 6. Frank Selvy. 7. Loyola Marymount beat U.S. International 181-150 for 331 combined points. 8. Kevin Bradshaw. 9. Georgetown coach John Thompson. 10. Kentucky.

Magic Numbers (Getting serious): 1. Years in which Kentucky won NCAA Tournament championships. 2. The top three single-season averages in Division I history, posted by LSU's Pete Maravich in his sophomore, junior and senior seasons. 3. The halftime score of the 1988 NCAA Tournament championship game—the 50th in history—between Kansas and Oklahoma. 4. The final records of the UCLA teams that won seven consecutive NCAA Tournament titles from 1967-73. 5. The record number of consecutive victories posted by UCLA from 1971-74. 6. The incredible field goal shooting performance of UCLA's Bill Walton in the 1973 NCAA Tournament championship game against Memphis State. 7. The record of the 1976 Indiana Hoosiers, college basketball's last undefeated NCAA champion. 8. The record scoring average of the run-and-gun Loyola Marymount team of 1989-90. 9. The record of North Carolina's Dean Smith, college basketball's all-time winningest coach, through the 1996-97 season. 10. Years in which Indiana won NCAA Tournament championships.

As Easy as U-C-L-A (Warming up): 1. Notre Dame. 2. Notre Dame. 3. Notre Dame. 4. Notre Dame's Dwight Clay. 5. Houston. 6. Houston's Elvin Hayes. 7. Alcindor's teams were 88-2; Walton's teams were 86-4 for a combined total of 174-6. 8. Patterson's Bruins were 57-3. 9. The coach was Larry Brown and the leading scorer was Kiki Vandeweghe. 10. Missouri.

As Easy as U-C-L-A (Getting serious): 1. Wilkes and Lee played with Walton. 2. Warren and Allen played with Alcindor. 3. Erickson and Goss played with McIntosh. 4. Meyers and Johnson played with Washington. 5. Schofield and Wicks played with Patterson. 6. Rowe and Shackelford played with Alcindor. 7. Hazzard and Goodrich played with Slaughter. 8. Meyers and Farmer played with Walton. 9. Bibby and Vallely played with Patterson. 10. Heitz and Wicks played with Alcindor.

Follow the Leaders (Warming up): 1. Danny Manning. 2. Dan Issel. 3. Don MacLean. 4. Calbert Cheaney. 5. Darrell Griffith. 6. Phil Ford. 7. Johnny Dawkins. 8. Glen Rice. 9. Lawrence Moten. 10. Sean Elliott.

Follow the Leaders (Getting serious): 1. Patterson succeeded Lew Alcindor at UCLA. 2. Polynice succeeded Ralph Sampson at Virginia. 3. Best succeeded Kenny Anderson at Georgia Tech. 4. Anderson succeeded Akeem Olajuwon at Houston. 5. Donnelly succeeded Magic Johnson at Michigan State. 6. Washington succeeded Bill Walton at UCLA. 7. Minniefield succeeded Kyle Macy at Kentucky. 8. Brown succeeded Isiah Thomas at Indiana. 9. Dalton succeeded Patrick Ewing at Georgetown. 10. Colescott succeeded Phil Ford at North Carolina.

Who's in Charge? (Warming up): 1. Georgetown coach John Thompson. 2. Former Kentucky coach Adolph Rupp. 3. Former UCLA coach John Wooden. 4. Saint Louis University coach Charlie Spoonhour. 5. Fresno State coach Jerry Tarkanian. 6. Indiana coach Bob Knight or former Alabama coach Wimp Sanderson. 7. Former Houston coach Guy Lewis. 8. Former St. John's coach Lou Carnesecca. 9. Former Western Kentucky coach Ed Diddle. 10. Mount St. Mary's coach Jim Phelan.

Who's in Charge? (Getting serious): 1. Army. 2. Ohio State. 3. Montana. 4. Fordham. 5. Minnesota. 6. Kansas State. 7. St. Joseph's. 8. Iowa. 9. Indiana State. 10. Creighton.

Tournament Talk (Warming up): 1. Kansas. 2. Temple. 3. Kansas. 4. Seattle. 5. West Virginia. 6. Ohio State. 7. Duke. 8. Princeton. 9. Utah. 10. Villanova. 11. Houston.

Tournament Talk (Getting serious): 1. Austin Carr (pictured with coach Johnny Dee on following page). 2. Elvin Hayes. 3. Bill Bradley. 4. Jeff Fryer. 5. Jerry Lucas. 6. U.S. Reed. 7. David Robinson. 8. Shaquille O'Neal. 9. Christian Laettner. 10. Oscar Robertson.

Finally, Four (Warming up): 1. Oregon defeated Ohio State. 2. Evanston. 3. Seattle. 4. Villanova, Georgetown and St. John's from the Big East. 5. None. 6. North Carolina. 7. California. 8. The Big Eight Conference. 9. Kentucky and Indiana. 10. Larry Brown, UCLA (1980) and Kansas (1988).

Finally, Four (Getting serious): 1. UCLA (11) and Kentucky (6). 2. Duke. 3. Houston. 4. UCLA (15) and North Carolina (13). 5. Oregon (champion), Ohio State (runnerup), Oklahoma (third place), Villanova. 6. Former championship teams that have changed their names. Oklahoma A&M now is Oklahoma State and Texas Western now is Texas-El Paso. 7. Schools that have won consecutive NCAA championships. 8. Teams that have won championships in their only Final Four appearances. 9. The only teams that could claim championships during UCLA's 12-year domination. 10. Teams with three or more NCAA Tournament titles.

En-titled (Warming up): 1. Jordan hit a 16-foot jump shot with 15 seconds remaining to give North Carolina a one-point victory over Georgetown. 2. Givens exploded for 41 points in Kentucky's victory over Duke. 3. Charles grabbed teammate Dereck Whittenburg's desperation airball and slammed it home with one second remaining, giving North Carolina State a shocking two-point upset victory over Houston. 4. Webber signaled for a timeout in the waning moments when Michigan was out of timeouts, securing North Carolina's victory. 5. Smart's 16-foot jump shot with five seconds remaining gave Indiana a one-point victory over Syracuse. 6. Imhoff's tip-in with 15 seconds remaining secured California's one-point victory over West Virginia. 7. Robinson sank two free throws with three seconds remaining in overtime to give Michigan a one-point victory over Seton Hall. 8. Goodrich scored 42 points in UCLA's easy victory over Michigan. 9. McClain scored 17 points and point guard McLain committed only two turnovers in Villanova's near-perfect 66-64 upset of Georgetown. 10. Rouse put back a missed shot with one second remaining to give Loyola of Chicago a two-point overtime victory over Cincinnati.

En-titled (Getting serious): 1. McGuire and Marquette defeated Smith and North Carolina. 2. Sloan and North Carolina State defeated McGuire and Marquette. 3. Crum and Louisville defeated Krzyzewski and Duke. 4. Haskins and Texas Western defeated Rupp and Kentucky. 5. Smith and North Carolina defeated Thompson and Georgetown. 6. Jucker and Cincinnati defeated Taylor and Ohio State. 7. Krzyzewski and Duke defeated Williams and Kansas. 8. Hall and Kentucky defeated Foster and Duke. 9. Ireland and Loyola of Chicago defeated Jucker and Cincinnati. 10. Wooden and UCLA defeated Durham and Florida State.

Matching Up: 1. UCLA, Henry Bibby. 2. North Carolina, Sam Perkins. 3. North Carolina State, Monte Towe. 4. Marquette, Butch Lee. 5. Ohio State, John Havlicek. 6. UCLA, Lucius Allen. 7. Villanova, Ed Pinckney. 8. Kentucky, Rick Robey. 9. San Francisco, K.C. Jones. 10. North Carolina State, Thurl Bailey. 11. Kentucky, Alex Groza. 12. UNLV, Anderson Hunt. 13. Michigan State, Jay Vincent. 14. UCLA, Keith Wilkes. 15. Duke, Grant Hill. 16. UCLA, Walt Hazzard. 17. Indiana, Quinn Buckner. 18. Louisville, Billy Thompson.

Home Sweet Home (Warming up): 1. Duke. 2. Georgetown. 3. Oklahoma. 4. Arkansas. 5. Purdue. 6. Temple. 7. Ohio State. 8. Missouri. 9. Clemson. 10. Memphis. 11. Louisiana State. 12. Louisville.

Home Sweet Home (Getting serious): 1. Indiana's Assembly Hall. 2. UCLA's Pauley Pavilion. 3. Syracuse's Carrier Dome. 4. Kentucky's Rupp Arena. 5. Houston's Hofheinz Pavilion. 6. Kansas' Allen Field House. 7. North Carolina's Dean Smith Center. 8. Notre Dame's Joyce Center. 9. UNLV's Thomas & Mack Center. 10. Maryland's Cole Field House.

Chapter 13: Pro Sports

Title Towners (Warming up): 1. 1975. 2. 1967. 3. 1981. 4. 1970. 5. 1988. 6. 1978. 7. 1956. 8. 1984. 9. 1960. 10. 1973.

Title Towners (Getting serious): 1. New York Knicks (NBA). 2. St. Louis Cardinals (MLB). 3. San Francisco 49ers (NFL). 4. Boston Bruins (NHL). 5. Baltimore Orioles (MLB). 6. Edmonton Oilers (NHL). 7. Portland Trail Blazers (NBA). 8. Minneapolis/Los Angeles Lakers (NBA). 9. Dallas Cowboys (NFL). 10. Detroit Tigers (MLB). 11. Pittsburgh Pirates (MLB). 12. Pittsburgh Steelers (NFL).

Common Knowledge (Warming up): 1. The 1933 and '34 Chicago Bears and the 1992-93 Pittsburgh Penguins. 2. New York Yankees, Green Bay Packers, Boston Celtics, Montreal Canadiens. 3. The Chicago Cubs (116) and Cleveland Indians (111). 4. The Detroit Red Wings won 62 games. 5. 17. 6. 16. 7. Los Angeles; New York. 8. Four—Edmonton, Montreal and Calgary in hockey and Toronto in baseball. 9. The

Chicago Blackhawks (1), Boston Bruins (2) and Philadelphia Flyers (2). 10. Boston Celtics center Bill Russell in 1969.

Common Knowledge (Getting serious): 1. Players who excelled in college in one sport and played professionally in another. 2. Teams that have won four or more consecutive championships. 3. League MVPs for Boston-based teams. 4. Prominent little men. 5. The best one-season records compiled by teams in the Big Four sports. The 1995-96 Chicago Bulls were 72-10; the 1906 Chicago Cubs were 116-36; the 1972 Miami Dolphins were 14-0, and the 1976-77 Montreal Canadiens were 60-8-12. 6. Teams that changed cities and nicknames. 7. Cities with four professional sports. 8. University of Minnesota products. 9. Teams that have won one championship. 10. Teams that have never won a championship.

Honors Roll (Warming up): 1. George Gervin. 2. Julius Erving. 3. Bobby Hull and Gordie Howe. 4. Cal Hubbard. 5. Frank Robinson. 6. Babe Ruth in baseball and Maurice "Rocket" Richard in hockey. 7. Bob Pettit and Jim Brown. 8. Oscar Robertson. 9. Boston teammate Jim Rice. 10. The Indiana Pacers.

Honors Roll (Getting serious): 1. Wayne Gretzky, Kareem Abdul-Jabbar, Gordie Howe, Bill Russell, Wilt Chamberlain, Michael Jordan, Eddie Shore. 2. Weeb Ewbank (Colts and Jets), Bill McKechnie (Pirates and Reds), Bucky Harris (Senators and Yankees), Sparky Anderson (Reds and Tigers), Alex Hannum (Hawks and 76ers), Scotty Bowman (Canadiens, Penguins and Red Wings), Tommy Gorman (Blackhawks and Maroons), Dick Irvin (Maple Leafs and Canadiens). 3. Doak Walker, Paul Hornung, Roger Staubach, O.J. Simpson, Earl Campbell, Tony Dorsett. 4. Don Shula, Connie Mack, Scotty Bowman, Lenny Wilkens. 5. Mike Piazza (Dodgers), Jerry Rice (49ers), Michael Jordan (Bulls), Ray Bourque (Bruins). 6. Ann Meyers (basketball) and Don Drysdale (baseball). 7. Lloyd and Paul Waner, George and Harry Wright, Al and Dick McGuire. 8. Tony and Phil Esposito, Bill and Bun Cook, Henri and Maurice Richard. 9. Bill Russell (11, Celtics), Henri Richard (11, Canadiens), Yogi Berra (10, Yankees), Sam Jones (10, Celtics), Jean Beliveau (10, Canadiens), Yvan Cournoyer (10, Canadiens), Joe DiMaggio (9, Yankees), Claude Provost (9, Canadiens). 10. John Wetteland, Yankees; Larry Brown, Cowboys; Michael Jordan, Bulls; Joe Sakic, Avalanche.

Double Jeopardy (Warming up): 1. Vic Janowicz, Bo Jackson. 2. Ernie Nevers. 3. Dave Winfield. 4. Deion Sanders. 5. Steve Hamilton (Yankees and Lakers), Gene Conley (Braves and Celtics). 6. Chuck Connors, who went on to star in the hit television series *The Rifleman*. 7. Tim Stoddard. 8. Charlie Ward. 9. Bob Hayes. 10. Scott Burrell.

Double Jeopardy (Getting serious): 1. Deion Sanders. 2. Bo Jackson. 3. Danny Ainge. 4. Brian Jordan. 5. Dave DeBusschere. 6. Ron Reed. 7. Gene Conley. 8. Steve Hamilton. 9. Dick Groat. 10. George Halas. 11. Jim Thorpe. 12 Carroll Hardy.

Family Ties (Warming up): 1. The Sutter brothers, hockey. 2. The Boyer brothers, baseball. 3. The Delahanty brothers, baseball. 4. The Jones brothers, basketball. 5. The DiMaggio brothers, baseball. 6. The Broten brothers, hockey. 7. The Perez brothers, baseball. 8. The Plager brothers, hockey. 9. The Barry brothers, basketball. 10. The Dineen brothers, hockey.

Family Ties (Getting serious): 1. Alou, McRae, Ripken Sr. and Dineen all coached or managed their son. 2. Griffey Sr. and Howe both played with their sons. 3. They are twins. 4. Calvin, Grant and Janet Hill. 5. Ann and Dave Meyers. 6. Lloyd and Paul Waner; Joe and Phil Niekro. 7. Father Bobby Hull, son Brett and brother/uncle Dennis. 8. Father Clay Matthews Sr. and sons Clay Jr. and Bruce. 9. Father Rick Barry and sons Jon, Brent and Drew. 10. Kansas City cornerback Dale Carter and Minnesota wide receiver Jake Reed. 11. Bobby and Barry Bonds. 12. Joey and Brian Mullen.

The Leader Board (Warming up): 1. Elgin Baylor. 2. Frank Thomas. 3. Craig Morton. 4. Larry Bird. 5. Steve Yzerman. 6. Karl Malone. 7. Thurman Munson. 8. Franco Harris. 9. Patrick Ewing. 10. Mark Messier.

The Leader Board (Getting serious): 1. 1986. 2. 1962. 3. 1973. 4. 1989. 5. 1960. 6. 1980. 7. 1954. 8. 1991. 9. 1982. 10. 1971.

City Slickers (Warming up): 1. Sandy Koufax and Magic Johnson. 2. Minnie Minoso and Bobby Hull. 3. Dave DeBusschere and Mike Bossy. 4. Ted Williams and John Bucyk. 5. Steve Carlton and Billy Cunningham. 6. Rusty Staub and Guy Lafleur. 7. Floyd Little and Dan Issel. 8. Mickey Mantle and Rod Gilbert. 9. Richie Ashburn and Bernie Parent. 10. Enos Slaughter and Bob Pettit. 11. Larry Doby and Otto Graham. 12. Luke Appling and Jerry Sloan.

City Slickers (Getting serious): 1. Philadelphia. 2. Chicago. 3. Boston. 4. New York. 5. Denver. 6. Detroit. 7. Los Angeles. 8. Dallas. 9. New York. 10. Philadelphia.

The Good, the Bad and the Ugly (Warming up): 1. Marv Throneberry. 2. Lakers stars Elgin Baylor and Jerry West. 3. Charles O. Finley, Al Davis, George Steinbrenner. 4. Anthony Young. 5. The 1972-73 Philadelphia 76ers finished 9-73 and the 1992-93 San Jose Sharks finished 11-71-2. 6. The Chicago/St. Louis/Arizona Cardinals. 7. The Aints. 8. Mike Keenan. 9. Denny McLain, Pete Rose. 10. Ted Williams.

The Good, the Bad and the Ugly (Getting serious): 1. The 1973-76 Philadelphia Flyers, who were known as the "Broad Street Bullies." The Flyers brawled their way to Stanley Cup championships in 1973-74 and 1974-75 before losing in the finals after the 1975-76 season. 2. Casey Stengel's 1962 Amazin' Mets, who lost a modern baseball-record 120 games. 3. The 1983 Chicago White Sox, who captured the American League West Division title by "winning ugly." 4. The first edition of Detroit's "Bad Boys," who won NBA championships in 1988-89 and 1989-90. 5. The "Darth Raiders" of the late 1970s, who won a Super Bowl and lived up to Al Davis' controversial Silver and Black tradition. 6. The 1972-73 Philadelphia 76ers team that compiled the worst record in NBA history—9-73. 7. The 1996 Detroit Tigers, who recorded the worst ERA (6.38) in American League history and surrendered a major league-record 241 home runs. 8. The 1994-95 New Jersey Devils, who ignored criticism of their boring neutral-zone trapping system and won a Stanley Cup championship. 9. The ever-controversial "Bronx Zoo" New York Yankees teams that won back-to-back World Series in 1977 and '78. 10. The St. Louis Cardinals' colorful 1934 Gas House Gang that beat the Detroit Tigers in the World Series.

The Name Game (Warming up): 1. The No-Name Defense. 2. El Birdos. 3. The Steel Curtain. 4. The Flying Frenchmen. 5. Showtime. 6. The Orange Crush. 7. We Are Family. 8. The Kraut Line. 9. Monsters of the Midway. 10. The Miracle Braves.

The Name Game (Getting serious): 1. The Three Amigos were speedy wide receivers who caught John Elway passes for Denver's 1987 and 1989 Super Bowl teams. 2. The Legion of Doom line was a virtual goal-producing machine for the 1995-96 and 1996-97 Philadelphia Flyers. 3. The Twin Towers anchored the Houston Rockets' frontcourt from 1984-85 through 1987-88. 4. The Hogs formed a powerful offensive line for the 1982 Super Bowl-champion Washington Redskins and beyond. 5. The Dream Team won a basketball gold medal in the 1992 Olympic Games at Barcelona. 6. Harvey's Wallbangers powered the Milwaukee Brewers to their only World Series appearance in 1982. 7. The Punch Line was a high-scoring unit for the Montreal Canadiens in the 1940s. 8. The Fearsome Foursome formed the defensive line of the Los Angeles Rams in the 1960s. 9. Murderer's Row was a murderer's row for the 1927 New York Yankees. 10. The Smurfs were diminutive wide receivers for the 1982 Redskins team that also featured the Hogs. 11. The M&M Boys powered the 1960-66 New York Yankees. 12. The Big Red Machine of Cincinnati won consecutive World Series in 1975 and '76.

Roots (Warming up): 1. St. Pats was the early nickname of the Toronto Maple Leafs. 2. The Syracuse Nationals evolved into the Philadelphia 76ers. 3. The Decatur Staleys evolved into the Chicago Bears. 4. Highlanders was the early nickname of the New York Yankees. 5. The Chicago Zephyrs evolved into the Washington Bullets. 6. The Seattle Pilots evolved into the Milwaukee Brewers. 7. The Colorado Rockies evolved into the New Jersey Devils. 8. The Portsmouth Spartans evolved into the Detroit Lions. 9. The Quebec Nordiques evolved into the Colorado Avalanche. 10. Titans was the early nickname of the New York Jets.

Roots (Getting serious): 1. The American Basketball Association, which existed from 1967-76. 2. The World Hockey Association, 1972-79. 3. The All-America Football Conference, 1946-49. 4. The ABA. 5. The World Football League, 1974-75. 6. The Federal League (baseball), 1914-15. 7. The WHA. 8. The United States Football League, 1983-85. 9. The Federal League. 10. The ABA.

Seasonal Offerings: 1. 1968. 2. 1977. 3. 1959. 4. 1983. 5. 1964. 6. 1988. 7. 1973. 8. 1948. 9. 1980. 10. 1955.

The Rookies (Warming up): 1. Bob Grim. 2. Peter and Anton Stastny. 3. Gale Sayers. 4. Walt Bellamy. 5. Wally Berger (Braves) and Frank Robinson (Reds). 6. Joe Juneau. 7. Ottis Anderson. 8. Kareem Abdul-Jabbar, Wilt Chamberlain, Wes Unseld, Larry Bird. 9. Benito Santiago. 10. Mario Lemieux.

The Rookies (Getting serious): 1. Tony Oliva for the Minnesota Twins. 2. Eric Dickerson for the Los Angeles Rams. 3. Teemu Selanne for the Winnipeg Jets. 4. Wilt Chamberlain for the Philadelphia Warriors. 5. Mark Fidrych for the Detroit Tigers. 6. Dan Marino for the Miami Dolphins. 7. Dale Hawerchuk for the Winnipeg Jets. 8. Oscar Robertson for the Cincinnati Royals. 9. Mike Bossy for the New York Islanders. 10. Fred Lynn for the Boston Red Sox. 11. George Rogers for the New Orleans Saints. 12. Elvin Hayes for the San Diego Rockets.

Who's the Boss? (Warming up): 1. Ten pennants and seven World Series. 2. Eight. 3. Nine. 4. Five. 5. Joe McCarthy, the 1936-39 Yankees; Scotty Bowman, the 1975-79 Canadiens; Al Arbour, the 1979-83 Islanders. 6. George Halas led the Chicago Staleys/Bears to titles in 1921, 1933, 1940, 1941, 1946 and 1963. 7. Sparky Anderson, Cincinnati (1975 and 1976) and Detroit (1984). 8. Don Shula. 9. Bob Johnson led the University of Wisconsin to three titles and the 1990-91 Pittsburgh Penguins to a Stanley Cup. 10. John Kerr coached the 1966-67 expansion Chicago Bulls and the 1968-69 expansion Phoenix Suns.

Who's the Boss? (Getting serious): 1. 1983. 2. 1970. 3. 1954. 4. 1978. 5. 1966. 6. 1988. 7. 1947. 8. 1968. 9. 1976. 10. 1957. 11. 1991. 12. 1963.

Chapter 14: Nicknames

Misters: 1. Baseball's Ernie Banks. 2. Baseball's Reggie Jackson. 3. Baseball's Joe DiMaggio. 4. Hockey's Glenn Hall. 5. College football's Doc Blanchard. 6. College football's Glenn Davis. 7. Hockey's Gordie Howe.

Big and Little: 1. Baseball's Christy Mathewson. 2. Baseball's Walter Johnson. 3. Baseball's Paul Waner. 4. Baseball's Lloyd Waner. 5. Basketball's Nate "Tiny" Archibald. 6. Baseball's Pee Wee Reese. 7. Basketball's Antoine Carr or Glenn Robinson. 8. Basketball's Oscar Robertson. 9. Basketball's Elvin Hayes. 10. Hockey's Don Saleski. 11. Basketball's Cliff Hagan. 12. Baseball's Randy Johnson. 13. Baseball's John McGraw. 14. Football Gene Lipscomb. 15. Hockey's Frank Mahovlich. 16. Basketball's Bill Walton. 17. Baseball's Frank Thomas.

Fierce Creatures: 1. Baseball's Dave Kingman. 2. Baseball's Greg Luzinski. 3. Basketball's Marvin Webster. 4. Football's Frank Kinard. 5. Football's Red Grange.

6. Hockey's Bob Kelly. 7. Basketball's Marvin Barnes. 8. Football's Randy White. 9. Baseball's Jimmie Foxx. 10. Hockey's Curtis Joseph. 11. Football's Ken Stabler. 12. Baseball's Jesse Burkett. 13. Basketball's Darryl Dawkins. 14. Hockey's Dominik Hasek. 15. Baseball's Al Hrabosky. 16. Football's Clyde Turner.

Animals: 1. Baseball's Harry Brecheen. 2. Baseball's Harvey Haddix. 3. Baseball's Bill Skowron. 4. Baseball's Ron Cey. 5. Baseball's Joe Medwick. 6. Baseball's Mark Fidrych. 7. Basketball's Billy Cunningham. 8. Baseball's Doug Rader. 9. College football's Paul Bryant. 10. Football's Alan Ameche. 11. Football's Y.A. Tittle. 12. Hockey's Jacques Plante. 13. Football's George Halas. 14. Baseball's Orlando Cepeda. 15. Baseball's Jim Grant. 16. Football's Lance Alworth. 17. Baseball's Pepper Martin. 18. Hockey's Ed Belfour.

Colors: 1. Baseball's Tris Speaker. 2. Basketball's Walter Davis. 3. Hockey's Brett Hull. 4. Football's Billy Johnson. 5. Baseball's Rusty Staub. 6. Baseball's Josh Gibson. 7. Hockey's Bobby Hull. 8. Baseball's Red Schoendienst. 9. Football's Donnie Anderson.

Authority Figures: 1. Baseball's Hal Newhouser. 2. Baseball's Casey Stengel. 3. Basketball's Julius Erving. 4. Basketball's John Wooden. 5. Baseball's Ozzie Smith. 6. Baseball's Willie Stargell. 7. Baseball's Jesse Haines. 8. Hockey's Wayne Gretzky. 9. Baseball's Branch Rickey. 10. Baseball's Elwin Rowe. 11. Basketball's David Robinson. 12. Hockey's John Bucyk. 13. Baseball's Frank Chance. 14. Basketball's Darrell Griffith. 15. Football's David Jones.

Sugar and Spice: 1. Basketball's Ed Macauley. 2. Basketball's Earl Monroe. 3. Basketball's Hakeem Olajuwon. 4. Hockey's Guy Lafleur. 5. Baseball's Jim Bottomley. 6. Baseball's Ty Cobb. 7. Basketball's Donald Watts or baseball's Andy Van Slyke. 8. Basketball's Walt Bellamy. 9. Basketball's Bobby Smith. 10. Baseball's George Selkirk. 11. Baseball's Marv Throneberry. 12. Baseball's A.B. Chandler. 13. Basketball's Lou Hudson. 14. Football's Walter Payton. 15. Basketball's Jamaal Wilkes. 16. Baseball's Charley Grimm.

Joes and Sams: 1. Baseball's Joe Jackson. 2. Baseball's Sam Jones. 3. Baseball's Joe McCarthy. 4. Baseball's Sam McDowell. 5. Football's Sammy Baugh. 6. Football's Joe Greene. 7. Football's Joe Namath. 8. Baseball's Sam Crawford. 9. Basketball's Joe Fulks. 10. Detroit's Joe Louis Arena.

"The" Men: 1. Basketball's Dominique Wilkins. 2. Baseball's Ralph Garr, hockey's Yvan Cournoyer. 3. Baseball's Hank Aaron, hockey's Dave Schultz, football's Fred Williamson. 4. Baseball's Roger Clemens, hockey's Maurice Richard. 5. Baseball's Sal Maglie. 6. Baseball's Harmon Killebrew. 7. Baseball's Larry Jaster. 8. Baseball's John Montefusco. 9. Baseball's Bill Klem. 10. Baseball's Duke Snider. 11. Baseball's Eddie Stanky. 12. Baseball's Nolan Ryan. 13. College football's Jack Thompson. 14. Baseball's Phil Regan. 15. Football's Daryle Lamonica. 16. Football's Brian Bosworth. 17. Baseball's Dave Parker. 18. Baseball's Andre Dawson. 19. Baseball's Dick Radatz. 20. Basketball's Allen Iverson. 21. Baseball's Will Clark. 22. Football's Ted Hendricks. 23. Baseball's Connie Mack. 24. Baseball's Marty Marion. 25. Baseball's Clark Griffith. 26. Baseball's Al Schacht. 27. Basketball's Shawn Kemp. 28. Baseball's Bucky Harris. 29. Baseball's Lou Gehrig. 30. Basketball's Gary Payton. 31. Baseball's Ted Williams. 32. Basketball's Karl Malone. 33. Baseball's Charley Gehringer. 34. Basketball's Chet Walker. 35. Football's William Perry. 36. Basketball's Charles Barkley. 37. Basketball's Clyde Drexler. 38. Baseball's Honus Wagner. 39. Basketball's Larry Bird. 40. Baseball's Mickey Mantle. 41. Baseball's Frank Frisch. 42. Baseball's Ernie Lombardi. 43. Baseball's Mike Hargrove. 44. Football's Christian Okoye. 45. Baseball's Joe DiMaggio. 46. Hockey's Henri Richard. 47. Baseball's Leo Durocher. 48. Basketball's George Gervin. 49. Baseball's Harry Walker. 50. Basketball's Dennis Rodman. 51. Baseball's Carl Hubbell. 52. Basketball's Wilt Chamberlain. 53. Football's Lou Groza. 54. Baseball's Jimmy Wynn. 55. Baseball's Babe Ruth.

One-Namers: 1. Baseball's Pepper Martin, football's Franklin Rodgers. 2. Basketball's Isiah Thomas. 3. Baseball's Dwight Gooden, basketball's Glenn Rivers. 4. Baseball's Lefty Gomez. 5. Baseball's Bob Hazle. 6. Baseball's Bill Monbouquette. 7. Baseball's Ryne Sandberg. 8. Baseball's Frank Howard, basketball's John Havlicek. 9. Baseball's Harry Heilmann. 10. Baseball's Dan Quisenberry. 11. Baseball's Sam Jones. 12. Baseball's Archie Graham. 13. Baseball's Zoilo Versalles. 14. Baseball's Jerry Koosman. 15. Baseball's Roy Campanella, baseball's Bert Campaneris. 16. Baseball's Lawrence Berra. 17. Baseball's Frank Robinson. 18. Hockey's Doug Gilmour. 19. Basketball's Tom Sanders. 20. Basketball's Earvin Johnson. 21. Baseball's Travis Jackson. 22. Football's O.J. Simpson. 23. Basketball's Walt Frazier. 24. Basketball's Shaquille O'Neal. 25. Basketball's Tyrone Bogues. 26. Hockey's Jim Carey. 27. Baseball's Jay Hanna Dean. 28. Football's Craig Heyward. 29. Football's Howard Cassady. 30. Hockey's Lorne Worsley. 31. Baseball's Walter Alston. 32. Baseball's Rogers Hornsby. 33. Basketball's Eric Floyd. 34. Baseball's Carl Yastrzemski. 35. Football's Bob Hayes. 36. Basketball's Michael Jordan. 37. Basketball's Anthony Webb. 38. Hockey's Phil Esposito. 39. Basketball's Slater Martin. 40. Baseball's Al Lopez. 41. Basketball's Jerry Lucas. 42. Baseball's Marty Marion, hockey's Glen Sather. 43. Baseball's Willie McCovey. 44. Baseball's Enos Slaughter. 45. Hockey's Derek Sanderson. 46. Baseball's Emil Meusel. 47. Hockey's Hector Blake. 48. Baseball's Lenny Dykstra. 49. Baseball's Brooks Robinson. 50. Baseball's Carl Furillo. 51. Baseball's Harry Simpson. 52. Baseball's Bill Lee. 53. Baseball's Bill Mazeroski. 54. Baseball's Paul Blair. 55. Baseball's Bill Wambsganss. 56. Baseball's Allie Reynolds. 57.Baseball's Phil Niekro. 58. Basketball's Cedric Maxwell. 59. Baseball's Leroy Paige. 60. Football's Earle Neale. 61. Hockey's John Vanbiesbrouck. 62. Football's Byron White. 63. Basketball's Anfernee Hardaway. 64. Baseball's Al Simmons. 65. Football's Elroy Hirsch. 66. Hockey's Gerry Cheevers. 67. Hockey's Stan Mikita. 68. Baseball's Jim Hunter. 69. Basketball's Fred Brown. 70. Basketball's Len Robinson. 71. Football's Carl Reynolds.

Significant Others: 1. Baseball's William Jacobson. 2. Baseball's Hughie Jennings. 3. Baseball's Carl Furillo. 4. Basketball's Bryant Reeves. 5. Baseball's Mitch Williams, hockey's Al Iafrate. 6. Basketball's Bill Bradley. 7. Baseball's Tony Oliva, hockey's Tony Esposito. 8. Baseball's Ron Guidry. 9. Baseball's Dick Stuart. 10. Baseball's John Candelaria. 11. Basketball's Bob Cousy. 12. Baseball's Leon Wagner. 13. Baseball's Tommy Henrich. 14. Football's Earl Campbell. 15. Baseball's Mickey Rivers. 16. Baseball's Wilmer Mizell. 17. Baseball's Grover Cleveland Alexander. 18. Baseball's Willie Mays. 19. Basketball's Rod Hundley. 20. Baseball's Bob Feller. 21. Hockey's Pavel Bure. 22. Football's Tony Dorsett. 23. Baseball's Stan Musial. 24. Hockey's Mario Lemieux. 25. Baseball's Billy Hamilton. 26. Baseball's Mordecai Brown. 27. Hockey's Teemu Selanne. 28. Hockey's Eddie Giacomin. 29. Baseball's George Kelly. 30. Baseball's Frank Baker. 31. Baseball's Pete Reiser, basketball's Pete Maravich. 32. Baseball's Wilbert Robinson. 33. Baseball's Tom Seaver. 34. Baseball's George Hendrick. 35. Baseball's Jimmie Foxx. 36. Baseball's Steve Balboni. 37. Baseball's Allan Lewis. 38. Baseball's Walt Williams. 39. Baseball's Burleigh Grimes. 40. Football's Nolan Smith. 41. Basketball's Dennis Johnson. 42. Baseball's Dennis Boyd. 43. Baseball's James Bell. 44. Baseball's Pete Rose. 45. Baseball's George Hendrick. 46. Hockey's Bernie Geoffrion. 47. Football's Dick Lane. 48. Football's Lawrence Taylor. 49. Football's Charlie Justice. 50. Basketball's Xavier McDaniel.

Chapter 15: College Sports

What's in a Name? (Warming up): 1. Arizona State vs. Siena. 2. Notre Dame vs. Pennsylvania. 3. Florida vs. Oregon. 4. Iowa State vs. Hawaii. 5. Western Illinois vs. Centenary. 6. Marshall vs. St. Peter's. 7. Oregon State vs. Indiana State. 8. Penn State vs. Texas Christian. 9. Florida A&M vs. Richmond. 10. Montana vs. South Carolina.

What's in a Name? (Getting serious): 1. Duke vs. Delaware. 2. St. John's vs. Marist. 3. Rutgers vs. Alabama. 4. Maine vs. Long Island University. 5. Minnesota vs. Kent. 6. Georgia Tech vs. Syracuse. 7. Tulane vs. Loyola (Md.). 8. DePaul vs. Creighton.

Conference Calls (Warming up): 1. The Pacific-10—UCLA 10, USC 4. 2. Ohio State. 3. Missouri and Texas Tech. 4. Northwestern. 5. Vanderbilt and South Carolina. 6. Arizona State. 7. None. 8. Boston College and Virginia Tech. 9. The Atlantic Coast Conference (5). 10. Penn State (2), Miami (3) and Notre Dame (1).

Conference Calls (Getting serious): 1. Minnesota (FB), Wisconsin (BB). 2. Michigan State (FB), Indiana (BB). 3. Auburn (FB), Kentucky (BB). 4. Southern California (FB), UCLA (BB). 5. Southern California (FB), UCLA (BB). 6. Southern California (FB), UCLA (BB). 7. Clemson (FB), North Carolina (BB). 8. Georgia Tech (FB), Duke (BB).

The Winning Formula (Warming up): 1. Chamberlain. 2. Maravich. 3. Griffin. 4. Ford. 5. Testaverde. 6. Robertson. 7. Elway. 8. Baylor. 9. Rozier. 10. Mikan. 11. Staubach. 12. Young.

The Winning Formula (Getting serious): 1. Oklahoma A&M. 2. Kentucky. 3. California. 4. Michigan. 5. UCLA. 6. Michigan. 7. Notre Dame. 8. Georgia. 9. Oklahoma. 10. Michigan. 11. Arkansas. 12. Michigan.

Crossing the Line (Warming up): 1. Amos Alonzo Stagg. 2. Charlie Ward. 3. Bruce Walton, older brother of Bill Walton. 4. Tony Gonzalez. 5. Joe Kapp. 6. Ohio State was the 1961 football co-champion and the NCAA Tournament runner-up in 1961 and 1962. 7. Rusty LaRue. 8. One, 1978. 9. Ohio State's John Havlicek. 10. Nebraska in 1995-96.

Crossing the Line (Getting serious): 1. Lew Alcindor, Bill Walton, basketball; Kenny Easley, Kenny Washington, Gary Beban, Jerry Robinson, football. 2. Paul "Bear" Bryant, Fran Curci, Bill Curry, football; Adolph Rupp, Joe B. Hall, Eddie Sutton, Rick Pitino, basketball. 3. Angelo Bertelli, Leon Hart, Paul Hornung, Walt Patulski, football; Austin Carr, basketball. 4. Jim Brown, football. 5. Billy Cannon, football; Pete Maravich, Shaquille O'Neal, basketball. 6. Cornelius Bennett, football; Derrick McKey, Jim Farmer, basketball. 7. Cazzie Russell, basketball; Gerald Ford, Tom Harmon, Ron Kramer, football. 8. Gale Sayers, football; Wilt Chamberlain, basketball. 9. Kevin Butler, football; Dominique Wilkins, basketball. 10. Gary Moeller, Mike White, John Mackovic, football; Gene Bartow, Lou Henson, basketball.

Seasonal Offerings: 1. 1964-65. 2. 1973-74. 3. 1981-82. 4. 1986-87. 5. 1969-70. 6. 1977-78. 7. 1984-85. 8. 1990-91. 9. 1967-68. 10. 1975-76.

Chapter 16: Crossword Challenges

Baseball, page 274.

Pro Football, page 275.

Pro Basketball, page 276.

Hockey, page 277.

College Football, page 278.

College Basketball, page 279.

Baseball, page 280.

Pro Football, page 281.

Pro Basketball, page 282.

S	N	O	B		F	A	B	I		F	G	A
H	O	U	R		T	I	P	I	N		M	O	O	R
O	S	L	O		W	O	R	L	D		A	U	N	T
T	H	U	N	D	E	R		L	O	N	G	L	E	Y
			Z	O	N	E		F	O	A	L
	A	L	E	R	T			I	R	V	I	N	E
A	B	A		M	Y	A	T	T		Y	E	A	R	S
L	A	U			L	U	C			I	A	M
S	C	R	E	E		A	G	H	A	S		L	S	U
	K	A	R	E	E	M			T	E	A	S	E
	A	E	R	O		S	T	A	R
T	O	P	S	E	E	D		E	L	L	I	S	O	N
A	B	E	E		B	O	O	N	E		Z	E	K	E
R	O	A	R		U	M	A	S	S		I	T	A	S
K	E	L			S	E	R	E		N	A	Y	S

Hockey, page 283.

A	D	A	M	S		H	O	S	E		E	M	U	S
S	A	D	A	T		A	N	T	S		R	A	S	H
S	T	A	N	L	E	Y	C	U	P		I	R	B	E
N	A	M		O	R	E	E		O	N	C	A	L	L
		T	U	G	S		U	S	H	L
M	A	T	H	I	S		U	T	I	L	I	T	Y
A	C	H	E	S		G	L	U	T		N	E	E	D
T	R	I	G		M	A	C	R	O		D	E	M	O
S	E	E	R		O	M	E	N		A	R	M	E	D
	S	L	E	E	P	E	R		S	T	O	U	N	D
	A	M	U	R		V	O	L	S
S	U	I	T	U	P		I	O	L	A		H	A	S
E	R	G	O		M	I	S	C	O	N	D	U	C	T
A	G	O	N		A	T	L	A		T	E	G	L	A
M	E	R	E		N	O	E	L		A	M	O	U	R

Five's a Crowd

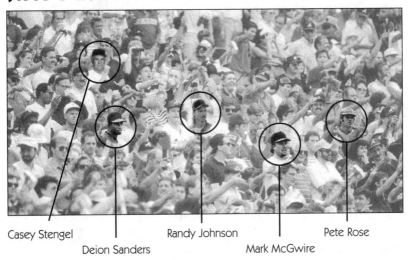

Casey Stengel

Deion Sanders

Randy Johnson

Mark McGwire

Pete Rose

Photo Credits

Contributing Photographers

Joe Angeles: Page 50 (Hull); **Associated Press:** Pages 79 (Bernie Brewer), 156 (J. Robinson), 173; **Bruce Bennett:** Pages 51 (Jagr), 128, 137; **Tom Berg:** Pages 42 (Taylor), 45 (Sanders); **Tom Bingham:** Page 152 (Lofton); **Frank Bryan:** Page 30 (Bench); **Jeff Carlick:** Pages 39 (Pena), 48 (Abdul-Jabbar), 49 (M. Johnson), 71; **Robert Christian:** Page 44 (Schottenheimer); **John Cordes:** Pages 33 (Winfield), 37 (R. Johnson); **Albert Dickson/THE SPORTING NEWS:** Pages 80 (Jacobs Field scoreboard), 80 (Mile High Bronco), 81 (Ralphie), 82 (Coors scoreboard), 83 (Barrel Man), 176; **Malcolm Emmons:** Pages 38 (Clemente), 49 (Knight), 65, 67, 158 (Warren), 171, 189, 267; **Jeff Fishbein:** Page 48 (Mullin); **Earnie Glazener:** Page 83 (Arlington Stadium scoreboard); **Pete J. Groh:** Page 74 (Dawg Pound); **Phil Hoffmann:** Page 75 (Navy goat); **Mark Johnson:** Page 42 (Shula); **Kansas City Royals:** Page 73 (Fountains); **Los Angeles Dodgers:** Page 74 (Brito); **Fred Kaplan:** Page 31 (Yastrzemski); **Robert Kingsbury:** Page 48 (Maravich), 104; **Mitchell Layton:** Pages 33 (E. Davis), 35 (Franco), 68 (Rogers); **Ed Mailliard:** Page 38 (Niekro); **Vic Milton:** Page 41 (Seaver); **Ronald L. Mrowiec:** Page 46 (Chamberlain); **Norm Perdue:** Page 48 (Jordan); **Russ Reed:** Page 39 (Palmer); **Kevin W. Reece:** Page 46 (Bird); **Louis Requena:** Pages 51 (Dryden), 80 (Mets Apple); **Janis Rettaliata:** Pages 31 (Quisenberry), 56; **Bob Rosato:** Page 44 (Perry); **Betsy Peabody Rowe:** Page 49 (McHale); **Steve Schwartz:** Page 43 (Paterno); **David Seelig:** Page 31 (Boggs); **Bill Setliff:** Page 33 (Mattingly); **Owen C. Shaw:** Page 47 (Bol-Bogues); **Carl Skalak:** Page 44 (Simpson); **Robert Skeoch:** Page 34 (Fielder); **Chuck Solomon:** Page 41 (Washington); **The Sports Group:** Page 42 (Favre); **Robert Stinnett:** Page 84 (Rabbit); **Noren Trotman:** Page 47 (Erving); **Greg Trott:** Page 32 (Eckersley); **United Press International:** Pages 32 (Berra-Larsen), 40 (B. Robinson), 78 (Busch beer wagon), 80 (Aints), 101, 175, 265. **Mike Valeri:** Page 47 (Auerbach); **Bob Vedral:** age 102; **Gary Weber:** Pages 32 (Parker), 41 (Strawberry), 103; **John Williamson:** Pages 34 (McGriff), 38 (Puckett), 45 (Seifert).

Colleges and Universities

Clemson: Page 74 (Howard's Rock); **Denver:** Page 148 (Sinbad); **Eureka:** Page 156 (Reagan); **Florida State:** Page 84 (Chief Osceola); **Georgia:** Page 72 (Uga); **Harvard:** Pages 145 (T. Lee Jones), 151 (Kennedy); **Indiana Basketball Hall of Fame:** Page 152 (Dean); **Michigan:** Page 82 (Helmets) **Minnesota:** Page 149 (Winfield); **Missouri:** Page 148 (Fitzgerald); **Notre Dame:** Page 83 (Touchdown Jesus); **Pomona-Pitzer Colleges:** Page 152 (Kristofferson); **Princeton:** Page 147 (Bradley); **San Diego State:** Page 159 (Gwynn); **Southern California:** Page 159 (Selleck); **Stetson:** Page 156 (Cassidy); **Temple:** Page 146 (Cosby); **UCLA:** Page 158 (Harmon); **Washington:** Page 85 (Helmet Car); **Yale:** Pages 150 (Bush), 157 (Phillips).

The Sporting News Archives

Pages 8-9, 11, 13, 14, 15, 16, 19, 20, 21, 22, 23, 25, 26, 29 (Ruth), 30 (Carlton), 30 (Cobb), 30 (Berra), 31 (Young), 32 (Gaedel), 33 (Valenzuela), 24 (DiMaggio), 34 (Jackson), 35 (Gibson), 35 (R. Henderson), 36 (McCovey), 36 (Mantle), 36 (Mays), 37 (Koufax), 37 (Marichal), 37 (Mack), 38 (Musial), 39 (Gray), 40 (Schott), 40 (Williams), 40 (F. Robinson), 41 (Rose), 42 (Bryant), 43 (Four Horsemen), 43 (Montana), 45 (Dempsey), 46 (Mikan), 46 (Gilmore), 46 (B. Russell), 49 (Robertson), 50 (Howe), 51 (Blake), 54, 55, 57, 59, 60, 61, 62, 63, 64, 66, 68 (Riggins), 68 (Hornung), 72 (Astrodome), 72 (Sym-Phony Band), 72 (Fenway wall), 72 (Yankee Stadium facade), 73 (L.A. Forum), 73 (Bull Ring), 73 (Yankee Stadium Bat), 73 (Cleveland sign), 74 (Big A), 74 (Charlie O. and mule), 75 (Kansas City stands), 75 (Football Hall of Fame), 75 (Wrigley wall), 75 (San Diego Chicken), 76-77, 78 (Hilda Chester), 78 (Boston Garden rafters), 78 (Crown scoreboard), 78 (Ebbets Field scoreboard), 79 (Astronauts), 79 (Musial statue), 79 (L.A. Coliseum), 79 (Yankee Stadium monuments), 80 (Griffith Stadium wall), 81 (Laker Girls), 81 (Wrigley tower), 81 (New York skyline), 82 (Wrigley house), 82 (Crosley Field wall), 82 (Celtics leprechaun), 83 (Noc-a-homa), 83 (Indiana court), 84 (Hand holding cigar), 84 (Gehrig's locker), 85 (SkyDome), 85 (L.A. Coliseum screen), 85 (Sun Bowl), 86-87, 91, 93, 94, 95, 97, 98, 99, 100 (Williams), 100 (Bogues), 100 (Lewis), 102 (Abdul-Jabbar), 107, 108, 109, 110, 111, 112, 113, 114, 115, 116, 117, 118, 119, 120, 121, 122, 123, 124, 125, 129, 131, 133, 134, 135, 136, 138, 139, 140, 143, 146 (Boudreau), 146 (Beradino), 147 (Ainge), 147 (Brown), 148 (Elway), 148 (Connors), 149 (Dryer), 149 (Ford), 150 (Gehrig), 150 (Irwin), 151 (Groat), 151 (Halas), 153 (Jensen), 153 (Kemp), 153 (Karras), 154 (Majors), 154 (Marinaro), 154 (Mathias), 154 (Weathers), 155 (Nixon), 155 (Olsen), 155 (Reynolds). 157 (Robeson), 157 (L. Smith), 158 (Luciano), 159 (Wayne), 161, 162, 163, 164, 165 (Rodgers), 165 (Glover), 167, 170, 172 (Oaken Bucket), 172 (Kuharich), 174, 187, 191, 192 (C. Jackson), 192 (Moncrief), 193 (Heathcote), 193 (Knight), 194, 195, 197, 199, 200, 201, 203, 221 (Stoddard), 221 (Shore), 222, 224 (Conley and Conley), 225 (Baylor), 225 (Mantle), 226, 227, 228, 230, 233, 234, 235, 236, 238, 242, 244, 245, 247, 262 (Alcindor), 262 (Beban), 263 (Thompson), 263 (Browner), 264 (Phelps), 264 (Rockne), 264 (Parseghian), 269 (E. Davis), 269 (Coleman), 270, 271, 284-285, 286 (16 mug shots), 306-309 (34 mug shots).